Using
ANALOGIES
in Middle and Secondary
SCIENCE
Classrooms

Using ANALOGIES in Middle and Secondary SCIENCE Classrooms

The FAR Guide—
An Interesting Way to
Teach With Analogies

Edited by ALLAN G. HARRISON • RICHARD K. COLL

CORWIN PRESS
A SAGE Company
Thousand Oaks, CA 91320

For information:

Corwin Press
A SAGE Company
2455 Teller Road
Thousand Oaks, California 91320
www.corwinpress.com

SAGE India Pvt. Ltd.
B 1/I 1 Mohan Cooperative Industrial Area
Mathura Road, New Delhi 110 044
India

SAGE Ltd.
1 Oliver's Yard
55 City Road
London EC1Y 1SP
United Kingdom

SAGE Asia-Pacific Pte. Ltd.
33 Pekin Street #02-01
Far East Square
Singapore 048763

Printed in the United States of America

Library of Congress Cataloging-in-Publication Data

Using analogies in middle and secondary classrooms: the FAR guide—an interesting way to teach with analogies/editors, Allan G. Harrison, Richard K. Coll.
        p. cm.
Includes bibliographical references and index.
ISBN 978-1-4129-1332-4 (cloth)
ISBN 978-1-4129-1333-1 (pbk.)
    1. Science—Study and teaching (Secondary) 2. Analogy in science education.
I. Harrison, Allan G. II. Coll, Richard K. III. Title.

Q181.U85 2008
507.1'2—dc22   2007014770

This book is printed on acid-free paper.

07   08   09   10   11   10   9   8   7   6   5   4   3   2   1

Acquisitions Editor:	Allyson Sharp
Managing Editor:	Cathy Hernandez
Editorial Assistant:	Mary Dang
Copy Editor:	Marilyn Power Scott
Typesetter:	C&M Digitals (P) Ltd.
Indexer:	Pamela Onorato
Cover Designer:	Scott Van Atta

Contents

8. Effective Physics Analogies

Allan G. Harrison

The abstract and difficult nature of physics concepts means that analogies and models are ever present in teaching them.

9. Effective Earth and Space Science Analogies

Neil Taylor and Terry Lyons

The vast scale of events in the earth and beyond requires models and analogies to bring events down to a size students can see and understand.

Acknowledgments

We acknowledge the contribution of the authors and the following people who have made this book a success:

We thank Professor Mike Summers of the University of Oxford for permission to reproduce Figures 3.1, 3.2, 3.3, 3.4, and 3.7.

We thank NSTA for permission to reproduce Figure 3.5 from *The Science Teacher.*

We thank Norton Publishers and Cook-Deegan for permission to reproduce Figure 6.10.

A special thanks goes to our graphic designer, David Downer, of Central Queensland University. David drew many diagrams, especially the chemistry analogy figures for Chapter 7 and the detailed diagrams in Chapters 6 and 8.

We thank Photos Rock for the photographs of the stationary and rotating fan in Chapter 7.

We thank Springer publishers for permission to reproduce Figure 7.8 and the large quotations from the works of Aubusson and Fogwill (2006) and Ritchie, Bellocchi, Poltl, and Wearmouth (2006) in Chapter 5.

We thank Stephen Lyons for his assistance with a number of diagrams in Chapter 9.

Publisher's Acknowledgments

The contributions of the following reviewers are gratefully acknowledged:

David Brock, Science Teacher
Roland Park Country School, Baltimore, MD

Sandra K. Enger, Associate Professor
The University of Alabama in Huntsville, Huntsville, AL

Debra K. Las, Science Teacher
ISD #535 Rochester Public Schools, Rochester, MN

Douglas Llewellyn
St. John Fisher College, Rochester, NY

Sara Lynne Murrell, Instructional Coach
Bethel Elementary Coach, Simpsonville, SC

John D. Ophus, Assistant Professor of Biology/Science Education
University of Northern Iowa, Cedar Falls, IA

Chuck Perkins, Teacher
South Kitsap School District, Port Orchard, WA

Robert E. Yager, Professor of Science Education
University of Iowa, Iowa City, IA

About the Editors

Allan G. Harrison is Associate Professor of Science Education at Central Queensland University. He taught biology, chemistry, and physics to students in Grades 7–12 for 25 years before completing his MSc and PhD at Curtin University of Technology in Perth, Western Australia. He has taught science teachers for 10 years and has researched teaching and learning with analogies for 15 years and published articles on science analogies in all leading science education journals. He also studies the capacity of analogies to engender conceptual change. He brings to this book his personal practical experience in teaching with analogies in high school and his research on other teachers' use of analogies. He believes that analogies, when used well, enhance students' interest and knowledge in science. He hopes you will share with him his commitment to learning for understanding.

Richard K. Coll is Associate Professor of Science Education at the University of Waikato, New Zealand. He holds a PhD in chemistry from Canterbury University and an EdD in science education from Curtin University of Technology. His research interests are concerned with mental models of science concepts and a variety of aspects of work-integrated learning.

About the Contributing Authors

Terry Lyons is chair of the International Organization for Science and Technology Education. He was a high school science teacher for 14 years and currently lectures in science education at the University of New England, Australia. He is a researcher in science education with the National Centre for Science, ICT and Mathematics Education in Rural and Regional Australia (SiMERR Australia).

Neil Taylor is senior lecturer in science and technology education at the University of New England in Australia. He has worked as a high school science teacher in Jamaica and the United Kingdom and in science teacher education at the University of the South Pacific in Fiji and the University of Leicester in England.

David F. Treagust is professor of science education in the Science and Mathematics Education Centre at Curtin University in Perth, Western Australia. His research interests focus on understanding students' ideas about science concepts, analogies, and models and how these ideas contribute to conceptual change and are used to enhance curriculum design and teachers' classroom practice. He was president of the National Association for Research in Science Teaching (USA) from 1999 to 2001 and is currently managing director of the Australasian Science Education Research Association.

Grady J. Venville is professor in science education at the University of Western Australia, an appointment she accepted in 2006. Prior to accepting that position, she was associate professor in science and technology education at Edith Cowan University. She is a passionate advocate of strong links between school science, science teacher education, and research in science education.

Introduction

Teaching is both an art and a science. People expect teachers to know their subjects and know how to explain difficult ideas to their students. But teaching is more than explaining; good teaching excites students and makes them want to explore the world around them. Exploring the world is the basis of inquiry science, and to foster inquiry, science ideas need to be intelligible and make sense; they also need to be plausible and believable. But most of all, science ideas should be fruitful in the sense that the ideas, objects, and processes that students explore raise new questions and expose new horizons.

The art of science teaching is seen in the interplay between the teacher's knowledge and the students' questions and "what-if" propositions. Sometimes when teachers think that they have taught an idea well, they are surprised by the quizzical looks on the students' faces. The students don't understand something about the explanation, some of the assumed information is not there, the process is foreign to them, or it is counterintuitive. What can teachers do? They can reexplain the concept and add more background information, and sometimes this works; but if the concept is outside the students' experiences, an analogy or model is a good way to go. Analogies and models are common in everyday life. A road map is a model of the roads and streets in a town or state; a computer is like a person's mind because it can remember and calculate; and a show home represents what your new house could look like.

Analogies and models are thinking tools; they are not fixed representations of objects or processes. When teachers say that a cell is like a tiny box, they are helping their students "see" that a cell has a protective wall all round it, that it comes in a variety of shapes and sizes and can be used for different purposes. When other teachers say that a cell is like a house, they are asking students to think about the things that happen in a house to maintain a family (food input, storage and processing, waste disposal, water flow, parents making decisions, letters sent to friends, etc.). Analogies and models of this kind allow students to adapt the analogy to their knowledge and experiences and see how a cell is like a box, like a house, or like a factory.

This book is written to help teachers creatively explain difficult and abstract concepts. We have included analogies for cells, global warming,

1

multiple analogies for electric current, role plays for chemical reactions and the states of matter, and analogies for plate tectonics and DNA, to name a few. The analogies that teachers use are as varied as the topics we teach in science. For this book, we have collected the popular and reliable analogies that we have found during our work with teachers. Each analogy is explained in detail and then summarized in the Focus-Action-Reflection (FAR) Guide. We hope you find these analogies useful and interesting for you and your students.

Please avoid seeing our analogies and models as definitive: change them, adapt them, and look for ways that they can be improved, and always watch for the point where the analogy or model breaks down. Most of all, encourage your students to construct their own analogies and join in with them as they create and develop their analogies and models.

The FAR Guide

The book has two central themes: first, using analogies is an interesting and engaging way to explain science concepts. Analogies make difficult and abstract concepts familiar by comparing them to everyday objects and experiences. For analogies to work, the analog or everyday object or experience must be familiar. If a particular analog is not familiar, substitute an example that is well understood by your students.

Second, the ways in which the analog is *like* the science concept and the ways in which it is *unlike* the science concept should be discussed with your students. Teachers sometimes avoid analogies because they engender alternative conceptions, which arise when the analogy is taken too far or too literally.

The FAR Guide was designed to enhance the presentation and interpretation of analogies. The acronym stands for

Focus—Be sure of what your students know and why you want to use the analogy;

Action—Be sure to check that your students understand the everyday object or experience you plan to use and ensure that you always discuss how the analog is *like* the science concept and how it is *unlike* the concept; and

Reflection—Reflect on the analogy's usefulness; ask yourself, "Do I need to revisit this explanation and are there better ways to use the analogy next time I teach this content?" Maybe you will decide to use a different analogy next time. This is good teaching.

The steps in the FAR Guide for teaching with analogies are summarized in the following table and elaborated in Chapter 2.

The FAR Guide

Focus	
Concept	Is it difficult, unfamiliar, or abstract?
Students	What ideas do the students already know about the concept?
Analog	Is the analog something your students are familiar with?
Action	
Likes	Discuss the features of the analog and the science concept. Draw similarities between them.
Unlikes	Discuss where the analog is unlike the science concept.
Reflection	
Conclusions	Was the analogy clear and useful or confusing? Did it achieve your planned outcomes?
Improvements	In light of outcomes, are there any changes you need to make next time you use this analogy?

We hope your teaching with analogies is exciting and productive.

Teaching With Analogies in a Standards-Based Classroom

Teaching with analogies can be fun and motivating for students, and research suggests it also enhances student learning of scientific concepts. However, teachers are busy people held to account for meeting their students' learning outcomes. This often involves meeting national educational standards devised by educational authorities. Meeting some standards is problematic, and teachers often have to consider exactly how they might meet such standards. For straightforward concepts and ideas, conventional teaching approaches may work well, but as most teachers know, many concepts are challenging, especially those that form the basis of this book. The analogies we provide here were not developed arbitrarily; they were developed to address subjects the literature suggests teachers find difficult to teach.

The analogies presented in this book provide an excellent and efficient means of addressing science standards for a variety of topics. To show how teachers can use these analogies to meet educational standards, for each analogy presented in Part II of the book we have linked the concepts to some national standards. We have chosen the U.S.-based National Science Teachers Association's recommended standards (National Academy of Sciences, 1996) and linked the concepts to specific standards at a variety of grade levels, mainly the Science Content Standards. You will see that the same analogy can be used to satisfy standards at different levels and for different topics. So, for example, the Shared Water Flow Analogy can be used for Science Content Standard B Physical Science, at Grades 5–8 for the topic "energy is transferred" and "energy is an important property of substances and . . . most change involves energy transfer." But it also can be used for Physical Science at Grades 9–12, where it can be used to explain Ohm's Law and moving electric charges. This reflects the versatility of analogies as teaching tools. Of course, you should exercise your judgment as to how a given analogy best suits your teaching demands and the learning needs of your students.

The links to the National Academy of Sciences (1996) standards we have provided are logical to us, but again you should exercise your judgment with analogy use as with any pedagogical tool. You may see a better fit with another standard that you may have struggled to meet. Likewise, the analogies here can be linked to a variety of other national standards, and the links provided here thus serve to illustrate how analogies can be used to meet national educational standards rather than how they must be used.

PART I

How We Can Use Analogies to Improve Science Teaching

1

Teaching With Analogies

Friends or Foes?

Allan G. Harrison

CHAPTER OVERVIEW

- Analogies and models are excellent teaching and learning tools.
- Analogies help students visualize abstract concepts like atoms, energy, and genes.
- Scientists use analogies to construct new ideas.
- The familiar object is called the *analog,* and the science concept is called the *target.*
- The links between the analog, and the target are called *mappings.*
- Valid mappings are called *shared attributes;* invalid mappings are *unshared attributes.*
- Every analogy breaks down somewhere, so don't take analogies too literally.
- Analogies are most effective when students help design and elaborate them.

Introduction

The other day I sat in on a class and listened as a science teacher, whom I shall call Neil, described evaporation and condensation in a sealed bottle.

The students agreed that wet clothes dry in the air and water vapor condenses on cold drink cans; still, some of them were bothered by the idea of water molecules constantly escaping from and returning to the water's surface in the sealed water bottle. Neil saw their worried looks and realized that he needed a better explanation, so he told them his busy high-way analogy for physical equilibrium:

Neil: Most of you've got your Ls [learner's licenses], so you're behind wheels of cars?

Student: Yeah.

Neil: OK, where you live, your street runs into a major road [draws a map on the board]—[there are] three lanes in one direction and three lanes in the other way. Your parents taught you to drive at a quiet time. So here you are, at the stop sign, lined up ready to do a left-hand turn into traffic. If it's 2 a.m. in the morning, would that be an easy task?

Student: Yep.

Neil: Because the streets are free, [there are] no cars to block you. It's pretty much the same, [at] 5 a.m.: there's a couple of early birds off to work, maybe a few more. Let's draw a couple of cars in here, a couple there, one there. At 8 o'clock in the morn-ing, [how would it look] if this is the major road into the city?

Student: Packed—bumper to bumper.

Neil: Packed, cars everywhere heading into the city and a few going the other way. That's the real situation.

Student: You can't enter now.

Neil: Now for a real bizarre reason, you don't obey the stop sign, you don't look, you simply pull out, right at peak hour. What would happen to you?

Student: You'd be hit by a car, and roll it, really stack it.

Neil: Yeah, hit, roll, and you would be spun back off the road or somewhere like that. You'd cause complete traffic chaos [wouldn't you]? Now, I use this example because it demon-strates what happens when the amount of evaporated water above the liquid increases—vapor pressure increases till [the air] can hold no more. This is why we get condensation happening: after enough water's evaporated, it's full. When

> you're at the stop sign at 2 a.m. you just go straight out.
> There's nothing there to stop you—like when there's not
> much vapor in dry air. A few molecules [are around], but it's
> not crowded. So lots of cars can come out of this street and
> zoom into the road and go anywhere they want. Same thing
> happens at 5 a.m—[there are] a few more cars but the road
> isn't full—like there's still space for water to evaporate. But at
> 8 a.m. you get to the point where there's so many cars, the
> road's full [isn't it]? Can you turn in?

Student: Yea, when a car slows and pulls off.

Neil: Yep. One has to condense before another can evaporate—one
car leaves and then one can enter.

Neil has two favorite analogies for chemical equilibrium; the other is
called the School Dance Analogy and is summarized by Richard K. Coll in
Chapter 7 (for a fuller account of both, see Harrison & de Jong, 2005).

Neil carefully plans his stories because he knows that he needs to keep
his students interested if they are to engage with nonobserveable concepts. He tells stories, draws pictures, asks questions and talks his students
through each analogy. And near the end of each story, he explicitly links the
familiar experience with the science concept. For example, he points out
that in chemical equilibrium, the system must be closed, dynamic, and the
rate of the forward reaction must be equal to the rate of the reverse reaction.

Equilibrium is a difficult concept for science students at all grades. For
example, biologists tell us that plants and animals balance inputs and outputs to keep their internal environments constant. It's very important to
keep one's water content, salt and nutrient levels, and temperature constant. For mammals, keeping temperature constant is a matter of life and
death in the cold of winter and the heat of summer. If body temperatures
vary more than 2–3°C up or down, mammals can die. In summer, a fine
balance needs to be maintained between heat gain through the skin, evap-
orative cooling in the respiratory system, and heat produced by muscles.
The balance is different in winter, but healthy mammals balance heat gain
and loss, and they adapt their physiological balances to suit all seasons. We
call this *homeostasis*, and homeostatic equilibrium is dynamic, just like
chemical equilibrium. Thus in Chapter 6, Grady J. Venville uses the Student
Walking Up the Down Escalator Analogy to model homeostasis (the full
story is found in Harrison & Treagust, 1994b).

This book contains many analogies and models that teachers have used
to simplify and exaggerate important ideas. You'll even find a role play for
chemical reaction in Chapter 7. Role-plays are special analogies that can help
students see what happens in chemical reactions. And remember, the more
you involve your students in the elaboration and acting out of analogies, the
more likely they are to develop alternative conceptions from the ideas you

have in mind. In order to avoid these alternative conceptions, we need to discuss the learning theory behind teaching with analogies and models.

Teaching With Analogies

The attraction of analogies in science, mathematics, social studies, technology, and literature lies in the ability to explain abstract ideas in familiar terms. Teachers often say that an artery or vein is like a hose or tube; the earth is round like a ball; the eye works like a camera; and plants, animals, and microorganisms are classified into functional groups, like the separate sections for fresh foods, canned foods, stationery, and cleaning supplies in a supermarket (Grady J. Venville uses this analogy in Chapter 6). It is easy to see why analogies and models are important ways to describe and explain objects and processes, especially those that cannot be seen, like atoms and molecules.

We start by introducing some useful terms to simplify our discussion: in an analogy the everyday object, event or story that is well understood is called the *analog,* and the science concept to which it is compared is called the *target*. This terminology is itself a metaphor, like an analogy, because we all aim to reach targets; if you hit the target, you've succeeded. Explanations have aims so that when you understand the target (or science concept) it means you've achieved your aim.

The structural or functional links that can be made between the analog and the target are called *mappings*. Mappings can be

Positive: Having *shared attributes*—ways in which the target is like the analog

Negative: Having *unshared attributes*—ways in which the target is not like the analog

Neutral: When it is not clear whether the target is or is not like the analog

Teachers should always be sure of all the shared and unshared attributes for the analogies they plan to use with their students. Of course, students can suggest their own analogies, and when this happens, some of the mappings are neutral and the challenge is to work out whether they are shared, unshared, or irrelevant. Many teachers skip this step saying that they are short of time, but it's important to help students make sense of their original ideas. These are the moments when students think creatively, and such moments can be high points in their learning.

Some teachers say that they are wary of analogies because they cannot predict how their students will interpret them. This is a real problem, and Shawn Glynn (1991) called analogies *two-edged swords* because analogies can simultaneously build scientific understandings and alternative conceptions. While teachers are wary of analogies, they show few inhibitions when using models to describe and explain ideas. It seems that the concrete nature of scale models is somehow treated as true, whereas personalized stories are open to interpretation.

Models and analogies are both human inventions and should be taught with care. Ball-and-stick and space-filling molecular models are very popular in science and chemistry, but the distinction between shared and unshared attributes is almost as vague with these as in a verbal analogy. Do the sticks bonds in molecular models and ionic lattices stand for real submicroscopic objects? Of course not; but many students think they do. Studies in classrooms show that models are loaded with as many interpretive problems as verbal analogies; for instance, bouncing balls in kinetic theory models of solids, liquids, and gases lead students to think that molecules are solid.

Most Models Are Analogies

In this book we treat analogical models and verbal analogies in the same way, and we apply the recommendations for improving teaching analogies to analogical models. Indeed, the widespread scientific acceptance of analogical models sometimes desensitizes teachers to the problems students have when trying to interpret analogical models. For instance, a teacher once said that an earthworm is like a simple tube or a packet of LifeSavers. When the teacher who designed this analogy simplified an earthworm in this way, the idea was to help the students realize that the materials inside the gut are outside of the earthworm's body. Ideas like this are not necessarily obvious, so we need to point out the key ideas in our favorite analogies.

A model of an analogy is shown in Figure 1.1. The *analogy* box overlaps the *analog* and *target* to show that the analogy is a thinking tool that can vary in the degree to which it connects or merges with the analog and the target. Next, Figure 1.2 shows how a camera can be used as an analogy for the eye using the analog-target mappings. (You may be asking whether students have a reliable understanding of how a camera works. The camera-eye analogy is used here only because it is popular and highlights some of the problems involved in analogy use.)

Research says that it is important to guide students and help them work out when and how a science concept is *like* an analog and when and how the concept is *unlike* the analog (Duit, 1991). All analogies break down somewhere, and it is important to discuss which scientific knowledge can be derived from an everyday object, event, or story and which cannot. Analogies and models are human creations and should be adapted and improved to suit new situations and problems. Analogical thinking is an excellent example of *constructivist learning,* and rather than not use analogies because they are imperfect, use them in ways that encourage students to map each analogy, suggest ways to improve them, and even create their own. Indeed, Aubusson and Fogwill (2006) argue that *imperfect analogies* are excellent learning tools because they expose the difficulties and problems

Figure 1.1   A Model of an Analogy and an Analogical Model

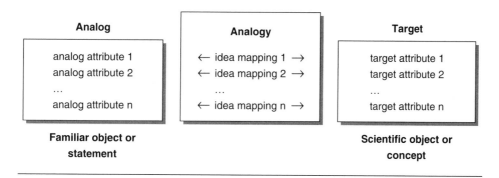

that arise when trying to describe and explain abstract ideas. Well-managed analogies make students think about what they are learning and help them craft better explanations.

Analogies and Scientific Discovery

Some people think that using analogies is a less-than-scientific way to explain natural phenomena. This ignores their popularity in explanations and the fact that some science concepts are unexplainable without analogies. For example, Harrison and Treagust (2000) watched an expert teacher use the wheels analogy to explain why light changes direction when it passes from air into glass (it bends towards the normal) and why it refracts the other way when it passes from glass into air (it bends away from the normal).

Have you noticed the distorted images caused by old window glass? Have you ever wondered why a pool of water looks shallower than it really is? Or have you seen a mirage on a paved road in summer? When I first thought about these effects, I said, "Surely there's a good scientific explanation for this bending—one that explains refraction in terms of atoms and molecules." Well, there isn't. The only explanation I found in the 56 textbooks I reviewed, from Grade 9 to third year of university, was analogical. Light "waves" bend or change direction for the same reason that water waves bend and change direction. Light changes direction because it slows down when it passes from air to glass (or water) and it speeds up when it goes the other way. This analogy is explained in detail in Chapter 8. Concepts like refraction help us understand why analogies are important thinking tools in science education—because they are thinking tools in science.

Thus, when David F. Treagust and I studied the types of explanation used in science classrooms, we realized that we needed to find an exemplary one to use as a model. The model explanation we found was Richard Feynman's first lecture—"Atoms in Motion"—in *Six Easy Pieces* (Feynman, 1994). Our analysis of this lecture showed that Feynman used 12 analogies to explain nonobserveable phenomena, and 5 of these analogies are listed in Table 1.1.

Figure 1.2   The Analogy: The Camera Is Like an Eye

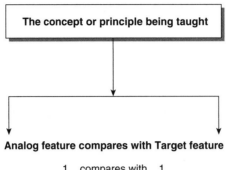

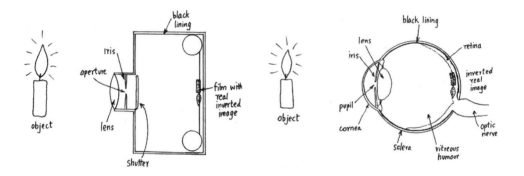

CAMERA is like the EYE

variable aperture suits brightness	pupil size varies to suit brightness
image recorded on the film	image on retina is sent to the brain
lens cap protects lens	eyelid protects the eye's cornea
can focus on near and far objects	can focus on near and far objects
black inside of camera stops reflections	black inside of eye stops reflections

CAMERA is not like the EYE

is limited to quite bright light	adapts to very low and very bright light
permanent single image	multiple nonpermanent images
one image	two images for binocular vision

Table 1.1   Five Analogies Used in *Atoms in Motion* (Feynman, 1994)

1. Paramecia are like "small football-shaped things swimming back and forth" (p. 4).

2. Molecules in water are moving "like a crowd at a football game seen from a very great distance" (p. 4).

3. "If an apple is magnified to the size of the earth, then the atoms in the apple are approximately the size of the original apple" (p. 5).

4. An atom hitting a moving piston in a cylinder is "like a ping-pong ball hitting a moving paddle" (p. 8).

5. Brownian motion is "like a game of push-ball" (pp. 19–20).

Scientists Using Analogies

The fact that Stephen Hawking (1988) used at least 74 everyday analogies in *A Brief History of Time* to explain astrophysics and quantum ideas shows their utility. To explain that the universe is expanding in all directions at once, he says "the situation is rather like a balloon with a number of spots painted on it being steadily blown up" (p. 45). On page 115 he muses that we could capture a black hole by "towing a large mass in front of it, rather like a carrot in front of a donkey." The noted physicist Robert Oppenheimer (whose team built the first atomic bomb) claims that most of the significant advances in science used analogy as a thinking tool. Numerous analogies can be gleaned from the history of science to show that scientific progress is helped by analogical thinking. For instance, thinking about the workings of a clock helped Johannes Kepler (1571–1630) develop his ideas of planetary motion, and Watson (1968) and his colleague Crick claim that they arrived at the double helix structure of DNA by making analogical models that fit the data. Richard K. Coll even begins his chapter on chemistry analogies by retelling the analogy Kekulé used: a *snakes biting their tails* analogy to suggest a molecular structure for benzene. A sample of other scientific discoveries that used analogical thinking is presented in Table 1.2.

Are Analogies Effective in Classrooms?

Ample evidence supports the claim that analogies and models are popular tools of trade for scientists, but the degree to which school students are able to understand and manipulate analogical models remains an open question. Students do not have the experience, knowledge, or time to create and test analogies like scientists do. But students are imaginative and can think

Table 1.2   Scientific Discoveries That Used Analogical Thinking
to Advance Science

Maxwell's mathematical descriptions of Faraday's electric lines of force used water pressure in tubes.

Robert Boyle imagined elastic gas particles as coiled springs.

Huygens used water waves to understand light phenomena.

Konrad Lorenz used analogy to explain streamlined motion in birds and fish.

In particle physics, analogical thinking led to the discovery of mesons.

Kekulé derived his idea for a benzene ring from an image of a snake biting its tail.

---

creatively, provided the problem is interesting and there are suitable analogs in their everyday experiences.

Still, what works for the investigative scientist may be of little value to students unless the teacher knows the benefits and pitfalls of analogy and monitors them. For example, Mark Cosgrove (1995) described science in the making when a class of 14-year-old boys proposed, applied, and modified their own analogies for electric current over a period of two weeks. Instead of teaching the scientific view, the teacher encouraged the students to suggest analogical theories, make and test their circuit predictions, and modify their analogies to fit the results. "The refinement of the student-generated analogy for electricity provided the students with a framework within which to reason" (p. 306), culminating in a scientifically acceptable model for current. This approach fits the curriculum aim of having students think and work scientifically. Analogy is a facile and friendly tool for students because it allows them to declare their preconceptions in a less judgmental context than having to commit themselves to right or wrong answers on biology, chemistry, or physics problems.

Nevertheless, some research suggests that while analogies are commonplace in human communication, they are not as effective in the classroom as might be expected (Duit, 1991). Uncritical use of analogies tends to generate alternative conceptions, and this is especially so when unshared attributes are treated as valid or where the learners are unfamiliar with the analogy. Indeed, in using any analogy, care needs to be taken to ensure that an impression is not conveyed that the analog is a true description of the target concept.

Analogies, Learning Theories, and the Personal Construction of Knowledge

Most analogy researchers agree that analogies promote learning through a constructivist pathway (Duit, 1991). Constructivism claims that people have rich mental environments that are made up of familiar experiences and knowledge; interests, events, and stories; and their own ideas of what counts as evidence and knowledge. The degree to which a new concept fits this mental environment determines its fit: whether it is accepted, modified, or rejected. Even young students have well-developed ideas of how they think the world works, and children's preconceptions can hinder learning in science. Four decades ago, David Ausubel (1968) pointed out that these "preconceptions [are] amazingly tenacious and resilient to extinction" (p. 336). Research since that time has shown that student preconceptions are so strong that, in some cases, they are preserved in the face of obvious and contradictory evidence (Osborne & Freyberg, 1985). Some students accept the teacher's science for the duration of the topic being studied and revert to their intuitive views following instruction. In other instances, students construct separate schema to accommodate the lesson content without altering their preconceived views.

Both preconceptions and learned misconceptions resist conceptual change (e.g., Nussbaum & Novick, 1982). Some teachers find this worrying, but the strength of all types of student conceptions means that acceptable conceptions, once learned, are robust and long lasting. Using analogies to learn science can be described as conceptual growth (the expansion of acceptable student conceptions) or conceptual change (revision of existing unscientific conceptions) or both. The teaching for conceptual change emerged around the same time as interest rose in analogical teaching. Most of the studies into conceptual change and learning with analogies were based, at least in part, on Piagetian theories (e.g., Curtis & Reigeluth, 1984; Glynn, 1991). Since the 1980s, researchers have interpreted learning with analogies using Piaget's equilibrium concepts (Gabel & Sherwood, 1980), Vygotsky's zone of proximal development (Cosgrove, 1995), Ausubel's meaningful learning (Harrison, Grayson, & Treagust, 1999), and social constructivist viewpoints. While most studies of analogy claim to be constructivist, few explicitly tie their theory and methods to theorists like Piaget and Vygotsky.

Piaget's stage development ideas suggest that younger children will benefit most from concrete analogies, analogs they can see and feel. It is reasonable to expect that the abstract thinking that emerges in Grades 8–10 will enhance the effectiveness of verbal and abstract analogies with older students who have begun to master mental models. Teachers should be cautious when using abstract analogies, as even some older students may not possess the necessary visualization skills. This is why teachers must ensure that their students understand the everyday object or experience that is the basis for the analogy. Vygotsky's (as cited in Cosgrove, 1995) theory recommends locating the analog in the students' zone of proximal development. Knowledgeable peers (other students) and adults (teachers) provide the "need to know" information that helps the student to correctly map the similarities and differences between the everyday analog experience and the target concept. Peers and teachers provide the knowledge that can be processed by the learner but is not yet known by the learner. As constructivists point out, it is the student who ultimately has to see and understand the shared analog-target attributes that lead to conceptual growth. Learning is the personal construction of new knowledge or the restructuring of old knowledge. Analogies help students learn and remember scientific ideas. Analogies also are powerful inquiry tools because they suggest new questions, relationships, and investigations.

Analogical learning does improve teaching. When Treagust, Duit, Joslin, and Lindauer (1992) surveyed analogy use in school science lessons, they found a low incidence of systematic analogy use, and they observed that no teacher whom they studied identified where the analogies they did use broke down. Ten years later, Harrison (2001) found that half the teachers that he studied, all drawn from the same community that Treagust et al. (1992) had studied, were discussing with their students where the analogies they used broke down.

Analogies That Enhance Concept Learning

Teachers who are aware of important and common alternative conceptions (well documented by Driver, Squires, Rushworth, & Wood-Robinson, 1994) often resort to analogies because they realize that it is much easier for students to accept a scientific idea if it agrees with something they already understand and accept. For example, students know that something is used up in a flashlight circuit because the batteries go flat. When they learn that a current flows from the battery to the light-bulb and back to the battery (see Figure 1.3), they conclude that more current flows out to the globe than flows back to the battery because something has to be consumed. Changing this idea has occupied many teachers and researchers who have come up with the following analogies for a series circuit:

> A continuous train that picks up people at one station (the battery) and drops them off at another station (the lightbulb; see Figure 1.4a)
>
> A bicycle whose continuous chain transfers energy from the pedals and gear wheel (battery) to the sprocket on the rear wheel (the light-bulb; see Figure 1.4b)
>
> A conveyer belt that picks up coal at the mine (the battery) and drops it into nearby railway wagons (lightbulb)
>
> A student who walks around a circle of other students (the circuit) giving jelly beans to three or four students who have correctly answered the teacher's questions (the teacher is the battery and the students the lightbulb; see Figure 1.4c)

Figure 1.3 The Battery, Globe, Switch, and Connections in a Flashlight

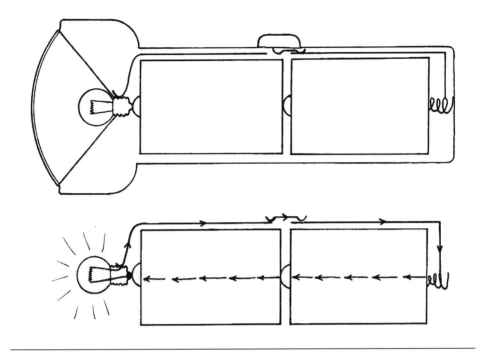

Figure 1.4a A Simple Series Circuit Is Like a Continuous Train

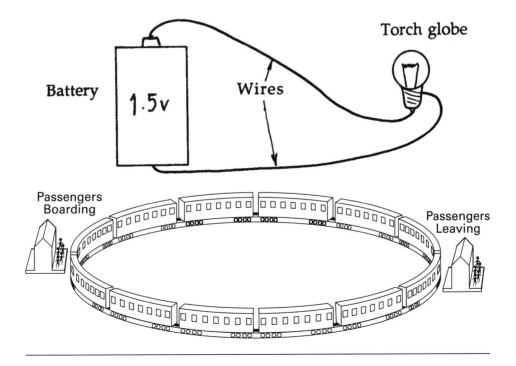

Figure 1.4b   A Series Circuit Is Like the Continuous Drive Chain on a Bicycle

Figure 1.4c   A Series Circuit Is Like Evenly Sharing Jelly Beans Around a Circle of Students

Rather than using just one of these analogies, using two or three similar analogies side by side or in consecutive lessons is much better. One analogy may work for one group of students, a different analogy can make sense to another group, and some students need multiple similar explanations before

they will accept the scientific conception that current is conserved but the energy the current carries is used up. The importance of multiple analogies is discussed in detail in Chapter 4.

Process Analogies Are More Effective Than Structural Analogies

Many teachers' analogies are used to describe structural similarities. For instance, "a molecule of gas is like a rubber ball," "an artery is like a hose," and "rock strata are like cake layers." Teachers often assume that the students understand the sense in which these comparisons are made. In the first example, the teacher has in mind the idea that a gas molecule is elastic, and when it collides with another molecule or the wall of its container, it will rebound with about the same speed and energy that it had before the collision. Unless students have this relationship explained to them, some may understandably visualize the molecule as just a round object while others may think of it as a moving elastic sphere. That is, they may pay more attention to the analogy's structural attributes and too little attention to the interaction effects.

Curtis and Reigeluth (1984) surveyed 26 science textbooks and found 216 analogies, which they classified into three types (see Figure 1.5). The most common type was the *simple analogy*, where the textbook writer made statements such as "a cell is like a small box" or "activation energy is like a hill." The grounds on which the comparison was based are not stated, and the student is left to interpret *how* a cell is like a box. (This analogy was used by Robert Hooke when he first described cork cells in 1665.) They also found a second type of analogy, where the grounds for the likeness were stated, and they called these *enriched analogies*. Take the example, "activation energy is like a hill because you have to add energy to the reacting substances to start the reaction." Enriching the analogy does more than tell the student under what conditions the analogy holds; it tells the student that the analogy is about processes, about dynamic functions and not limited to superficial structures. Indeed, the difference between a simple structural analogy and an enriched functional analogy is the addition of some form of causation: a simple analogy is descriptive, whereas an enriched analogy is more explanatory.

The final type identified by Curtis and Reigeluth (1984) is the *extended analogy*. Extended analogies contain a mix of simple and enriched mappings. The Eye Is Like a Camera Analogy is an extended one. The grounds on which an eye is like a camera are stated in each case, and there are multiple shared attributes in the analogy as well as some limitations or unshared attributes.

Dedre Gentner (1988) and her colleagues went further and studied the question, "Which types of analogy make the most useful learning tools?" Gentner's research showed that superficial structural similarities attract students to the analogy and help them recognize that useful similarities exist between the everyday situation and the science concept. However,

Figure 1.5   Simple Analogy Plus Three Levels of Enrichment for Textual
Analogies

Simple Analogy	Analog	←————————→	Target
Enriched Analogy	Analog	←grounds (limitations)→	Target
Extended Analogies		←grounds (limitations)→	
	Analog	←grounds (limitations)→	Target
		←grounds (limitations)→	
	Analog	←grounds (limitations)→	
	Analog	←grounds (limitations)→	Target
	Analog	←grounds (limitations)→	

SOURCE: Adapted from Curtis and Reigeluth (1984, p. 111).

she points out that if that is all we expect from the analogy, then students
will derive limited and unpredictable ideas from the pairing. For example,
one teacher I worked with decided to use The Continuous Train Analogy
to explain why current is conserved in an electric circuit. Partway through
the explanation in class, she found herself concluding that electric current
slows down when it reaches a resistor because the train slowed at a station
to drop off its load! Subsequent discussion showed that her problem partly
arose because she concentrated more on mapping the analog's structures
than its functions.

This is Gentner's (1988) point: structural analogy opens the door to
analogical possibilities, but it is only the functional relationships that can
build conceptual understanding. Her view is that analogy is much more
than similarity, and students benefit most when "not just shared relations
but shared higher-order relations" are recognized and understood (p. 76).
She claims that systematically related mappings (i.e., extended analogies)
are much more effective in achieving learning about the target than single
or simple mappings.

Analogy is an excellent strategy for explaining how science processes
work, and if we do not exploit this benefit of analogy, why use it? Analogy
requires considerable mental effort and teaching time, and analogies are
conceptually risky if the shared and unshared attributes are not carefully
mapped. So why use an analogy for structural outcomes when it requires
so much effort and vigilance? This warning is not an argument for not
using analogies; rather, it is an endorsement for using analogies in prepared and systematic ways that develop higher-order thinking. (This issue
will be taken up by Grady J. Venville in Chapter 2 when she explains the
FAR Guide.) Analogies are discovery tools in science, mathematics, and
social science and should be used because they are interesting and help

build knowledge. Also, we will never eliminate analogy from language because language is inherently analogical. The argument presented here is to think and plan your analogies carefully. If you choose analogies that help students understand science processes, you will be surprised by the learning gains your students will make.

IMPORTANT POINTS TO REMEMBER

- An analog should be *familiar* to the students and easy for them to visualize.
- Analog-target mappings should be systematic and begin with a simple structural analogy and extend to higher-order thinking.
- The *places where an analogy breaks down* should always be discussed.
- Teaching analogies should be interesting and suggest new ideas.

Conclusion

Analogy and analogical thinking is central to science and to thinking and working scientifically. Certain cautions should be observed when explaining with or developing an analogy: the analogy should be interesting and familiar, and the shared and unshared attributes need to be negotiated with students. Analogies are powerful higher-order thinking tools that help scientists and everyday people make sense of the natural phenomena that surround them. But analogies can be two-edged swords. Always point out to your students where the analogy breaks down.

The chapters that follow examine many of the popular analogies used in teaching biology, chemistry, earth science, and physics. Some analogies are effective knowledge-building tools; others have been found to encourage alternative conceptions if not used carefully. Thus, in Chapter 2, Grady J. Venville synthesizes 10 years of research into teaching with analogies and explains how to use the Focus-Action-Reflection (FAR) Guide. In Chapter 3, Neil Taylor and Richard K. Coll discuss analogies that increase student interest and show teachers how they can use analogies as motivational tools. In Chapter 4, Allan G. Harrison examines why multiple analogies are better than the one-size-fits-all analogy. Richard K. Coll and David F. Treagust use Chapter 5 to explore ways to encourage students and teachers to develop their own explanatory and understanding-widening analogies. Chapters 6 through 9 present sets of biology, chemistry, physics, and earth science analogies.

2

The Focus-Action-Reflection (FAR) Guide—Science Teaching Analogies

Grady J. Venville

CHAPTER OVERVIEW

- When using an analogy, it needs to be appropriate for the science content and the student.
- Teachers need to discuss where the concept is like the analog and where it breaks down.
- Teachers should use a systematic method when presenting analogies to their students.
- The FAR Guide is a systematic format for presenting analogies.
- Planning should focus on why the concept is difficult and what the students already know.
- The analogy should be familiar and interesting to the students.
- Teachers should reflect on how they presented an analogy and how their students responded.
- Planning analogies with students is an excellent way to enhance scientific thinking.

Teachers' Use of Analogies When Teaching Science

Analogies are a quick and interesting way to explain nonobservable science objects, such as atoms, and abstract processes, such as gene action. However, in their research, Venville and Treagust (2002) found that some popular analogies used by science teachers are ineffective. This was the impetus for the development of a model that can be used for improving teaching with analogies and that forms the basis for all the analogies presented in this book. For example, we observed one science teacher teaching introductory genetics; let's call him Jason. He explained that the nucleus of the cell is like a "computer" because it "controls the cell's functions." He said that the structure of DNA is like the lookout tower in King's Park (a DNA-inspired structure in a popular park in Perth, Australia; see Figure 2.1). He also described the genetic code as being like a blueprint or an architect's plan of what you are going to look like. Jason did not present a detailed description of any of these analogies, spending less than three minutes on all of them in total. He did not outline any specific features that were similar between

Figure 2.1   The DNA Tower in King's Park (Perth, Australia): Like One Strand of a DNA Molecule

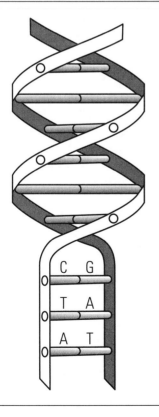

the analog and target or any features that might be different. Analogies used in this limited way, without extension, lose the potential for helping students with their understanding of scientific concepts.

It is also interesting to note that Richard Dawkins (1989) in his famous book, *The Selfish Gene,* pointed out that our modern knowledge of the way in which genes are expressed has rendered the concept of a genetic blue-print obsolete. He suggested that it would be better to visualize the genetic information as a recipe or series of instructions for creating an organism. The point to be made here is *that the appropriateness of the analog is a critical aspect of using analogies* that science teachers need to consider. Many science classes today are occupied by students from diverse backgrounds, and this compounds the issue of finding analogs that are familiar to all students.

As the vast majority of science teachers have no formal training in the use of analogies, it is not surprising that analogies are used less effectively than they could be. Our observations of teachers' use of analogies resulted in our recognizing the need for a teaching model for more effective presentation of science analogies. Such a model could be used for professional development and teacher training and as a template for teachers to improve the delivery of their favorite analogies.

IMPORTANT POINT TO REMEMBER

If analogies are to be used effectively by science teachers, a carefully planned strategy is required, one designed to make the analogies relevant to as many students as possible.

Teacher Involvement in Developing a Model for Teaching With Analogies

Our studies of teachers' use of analogies and the development of teaching models for more effective presentation of science analogies occupied at least 10 years. Because the studies often involved prolonged engagement with high school teachers and their students, many were reported as case studies (e.g., Venville & Bryer, 2002).

The first phase of the research involved scrutinizing the literature to identify any models for systematically presenting instructional analogies and running trials of the model's effectiveness in the classroom. Five experienced science teachers were involved in using the models from the literature to present their favorite analogies in their classrooms. The efficacy of these models was evaluated using in-class observations and postlesson interviews with students and teachers.

Analysis of the teachers' performances, their reflective comments, and evaluations of student understanding showed that the models neglected two important aspects of effective teaching, namely, lesson planning and postclass reflection. The researchers envisaged a model that encouraged teachers to think about analogies and their presentation before, during, and following lessons. This led to the development of a teachers' guide stressing the *Focus, Action, Reflection* aspects of teaching, and the model was called the FAR Guide for teaching with analogies.

The final phase of this process involved disseminating the FAR Guide through numerous workshops in schools and at local, national, and international conferences. The developers were aware of the need to remain sensitive to teachers' comments and to be ready to make minor adjustments to the model as the need arose. Preliminary evaluations of the FAR Guide consisted of seeking teachers' views about the Guide following workshops conducted at science teachers' conferences. This was followed by observations of six experienced teachers using the FAR Guide in their classrooms. The feedback provided by both groups led to refinements and resulted in the current form of the FAR Guide The contribution of practicing teachers to this development of the Guide is gratefully acknowledged and applauded. The critical views of the participant teachers provided invaluable information in the formative development of the FAR Guide, meaning we can have confidence about its use in teaching science using analogies.

The FAR Guide: An Effective Model for Presenting Science Analogies

The purpose of the FAR Guide is to help teachers maximize the benefits and minimize the problems when analogies arise in classroom discourse or in textbooks. The guide was designed, as much as possible, to reflect the skilled way in which exemplary, practiced teachers use analogies to teach about science. Because the three phases—Focus, Action, Reflection—are quite self-explanatory and epitomize good teaching, most teachers assimilate the FAR Guide into their practice with ease. The three phases of the Guide are summarized in Figure 2.2 so that teachers can quickly recall the necessary steps for effective analogy instruction. More detailed explanations of each of the phases follow:

1. **Focus**. In teaching with analogies, teachers should initially consider the difficult aspects of the concept to be taught (difficulties for both the teacher and the students). During this first phase, the teacher should explore whether or not the students already know something about the target concept and whether or not they have alternative conceptions. Questions about how the analogy can reinforce appropriate conceptions and challenge inappropriate conceptions can be addressed. This is the time for teachers to determine whether their students are familiar with the analog and plan how student familiarity and common understandings of the analog can be enhanced through the use of examples or descriptions. If teachers find that they cannot make the analogy work at this stage, then

the analogy should not be attempted in the class. This *focus* on analogical instruction should take place both before and within the early part of the lesson, depending upon the circumstances; however, some degree of focus before the lesson commences seems to be critical and essential to effective analogy use.

2. **Action**. The action phase of analogical teaching involves the teacher giving careful attention to the students' *familiarity* with the analog and the *like* and *unlike* attributes of the analog and the target. To achieve this, similarities are explicitly drawn between the features of the analog and target in a process called *mapping of shared attributes*. This is the essence of analogical instruction and should be extended, elaborated, argued, negotiated, dramatized, drawn, and written, as necessary, to help the students understand the higher-order principles that the target concept and the analog have in common. In addition to the mapping of shared attributes, the ways that the analog and target are unlike are also explicitly identified. This process can involve negotiating with the students where the analogy breaks down and determining the limitations of the analogy so that students do not extend the analogy beyond its usefulness.

3. **Reflection**. Following the presentation of the analogy, the teacher reflects on the clarity and usefulness of the analog as well as the conclusions drawn from it. Subsequently, the teacher should consider ways in which the analog, the mappings, or the analogy's position in the lesson may be improved. This *reflection* phase may take place during the lesson itself or after the lesson as later preparation occurs. In practice, these phases are not distinct but run into one another. Because reflection is a characteristic of all good teaching, competent teachers will likely implement this step as a matter of course.

The phases of the FAR Guide have become second nature to those teachers who have become familiar with them, and these phases have been usefully applied to the teaching of analogies.

An Example of How to Use the FAR Guide: The Cell Is Like a City Analogy

Introductory biology courses almost always include the interesting topic of the cell, and young students are fascinated with looking through microscopes at stained onion and cheek cells. The topic is less interesting, however, when the topic focuses on submicroscopic organelles (tiny structures inside cells) and the functioning of the cell. In this situation, an analogy between the cell and a city can be used to inject some fun into the learning as well as to create a window of opportunity for the students to learn about this abstract, unfamiliar, and seemingly inaccessible world. The FAR Guide

Figure 2.2   The FAR Guide for Teaching and Learning With Analogies

Focus	
Concept	Is it difficult, unfamiliar, or abstract?
Students	What do the students already know about the concept?
Analog	Is the analog something your students are familiar with?
Action	
Likes	Discuss the features of the analog and the science concept. Draw similarities between them.
Unlikes	Discuss where the analog is unlike the science concept.
Reflection	
Conclusions	Was the analogy clear and useful, or confusing? Did it achieve your planned outcomes?
Improvements	In light of the outcomes, are there any changes you need to make next time you use this analogy?

is used as a template to consider the teaching of the cell through the use of an analogy with a city.

Focus

Cells are microscopic and abstract entities. The most difficult aspect about cells for high school students is learning the functions of the various organelles and understanding that they are coordinated and function as a holistic unit. Students may already have appropriate or inappropriate concepts about the cell and organelles from previous classes, as this topic can be taught at different levels, particularly in elementary (primary), middle, and high school. Young students often get cells confused with atoms and molecules because all have nuclei.

An important question to consider with this analogy is whether the analog of the city is something your students are familiar with. Most students are familiar with a city or a town and working components of a city, such as the power station, roads, building sites, hospitals, and so on. Experience has shown that some students have limited experience with a city or town council, however, and may not fully understand what the local government is responsible for. Therefore, teachers need to explicitly teach this aspect of the analogy, if necessary.

Action

The action phase of this analogy can be implemented in one of two ways. The teacher can outline features of a city that are like features of a cell. For example, the teacher could explain the similar control and coordination functions of the nucleus of a cell and the city council; that the mitochondria in a cell are like the power stations in a city because they both provide energy; that the plastids are like warehouses because they store things and the Golgi bodies are like factories because they produce substances that are to be used outside the cell or city. The beauty of this analogy is that with a little imagination, it can be extended to help the students learn about many of the organelles of the cell and create a picture of an integrated, functioning unit. Don't be afraid to develop analogies like this further; just remember to do the mapping of both shared and unshared attributes.

Another way to approach the action phase is to have the students work together in groups to develop the analogy themselves. You can provide the students with a worksheet (see Figure 2.3 for an example) that encourages them to be creative and give full reasons why they feel some parts of the cell are like parts of a city.

With either approach it's very important to review the features of the analog and target that are not similar. For example, a city is much larger than a cell, cells tend to be packed much closer together than cities (at least in some countries), and there are various limitations for each organelle; for example, modern cities don't have a peripheral physical barrier like the cell membrane or cell wall.

Reflection

It is worthwhile for the teacher to talk to some of the students to check whether the analogy was clear and useful or was confusing. If group work was used, the teacher can check the worksheets or get the students to do a class presentation to ensure that the ideas generated by the students are appropriate. One student that I spoke to after this analogy was used in her classroom thought that the function of the nucleus was to clean the cell. This was due to her rather simple view that the city council was solely responsible for taking garbage and rubbish away. The teacher can reflect on student responses like this and make improvements or adjustments for the next time it is used.

How to Adapt Your Analogies to the FAR Guide

It is possible, and certainly advisable, for teachers to adapt their favorite and frequently used analogies to the FAR Guide. This is a straightforward process of working through the steps of the Guide (Figure 2.1) and answering or developing answers to each of the questions. We suggest that the analogy be written down in a similar way to the analogies presented in this book.

Teachers should initially *focus* to ensure that the concept is difficult and needs an analogy, to make explicit the students' preinstructional ideas, and to ensure that the analog is something their students are familiar with. At the very least, the like and unlike features between the analogy and the target

Figure 2.3   Sample Worksheet for Students Working in Groups to Map the Attributes of the Cell-City Analogy

Group Worksheet

The organelles of a cell have similar functions to some parts of a city. Work with the students in your group and think about the parts of a city that have similar functions to the organelles that you have learned about. Feel free to refer to your textbook. Write down the organelle, the part of the city that your group thinks is similar, and the function they have in common. Here is an example for you to follow:

CELL	FUNCTION	CITY
	How the Cell is LIKE a City	
Nucleus	The nucleus controls and coordinates all the cell's structures and functions so that all the parts work together.	The city council controls roads, buildings, shops, and parks by making laws and checking that the correct things are done.
	How the Cell Is NOT LIKE a City	
Cell wall	The cell has a wall that encloses the cell's contents.	Most cities do not have walls surrounding them.

should be written down before the analogy is used in the classroom. Finally, it is important for the teacher to *reflect* on the teaching sequence and decide whether the analogy was clear or confusing and to decide on improvements for future use.

Teachers' Views of Their Practice With the FAR Guide

Several teachers who participated in workshops on the FAR Guide were observed as they taught science with analogies in their classrooms. Subsequent interviews revealed that the FAR Guide had affected their use of analogies in the following ways:

Confidence and enthusiasm. Teachers felt renewed enthusiasm for using analogies to help students understand scientific concepts. More important, they had increased confidence in the validity of the use of analogies as a pedagogical tool after they had attended the workshops.

Student familiarity with the analog. Teachers found that the most important part of the FAR Guide was their increased awareness of the need to establish students' familiarity with the analog.

Delineating like and unlike features. One teacher found that the action phase, in particular, helped her to focus on the main points of the analogy. Other teachers recognized the need to be clear and explicit about the similarities and differences between the analog and target as this provided both teachers and students with a strong basis for further learning.

Reflection. Reflecting on their analogies helped teachers critique their explanations and guided plans to improve future presentations.

Teachers' content knowledge. Teachers often lacked the knowledge to clearly delineate the limitations of analogies used to explain concepts outside their specialized content areas. This problem can be addressed by careful personal research prior to using the analogy or by working with a teacher who has the expertise to answer the difficult questions that students ask. It is important for teachers to thoroughly understand the content that they intend to explain by the use of an analogy. (We address this aspect for a series of analogies presented in Part II.)

Training students to use analogies. Several teachers recommended training students to interpret analogies, to understand why analogies are important in science as well as their advantages and disadvantages. In their research, Venville, Bryer, and Treagust (1993) have shown the value of training students to use an analogy in order to highlight its limitations.

Using the FAR Guide in Science Teacher Education

Two areas where the FAR Guide has been successfully used are inservice and preservice teacher education. Both contexts appear to be suitable settings for enhancing teachers' presentations of analogies. Inservice education is a sensitive issue and requires, at the minimum, a clearly defined process, material and social support, teacher commitment to improvement, and ownership of the change process.

While the FAR Guide is mostly self-explanatory, productive outcomes have emerged from cooperative in-class partnerships. Individual teachers can accommodate the FAR Guide into their practice because it models preexistent expert practice, namely, prelesson focus, in-class action, and postlesson reflection. Our experience suggests that the best results emerge when two or more teachers work together using the FAR Guide to present their favorite analogies to each other and then to students. Cooperative planning, implementation, observation, and critical discussions about each other's use of the FAR Guide appear to maximize the benefits for both teachers and students.

IMPORTANT POINTS TO REMEMBER

- Some form of student training is needed if students are to understand and use analogies well.
- It is best if two or more teachers work together using the FAR Guide to present analogies.

The FAR Guide has also been used with final-year preservice teachers in Australia for several years. In a final-year science pedagogy unit, student teachers examine explanatory analogies and are confronted by many of the alternative conceptions that arise during uncritical analogy use. The FAR Guide is then introduced, explained and discussed, and pairs of students are asked to choose an appropriate concept to present to the class using an analogy. Each analogical microteaching episode is presented to the preservice group and treated as a school science lesson segment. The analogy, FAR Guide presentation, and the explanation are critically reviewed by the group and suitably modified for future use. The preservice students also are encouraged to present analogies in the FAR Guide format while on teaching practice so that their use of the FAR Guide and analogical explanations can be critiqued by experienced teachers and university supervisors.

Conclusion

Teachers who have used the FAR Guide in their classrooms agree that it enhances student understanding of the science concepts explained using analogies. Provided teachers spend time negotiating each analog's familiarity and establishing the analogy's similarities and differences vis-à-vis the target with their students, analogies are powerful and motivating learning tools. The FAR Guide does more than just establish analog familiarity and ensure valid shared and unshared mapping, it encourages teachers to regularly self-evaluate their teaching, and this should result in enhanced teaching and learning.

3

Using Analogies to Increase Student Interest in Science

Neil Taylor

Richard K. Coll

CHAPTER OVERVIEW

- Much of our thinking is done in pictures, and even young students have vivid imaginations that help them see objects, stories, and situations in their mind's eyes.
- Adults and students enjoy making sense of new situations by seeing problems and scenarios in everyday terms.
- An additional value of analogy and analogies is that they are often used to raise interest in stories and jokes.
- Learning about nonobservable phenomena in science is enhanced when we can see and think about objects and processes in terms of everyday objects and events.

Analogies can link unfamiliar and abstract scientific concepts to familiar and concrete analogs that help students understand science objects and processes. Remember that in an analogy, the familiar object or event is called the *analog* and the science object or process is called the *target*. It is important to remember that an analog tells us something—but not everything—about the target concept. Effective analogies have a number of qualities: they are appropriate to the science, they are familiar and interesting, and they stimulate students' high-level thinking abilities. Analogies are excellent ways to explain science concepts like biological and chemical equilibrium and kinetic theory because students not only see how the science concept works, but they also realize that the science processes occur in their everyday lives.

Seeing an Analogy

When learners see the analogy between a familiar object or process and a difficult or nonobservable object or process, they make links between the object's parts and actions. Analogies are believed to increase students' interest and understanding by helping them visualize abstract concepts and by helping them compare similarities from the real world with the new concepts. While it is important that analogies be informative, they should not be trivial. Analogies are most effective when they explain processes and stimulate high-level thinking rather than just dealing with superficial similarities (Gentner, 1983). Thus describing in depth the scenario where a person walking up the down escalator is an analogy for homeostasis (Harrison & Treagust, 1994a) is more useful to a student's understanding than just stating superficially that an atom is like a ball. The conditions under which the analogy is seen to be correct do need to be discussed with students.

Motivation and interest are essential ingredients in effective learning. If students are not attracted to a concept or context, learning will almost certainly be limited. It is the student who decides whether or not to engage in concept learning, and this choice is almost always based on the question, "Do I want to learn this stuff?" Students choose to be involved in a topic for a variety of reasons, including interest in the task, rapport with the teacher, perceived value and utility of the knowledge, self-efficacy, and the social climate. This last factor is often ignored when teaching with analogies, but it is important. Classrooms are social settings, and Vygotsky's (1986) learning psychology helps us understand why social interaction is useful and suggests ways teachers can enhance their planning and teaching (e.g., by choosing analogies that are located in a student group's *shared* "zone of proximal development"). Social knowledge and experience is the most effective source of teaching analogies, and analogs *must be familiar* to the students (drawn from *their* life-world). Simply put, if an analog is not familiar or interesting, it should not be used.

Analogies can motivate students only if they are relevant and provide students with strong visual images that can be readily linked to abstract concepts. In many cases *humor also adds to the appeal of analogies* and helps students to remember both the analogy and the underlying concept. A male teacher we work with discusses most of his analogies in the contexts of sport, games, cars, and boy-girl relationships. He often tells stories that have the students laughing—at him and at his mistakes. But they like and remember his analogies and understand many of the concepts he explains through these highly motivational analogies.

The motivational dimension of analogies has often been overlooked. In this chapter we examine a number of analogies that provide strong visual representations, relevance, and, in some cases, incorporate humorous scenarios that are much more likely to engage students and increase their desire to learn. We have chosen analogies related mainly to the teaching of kinetic theory, a concept that is central to students' scientific understanding of a wide range of particle topics. This theory is particularly important for explaining the macroscopic properties of matter—solids, liquids, and gases. Kinetic theory emerged from the efforts of Robert Boyle and the nineteenth-century scientists who wanted to describe and explain the ways in which solid, liquid, and gas particles relate to each other. But published research suggests that kinetic theory is difficult for many students to understand. The most likely reason for this is that it deals with submicroscopic phenomena that are inaccessible to students. Before going on to tell you about some pertinent analogies, we outline the main points of kinetic theory.

Kinetic theory is used to explain the macroscopic behavior of the three phases of matter and the order-energy relationships between these phases. According to kinetic theory, solids have a fixed shape and volume, and the particles *vibrate* about fixed positions. In the liquid phase, matter still has a fixed volume but liquids take the shape of their container—because the particles, although still close together as in solids, are able to *move* or slide over one another. In solid and liquids, then, the particles are close enough to each other for the attractive forces between them to be important. Gases are different; they have variable volume and shape. In gases the particles are so far apart that interparticle forces can effectively be ignored, and the particles move in straight lines, colliding elastically with each other and also with the walls of the container.

In essence, kinetic theory requires students to think in pictures. Students need to visualize particles and understand the relationship between particles and their energy and realize that matter consists of tiny particles, called atoms and molecules, that are constantly in motion. Students need to visualize that particles in solids, liquids, and gases all have spaces between them. Andersson (1990) explains that the relative spacing of particles in the solid : liquid : gas phases is about 1 : 1 : 10. He also found that the dynamic picture of atoms and molecules in never-ending motion in empty space is not understood by many students, because they think that matter is continuous rather than particulate in nature. If students visualize solid particles as touching, it is hard for them to visualize liquid particles that move around in relation to each other as being the same distance apart as solid particles.

Harrison and Treagust (1994b) point out that it is very difficult for students to visualize how atoms and molecules are arranged and behave in these three phases because it is impossible for anyone to see even a very large molecule. For most students, matter can exist only as it is—as macroscopic "stuff," and this also prevents them from meaningfully understanding what happens in transitions between phases (e.g., from liquid to gas). Other research has shown that a lack of understanding of chemical concepts may be linked to students' inability to build complete mental models that represent particulate behavior (Williamson & Abraham, 1995).

Students Need to Think in Pictures

Clearly, for students to develop a meaningful understanding of many topics in the physical, life, and Earth and space sciences, they need to develop a robust conception of kinetic theory, and analogies are an effective way to achieve this.

Below are some interesting and amusing analogies that you can use to help guide your students toward the scientific conceptualization of kinetic theory. The point here is to show you how to increase student interest in a fun way.

The Beach Analogy

The beach is a place that most students can easily relate to, and it is also a place that students generally have positive feelings about; summer, the beach, friends and family, school holidays and breaks, all add up to excitement and fun. Hence the beach provides an excellent and interesting source of analogy, particularly for young people. The beach analogy described below (adapted from Pendlington, Palacio, & Summers, 1993), helps students visualize how a solid, which appears to be continuous, is in fact made up of very tiny particles that the eye simply cannot see.

Imagine that you are looking down on a white sandy beach from a high cliff. Can you see the individual grains of sand?

No, you can't. If you want to see and feel the sand, you must walk down onto the beach and get much, much closer before you can see the grains of sand. Imagine now that you are standing on the beach. Look down at the sand. Can you see the grains of sand now? Yes, you can now see, and touch, the grains of sand—and even feel them between your toes. See Figure 3.1.

Figure 3.1   The Beach Analogy

SOURCE: Reprinted with permission from Mike Summers.

So here we relate the particles of kinetic theory—something students find hard to understand or relate to—to the grains of sand, something almost all students will understand and will have experienced physically. You must always remember that the analog must be accessible to your students so that the target will be understandable. So if you live inland, miles away from a beach, then a desert or other sandy area might be a better analogy. The idea is much the same; the distance from the beach or sand dunes makes it hard to see the grains of sand. But when we get up close and personal, we can easily see the grains (i.e., the analog), which helps the students think of the particulate nature of substances (i.e., the target). Of course as we have noted before, you need to *think of ways in which the analog and target are not similar*, lest you introduce alternative conceptions at the same time. Here we are building up the notion of fine structure and, by using this analogy, we make the idea of the fine structure accessible to students, letting them realize that even though we cannot see individual molecules (or grains of sand from a distance), they nonetheless exist when we look at them more closely. But remember, grains of sand are not molecules; in this analogy the grains are *like* molecules just in that one aspect.

In some circumstances, the beach or desert analogy may not be suitable at all. In that case, we can develop this analogy using a similar idea: remember to tailor your analogy so that the analog is accessible to your students. For example, the beach or desert analogy can be developed further or replaced by providing students with tightly woven pieces of cloth and a magnifying glass or hand lens. Held at a distance the cloth appears to be continuous, but examined with a hand lens, the individual stitches of the weave are clearly evident. In this case, the weave is the analog of the particle rather than the grains of sand. This has the added benefit of giving you the opportunity to get your students to do a physical activity, rather than just telling them about something, like the beach or desert.

Another way to demonstrate this idea uses a printed color picture in a magazine. Look at the picture as if you are reading the magazine, then look at the picture using a 10x hand lens and finally with a microscope (e.g., 100x). You will see the tiny color dots that make up the picture, like the pixels on your TV screen. Now the dots of the color are the analog of the particles of the molecular substance.

These analogies allow students to link the very abstract concept that solids comprise tiny particles called atoms and molecules to concrete experiences that are familiar, relevant and interesting. The analogy helps them realize that even though they cannot see the particles of sand on the beach or the dots in the picture, the fine detail is there if we delve deeply enough. So too, solids, liquids and gases are made up of particles even though we cannot see them. Furthermore, these analogies are very visual and help students move toward a more particulate model of matter.

Using People to Model Energy

Understanding kinetic theory also requires students to think about the relationship between particles and energy. In other words, students must understand the scientific view that all particles can gain or lose energy. Energy is a very abstract concept with no obvious physical characteristics (although it manifests in many exciting ways). Students need to be aware of the impact energy can have on matter, particularly at the molecular level, if they are to understand physical and chemical change. Once again the use of analogy can provide the necessary stimulus to understand this crucial concept. Used in conjunction with compatible pedagogies, analogy can develop students' mental model of energy by helping them visualize the energy-particle relationship. The "What Is Energy?" analogy (Pendlington et al., 1993) provides an excellent way to help students understand this relationship.

In some respects, the idea of energy is like enthusiasm. When scientists say "particles have energy," it is *like* saying that people have enthusiasm (see Figure 3.2).

Anthropomorphic analogies, like the people analogy used here, are often used to teach kinetic theory's abstract explanation for the three phases of matter (e.g., Coffman & Tanis, 1990). Harrison and Treagust (1994b) also described an analogy for change of phase based on a classroom scenario that they have embedded within a modified version of the Teaching-With-Analogies Model developed by Glynn (1991). The activity (in this case, enthusiasm) of the individual is the analog of the energy of the particle—for which the person is the analog.

Students' understanding of kinetic theory's model for change of phase also can be developed through other similar anthropomorphic analogies that are pictorial in nature. The cartoons in Figure 3.3 again represent particles as people and show how changing the amount of energy the "particles"

Figure 3.2   Energy Is Like Enthusiasm

SOURCE: Reprinted with permission from Mike Summers.

Figure 3.3   Solid Particles Are Like Dancers

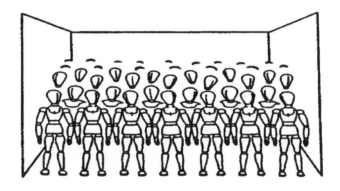

SOURCE: Reprinted with permission from Mike Summers.

have can lead to transformations at the macro level that are visible as change of phase—in this case, changes in a group of people's behavior.

Using People to Model Energy and Particle Relationships in a Solid

Kinetic theory provides scientists with a good picture of the energy relationships and interaction between particles; and although very simple, the theory provides a useful predictive model for the behavior of matter in its three different phases. The analogy builds on students' experiences and interests. It uses a familiar and positive real-world example that is accessible and entertaining.

Let's start with the solid phase and then go on to look at the other phases of matter as detailed by kinetic theory.

The Solid Phase—A Packed Nightclub or Dance Floor

Imagine a nightclub packed with people. It is so packed that the dancers are unable to move around and have very little enthusiasm for dancing. They can shake their heads, bob up and down, and sway slightly from side to side, but larger movements are not possible. These dancers are behaving like solid particles (Figure 3.3).

So here we present the key aspects of the solid phase as understood by kinetic theory: particles have low energy, little movement, and high order. The analog is reasonably simple: the dancers are the particles; they are in fixed positions (i.e., high particle order) because the place is crowded, so there is high order, and finally, particles can only vibrate, so like the dancers, they have little opportunity to move.

The Liquid Phase—A Closely Packed Nightclub or Dance Floor With Excited Dancers

We can build on the packed-dance-floor analogy to explain the next phase of matter, the liquid phase. We need to be wary of traps like unshared attributes, where the analogy breaks down. But let's look at the next use of this analogy, and then we can consider the traps.

The dancers are still closely packed but they have more enthusiasm than those in the analogy used for the solid. They are not fixed in one spot but can squeeze round each other, sliding around the dance floor and changing places. These dancers are like the particles of a liquid, close together but freer to move. So now the particles, while still close together, are able to move around and slide past each other. This is the key difference between the solid phase and liquid phase in the kinetic theory model. The spacing is much the same in the two phases, the interaction and extra movement are the differences. You must be careful of one of the real traps in student thinking here, the idea of spacing between particles in a solid. The spacing between liquid-liquid and solid-solid particles is almost the same (in fact, in the case of water and a few other substances, the molecules are closer together in the liquid phase). It is important to emphasize here that the difference in model and behavior is not due to spacing but to interactions, specifically, *attractions:* interparticle interactions in kinetic theory and interpersonal interactions in the analogy.

The Gas Phase—A Sparsely Populated Nightclub or Dance Floor With Very Excited Dancers

Let's now move on and use the dance floor analogy to explain the final phase of matter, the gaseous phase.

This time imagine the nightclub with just a few dancers and very good music. There is plenty of room, and they have lots of enthusiasm. They can dance wherever they like. They love the music so much they are dancing

Figure 3.4 Gaseous Particles Are Like Leaping Dancers

SOURCE: Reprinted with permission from Mike Summers.

very excitedly and can use up the entire room, including leaping up to the ceiling. These dancers are like the particles of a gas (see Figure 3.4).

The series of analogies presented here (adapted from Pendlington et al., 1993) can help students visualize the relative energy and spacing in the different phases of matter. As well as being highly visual in nature, they use a humorous nightclub or school dance floor scenario that students should be able to relate to very easily, particularly socially active teenagers. However, as with any analogy or series of analogies, teachers should remember the potential two-edged sword effect referred to in Chapter 1, and considerable care must be taken in the way in which the analogies are presented. You must always *be sure to map the shared and unshared attributes*. For example, students are much larger than molecules or particles, and there are many more molecules or particles present in even a tiny amount of substance than the number of people that could fit on even the largest dance floor, and so on.

Using Role-Playing to Make Analogies More Interesting and Fun

The pictorial analogies we have described are fun and relevant for students. But we can build on such analogies further and use actual physical activities, which students find even more interesting. For further effect, we can dramatize all of these analogies, for example, by asking students to act out particulate behavior as energy is applied or removed. This adds to the analogies' relevance and makes them more fun and thus more memorable. For example, the concept of condensation (changing from the gaseous to liquid phase) is, for many students, the most difficult phase change to explain. They find it much easier to understand when they have acted out striking a cold surface and losing energy.

Jarvis, Taylor, and McKeon (2005) have used this type of activity with preservice elementary teachers and found role-playing to be extremely effective in improving their understanding of kinetic theory. This was borne out by comparison of their preinstruction and postinstruction explanations of various changes of kinetic state. Clearly, activities like these need to be controlled, but the activity helps students to remember the experience and aids their understanding and retention of the underlying concepts.

Using Amusing Analogies for Other Abstract Physical Science Concepts

When building on the concept of kinetic theory, teachers may look at how atoms combine to form molecules and examine the bonds that hold these various bodies together. Once again these concepts present teachers of science with significant problems, as submicroscopic particles are extremely abstract and remote from students' everyday experiences. Generally the more humorous and relevant the analogy, the more memorable it will be and the more impact it is likely to have.

Chemical bonding is a very difficult area for many students. Like many other science areas, it deals with submicroscopic things, but in addition, the concept of bonding often involves the use of many other models that are themselves complex. The notions of the atom, molecules, and particles are all embedded in the various models for chemical bonding. Chemical bonding is usually introduced in the latter stages of high school, and students are faced with several theories. The main teaching model used at this level is based on the octet rule, and students also are introduced to ionic bonding and covalent bonding, both of which prove problematic. The analogy that follows has been developed by Licata (1988) to help explain the formation of a covalent bond, and it very effectively combines humor and relevance.

Using Food Analogies to Aid Understanding of Covalent Bonding

Here is an interesting and amusing analogy that we can use to help students understand covalent bonding. Again we use an amusing and topical analogy, one every student can relate to: food.

You are sitting in a cafeteria; the person next to you says, "I'll give you half of my cheese sandwich if you'll give me half of your peanut butter sandwich."

The sharing of one's lunch can be used to explain the sharing of electrons: the sandwiches that make up two students' lunches are mapped as the shared electrons that go to make up a covalent chemical bond. Again, you can build on this analogy and talk about polar covalent bonds, where

Figure 3.5   Covalent Bonding Is Like Sharing Your Lunch

SOURCE: Licata, P. K. (1988). Chemistry is like a. . . . *The Science Teacher, 55*(8), 41–43. Used with permission of the publisher.

the sandwich is unequally shared, and dative bonds, where a student steals another student's lunch.

Using Analogies to Aid Understanding of Intermolecular and Intramolecular Bonding

Teachers can build on simple, amusing analogies and use them to explain even difficult topics like distinguishing intramolecular and intermolecular forces. These forces are generally seen as uninteresting to students, particularly when they are taught in a didactic manner. When an amusing and motivating analogy is used, we can quickly help students relate to these and similar concepts. Let's use a derivation of the previous pictorial analogy for kinetic theory to show how we can help students understand the difference between intermolecular and intramolecular bonding in molecular substances.

Imagine groups of three students tied together with rope. Then imagine that these groups of three are connected by some students holding hands with members of other groups (see Figure 3.6). In a similar manner, a molecule is a number of atoms joined together. Some molecules have just two or three atoms, some have many, many atoms. The three children tied together represent the strong intermolecular bonds; the hand-holding

Figure 3.6   Groups of Students Holding Hands Is Like Intramolecular
                   Bonding

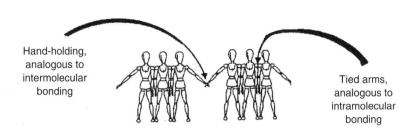

Hand-holding,
analogous to
intermolecular
bonding

Tied arms,
analogous to
intramolecular
bonding

SOURCE: Reprinted with permission from Mike Summers.

students represent the weaker intramolecular bonds. An example of intramolecular bonding is the hydrogen bonding between water molecules H–O–H, bonded like the three hand-holding students. Which bond type is easier to break? Hand-holding bonds are easily broken and reformed while the tied-together bonds are much stronger. The intramolecular bonds will always give way before the intermolecular bonds.

Clearly there are many ways you can build on this analogy. You could, for example, use two students together to analogize a diatomic molecule like dihydrogen (H_2) or dichlorine (Cl_2) or use students to show heteronuclear diatomics, like hydrogen chloride (HCl). Water could be exemplified by two boys vying for the same girl or two girls both wanting the same boy. You can make very big molecules made of many boys and girls and show how, by holding hands, they can still form intermolecular bonds between big and small molecules. This analogy has plenty of potential for role-playing, just like the analogies for kinetic theory. The appeal of this analogy can be increased further by getting the students to once again act out this analogy by binding the groups of three students in the molecule with string or rope. The greater the *active engagement* of the students, the more likely it is that they will think about and understand what is being taught by the analogy.

Fun Analogies in Other Subjects

The use of analogies is popular in the practice and teaching of both chemistry and physics. This is probably because for these two subjects, teachers often struggle to explain macroscopic properties and phenomena with models and theories based at the microscopic level. But we don't want you to think that analogies are restricted to these two disciplines, and so we want to tell you about some entertaining analogies in other subjects. Let's look at an example from the biological sciences.

Many students feel comfortable about studying biology-related subjects because they are dealing with things that they can relate to easily: animals and plants. Students will already have had some experiences with plants and animals and, unlike the atoms and molecules of chemistry and physics, biology classes deal with comfortable and familiar ideas and artifacts. But research has shown that there are also many concepts in the biological sciences that students struggle to understand. Again these are often abstract, microscopic things with some basis in or links to physics and chemistry. A couple of well-known examples are genetics and photosynthesis. We can help students relate to genetics and chromosomes by comparing the scientific concepts with more familiar concepts like language and words. But the example we want to look at here is photosynthesis, which uses a food-making analogy. Food making in plants can be likened to making a cake (Lenton & McNeil, 1993; see Figure 3.7). In each case some basic ingredients are needed, and the final product is food, which both plants and humans use to keep alive. We can tell our students that a cake, being food, is made up of ingredients such as flour, sugar, eggs, and milk. To make the cake we need to provide energy in the form of heat and mechanical energy in the mixing of ingredients before we bake the cake. In the plant we also have basic ingredients—in this case, simple chemicals like carbon dioxide and water. The plant makes the food in a similar way to a cook baking a cake. The plant uses the process of photosynthesis and uses energy in a different form, light energy, which it gets from the sun: the end product is plant food in the form of sugars and starch.

Again you can see how you might build on this analogy in the classroom, using or even baking a cake. And of course we need to be careful, since like all analogies, the cake analogy for photosynthesis needs careful mappings, showing students where the analogy is like the target and where it is not.

How to Develop and Use Interesting and Amusing Analogies in the Classroom

We hope that you can see that the rules for using interesting and amusing analogies are similar to the rules for using all types of analogies. The analog must be accessible to the students, and teachers must carry out appropriate mapping and point out or discuss where the analogy breaks down. If you use amusing and stimulating analogies, you build on all the other advantages of analogy by adding a fun element. This makes the analogy more vivid and accessible and means that your students will likely remember it more easily.

Harrison (2002) makes the important point that many students do not fail science, but rather it is science that fails them because it does not excite

Figure 3.7   Baking a Cake Is Like the Way a Plant Makes Food

their interest. He goes on to observe that school science no longer has an elitist mandate to select those students who are capable of higher-level learning. Disinterested students cannot be ignored as lacking in knowledge or ability. School science has a warrant to engage students in exploring the science knowledge that affects their lives. The effective use of engaging analogies is one strategy that helps achieve this extra dimension, the ability to capture students' interest and involve them in challenging science concepts in a fun way.

Always remember that analogies can act as two-edged swords and may introduce alternative conceptions if used inappropriately. It is important not to assume that an analogy that links to a popular real-world activity will benefit all students. A familiar alternative is needed. For instance, an alternative analogy, based on the proximity of each student's home to the school and different-sized sport balls, was used to model the nucleus, electron, and the space between them in a hydrogen atom. Teachers are good at improvising, and this skill is very important when using analogies.

It is important also to realize that analogies may not transfer effectively across cultural boundaries, and teachers need to be aware of and adapt analogies to their students' interests and background knowledge. Where possible, a range of analogies should be used to target a particular concept. The next chapter examines the need for multiple analogies.

4

Multiple Analogies Are Better Than One-Size-Fits-All Analogies

Allan G. Harrison

CHAPTER OVERVIEW

- Multiple analogies use sets of familiar objects, processes, and events to explain a concept.
- Analogies can generate alternative conceptions when they are used to explain too many aspects of the target concept.
- Multiple analogies reduce the use of single analogies past the point where they break down.
- Multiple analogies are effective because each analogy explains only the ideas where it works well, and students can choose the analogies that best suit their experience and thinking needs.
- Multiple analogies for homeostasis and cell structure and function are proposed.
- A set of multiple analogies for physical and chemical equilibrium is summarized.
- Multiple analogies for electric current are presented, discussed, and compared.

Introduction

As discussed earlier, analogies help students understand the unknown by drawing on knowledge they own and trust. They enable students to visualize abstract concepts, and visualization is particularly strong when mental models of everyday objects and processes are used to build scientific mental models. This reduces the mystique of science and helps students explain difficult concepts in terms of their existing knowledge.

Some students need several reasons to change conceptions, and in a class of 20 or more students, not all students will have the same set of experiences on which to build analogical reasoning. Multiple analogies are especially useful because they accommodate student differences, offer students choice, and provide multiple reasons for changing conceptions. Giving students choices enhances their understanding and interest. Analogies are motivating when students feel that their interests have been taken into account, and only multiple analogies can provide these choices for a class of students.

IMPORTANT POINTS TO REMEMBER

- Not all students have the same set of experiences on which to build or relate to analogies.

- Analogies are more motivating when students feel their ideas and views have been incorporated into analogy construction.

- Multiple analogies allow the full gamut of student experiences to be utilized.

Some concepts are particularly well suited for explanation by multiple analogies. For instance,

- In physics, current conservation in electric circuits
- In biology, homeostasis and cell structure and function
- In chemistry, chemical equilibrium and models of bonding
- Also in physics, electric circuits and balanced forces

Biology: Multiple analogies useful for explaining homeostasis

1. The analogy of the student walking up the down escalator (the student's level neither rises nor falls, which models constant temperature when heat production equals heat loss; Harrison & Treagust, 1994b)

2. The analogy of the balanced household budget (income equaling expenditure means happiness for all)

3. The analogy of the regularly watered, fertilized, and mowed lawn (it grows as fast as it is trimmed, provided a time span of two to three weeks is considered)

4. The analogy of the car cooling system, in which a thermostat is employed (heat generated by the engine equaling heat lost through the radiator results in a constant motor temperature)

Biology: Multiple analogies useful for explaining cell structure and function

1. A cell is like a family living in a house (food, water, waste, people, furniture, doors, and walls model the organelles and their functions)

2. A cell is like a factory (workers, management, material inputs and outputs; products and waste can be interpreted like the analogy of the family living in a house)

3. A cell is like a city (elaborates in ways similar to the city and house analogies)

4. Candy model (students can build a confectionary cell using their knowledge of cell structures)

Chemistry: Multiple analogies for molecular structure and bonding

1. Chemical formulae using chemical symbols and numbers

2. Ball-and-stick representations of molecules with single, double, and triple covalent bonds

3. Space-filling molecular models that show the relative sizes of atoms and orientations in a molecule

4. Lewis electron dot diagrams and Lewis 2D representations

These four molecular analogical models are used side by side and interchangeably in middle school and high school chemistry textbooks. These representations are analogical models (Pimentel, 1970), but very few textbooks talk about the shared and unshared attributes and where the models break down. Teachers assume that students understand the shared and unshared attributes, but students often wonder how and why these models represent the same molecules. Multiple molecular models are needed in chemistry, and research recommends that teachers spend some time explaining the benefits and weaknesses of each model type (Harrison & Treagust, 2000). This will make them more effective as teaching tools.

Chemistry: Multiple analogies for equilibrium (physical and chemical)

1. The analogy of the school dance, in which a limited proportion of students attending a dance pair off, bond, and then some pairs break

up. This analogy introduces simultaneous forward and reverse reactions (revisited in Chapter 7)

2. The analogy of excess sugar in a teacup. For a molecule to dissolve, a dissolved molecule must first crystallize out of solution. This introduces balanced forward and reverse reactions.

3. The analogy of curry simmering in a pot. The rate of water molecules evaporating equals the rate of molecules condensing, showing that equilibrium systems are closed.

4. The analogy of the busy highway or full parking lot. A car must leave the highway or parking lot before another car can enter or park, respectively—this shows that equilibrium reactions are dynamic (these four analogies are described in Harrison & de Jong, 2005).

Physics: Multiple analogies for current conservation in a simple series circuit

1. The analogy of the continuous train. Passengers (energy) board at the battery and alight at the lightbulb while the moving train (current) is conserved (Dupin & Johsua, 1989; see the detailed version in Chapter 8).

2. The analogy of the bicycle chain, where the moving chain (current) is conserved but transfers energy from the pedals to the back wheel.

3. The analogy of the conveyer belt, in which the conveyer belt (current) is conserved while the material placed on the belt at its start (battery energy) leaves at the other end of the belt (energy converted to light at the lightbulb).

4. The analogy of the M&M's circle. Students moving around in a continuous circle (current) are given two M&M's each. They eat one to move them around the circuit, and the other is eaten at the lightbulb to make it light up.

5. The Field Analogy can then be used to explain how lightbulbs in a series circuit know that there is another lightbulb in the circuit with which they must share the current and the energy it carries.

Physics: Multiple analogies for balanced forces—bridging analogies (Clement, 1993)

This is a different type of multiple analogy. A set of carefully sequenced analogies bridges the cognitive gap between a book sitting on the table (many students recognize only the downward weight force) and scientists' conception that the table is exerting an equal and opposite force to the book's weight. The bridging analogies are illustrated in Chapter 8 and comprise the following:

1. A book sitting on a table is compared to a spring being squeezed between finger and thumb.

2. The book on the table and the spring between finger and thumb is then compared to a book sitting on a soft cushion (the book deforms the cushion).

3. The book on table, the spring between fingers, and the book deforming the cushion is compared to a book bending a thin board (model table) on which it is placed.

4. Thus, the book on the table (but not deforming the table) is now seen to be like a book sitting on and bending the thin board (analogous to the table). At this point, most students conclude that a book on a table does exert a force on the table and the table exerts an equal and opposite reaction force on the book.

Bridging analogies are multiple analogies, and some are elaborated in later chapters. They are valuable in bridging cognitively distant concepts because each step is cognitively shorter than the total conceptual leap. They also offer the benefit of providing students with cognitive choices, multiple explanations, and reinforcements of abstract concepts. Most of the *multiple analogy sets have been well researched*, and the conceptual changes are quite striking. Clement's (1993) bridging analogy raises the question of whether all multiple analogies are, in some way, bridging analogies.

Multiple Analogies for Electric Current

To begin with, it helps to know which science concepts are consistently difficult for students to understand and which concepts need single analogical explanation and which need multiple analogies. Some of the concepts we are about to discuss challenge scientists and teachers, so don't be too worried if you conclude: "Hey, that's what I thought." Roger Osborne and Peter Freyberg (1985), David Shipstone (1985), and Lillian McDermott (1993) studied and documented the conceptual problems that students have with understanding electricity. And remember, some of these conceptions arise time and again and across elementary and secondary grades.

The most common problem students have is the belief that the current in a circuit is used up as the battery goes flat. Diane Grayson (1994) explains why this idea is intuitively appealing:

After all, batteries go flat or die after a while. How can the current *not* be used up? Frequently, instruction stops here, but I believe this is a dangerous state in which to leave a student. Because they have not really resolved the issue of what was wrong with their own preconceptions, students might not make the conceptual change to believing that current is not used up, or they might appear to accept the new ideas for a time and revert to their previous ideas some time later. . . . This is the point where I introduce concept [of] substitution. Students are told that they were *right* to say that something is "used up," as evidenced by the fact that the batteries do go flat, but the "something" that is used up is "energy" and not current . . . the instructor introduces the correct physics term at the time that the apparent misconception arises, even though the term may not have been encountered before in the course. (pp. 5–6)

But we can do much more than just tell the students the correct physics term; we can use analogies from their everyday world that help them visualize and understand how circuits use the electric current to carry energy from one point to another. After all, the idea of trains, bicycle chains, and lines of people carrying food, energy, or objects from one place to another is easy to model and explain.

Electric Circuits

Inquiring About Electric Circuits

When students make simple circuits, their observations sometimes don't match their predictions. For example, when one lightbulb in Figure 4.1 is connected to one battery, it glows brightly; but in Circuit 2, when two identical globes are connected to the same battery, the lightbulbs are less than half as bright. What's happening?

Several problems arise when students make these circuits.

Problem 1: Students think that the current flowing from the battery to the lightbulb is greater than the current returning to the battery. This is called the "consumed current" model and is best corrected by using two or three visual conservation analogies, like the continuous train, the bicycle chain, and the M&M's circle.

Problem 2: Students think that the same amount of electricity as flowed through one lightbulb in Circuit 1 will be shared between the two lightbulbs in Circuit 2. But when identical batteries are used, the brightness of Circuit 2's lightbulbs suggests that less electricity is shared between two lightbulbs than flowed in Circuit 1. And if you connect each circuit to a new battery, Circuit 2 will glow three to four times longer than the battery in Circuit 1 took to go flat. So how much electricity flows in Circuit 2, and why is it less than half the current in Circuit 1?

Problem 3: Some students predict that the electricity flowing in Circuit 2 is shared unevenly. After deciding on the electricity's direction, they predict that the lightbulb that the electricity passes through first gets

Figure 4.1   A Simple Circuit With One Lightbulb and a Series Circuit With
Two Lightbulbs

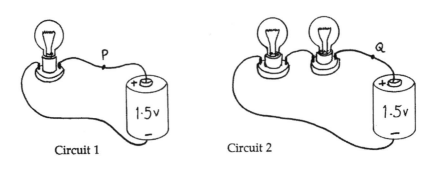

Circuit 1   Circuit 2

more of the electricity and glows brighter than the second lightbulb. This prediction indicates that these students think that the current is partly used up by lightbulbs and motors.

Problems 2 and 3 can only be explained satisfactorily using the electric-field analogy. Use this analogy with students who are used to models and have a sound practical knowledge of inquiry science circuit phenomena.

Problem 4: Students also are perplexed when they set up the circuit shown in Figure 4.2. How can they explain why all the lightbulbs are equally bright after seeing what happened in Figure 4.1?

Problem 4 is best explained using the analogy of a crowd leaving the school hall with one or two doors opened.

Electricity concepts are difficult to explain, and analogies are an effective way to help students understand and visualize what they see happening. But once again, be careful: Analogies and models can mislead, especially when the analogy is taken too far. Alternative conceptions that are generated by poor analogies are difficult to correct because analogies use everyday experiences that build strongly held conceptions. Inappropriate mental models are as strongly misleading as appropriate mental models are beneficial. Strong visualization can work for you and against you.

This is why analogies are often called two-edged swords (Glynn, 1991). Some teachers respond by saying, "If I don't use any analogies, I won't mislead my students." But disavowing analogies takes away one of your best teaching strategies. And some science concepts, at least in middle school, can be explained only by analogy (e.g., refraction of light and the field explanation for current sharing in circuits). A better resolution is to

Figure 4.2   A Simple Circuit With One Lightbulb and a Parallel Circuit With
Two Lightbulbs

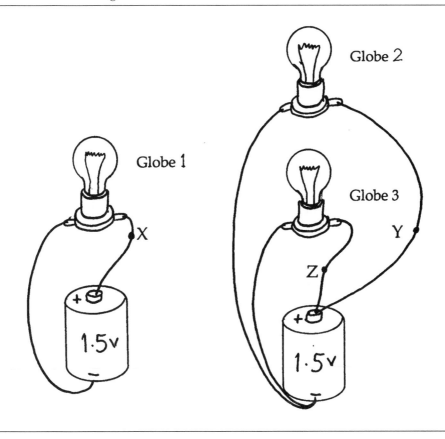

choose effective analogies and thoroughly discuss their shared and
unshared attributes with your students. Better still, encourage your
students to build and interpret their own analogies, guide them in this
enterprise, and help them role-play some key analogies.

In my experience it is better to use two or three analogies than stretch
just one. A good rule is to keep each analogy and model simple.

IMPORTANT POINTS TO REMEMBER

- Alternative conceptions generated by poor analogies or inappropriate use of
  analogies are very hard to extinguish.
- Some science concepts can be explained only by analogy.

Multiple Electricity Analogies

The recommended set of multiple analogies for electricity concepts comprises all or part of the following list:

1. The flowing water analogy for a simple series circuit teaches that electricity flows in a circuit like water flows through pipes (an example of a simple analogy; see Chapter 1). This analogy can be enriched and extended by explaining the ways a water filtration circuit in a classroom aquarium is like a simple series circuit (see Chapter 8). But take care: Students may conclude that this analogy teaches that electricity is a physical substance and that electricity will leak out of an electric socket that has no plug in it. Once students understand that electricity flows, it's important that they do not think that the electric current is wholly or partly consumed by a lightbulb or motor. That's why some of the next three analogies should accompany the flowing water analogy.

2. The Continuous Train Analogy (Figure 4.3) demonstrates that current is conserved while energy is transferred from the battery to the lightbulb, where it changes into heat and light (Dupin & Johsua, 1989). The passenger train picks up passengers at one station (the battery) and drops them off at another station (the lightbulb).

   Analogies that reinforce the idea that current is conserved help overcome the persistent misconception that current is consumed (Osborne & Freyberg, 1985). We recommend reinforcing this idea with another analogy like one of the following:

3. The Bicycle Chain Analogy demonstrates current conservation (Figure 4.4). The chain is obviously not used up as it transfers energy from the pedals (battery) to the back wheel that, in turn, moves the bicycle forward (like the lightbulb producing heat and light).

Figure 4.3   The Continuous Train Analogy Showing That Current Is Conserved

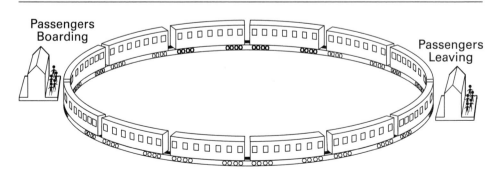

Figure 4.4   The Bicycle Chain Analogy for Electric Current

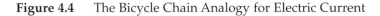

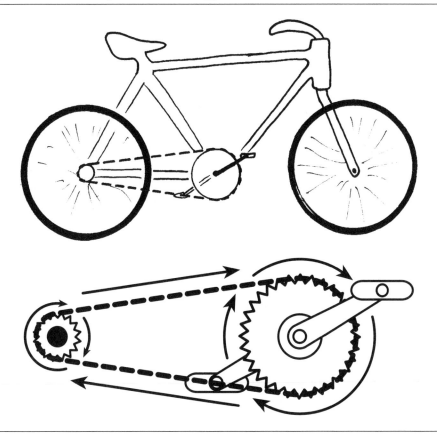

4. The student M&M's Circle Analogy (Figure 4.5). A group of students form a circle and the teacher or another student (called "the battery") gives each student two M&M's and a small push (to rotate the circle). Each student immediately eats one M&M (to keep the circle moving) and eats the other M&M on arrival at a box to be stepped over that represents the lightbulb. The second M&M does the work that pushes the electric current (the stepping up student) through the lightbulb filament, thus converting the M&M's energy into heat and light.

Summary

The multiple analogies that explain current conservation are the continuous train, bicycle chain, and M&M's. Collectively, they reinforce the concept that current is conserved and use a variety of contexts and mechanisms to show that it is the battery's energy that is transformed into light. This provides students with multiple explanations of how current is conserved and provides cognitive options for students who lack the experiential knowledge for one or more of the analogies. Current conservation is too important a concept to rely on just one analogy.

Figure 4.5   The M&M's Circle Analogy for Electric Current Conservation

Extending Concepts

Once students understand that current is conserved, teachers then need to explain the other key concept in electric circuits—voltage. Voltage is another abstract concept that depends heavily on analogy for its understanding and visualization. This explains the popularity of the analogy that voltage is like water pressure in a tank (see Figure 4.6). Water pressure is the best everyday concept for helping students visualize electrical *pressure*. The pressure metaphor highlights the essential role of analogy in these explanations. It is worth restating the warning to not apply the water analogy past its breakdown point: The Water Pressure Analogy can result in the misconception that electricity is a substance.

The number of open doors in the school gymnasium is an appropriate analogy for explaining the brightness of two lightbulbs in parallel circuits as opposed to two dull lightbulbs in series circuits, when the same lightbulbs and battery are just connected in different ways (see Figure 4.7). The analogy is elaborated in Chapter 8.

The Electric Field Analogy

All these analogies are, however, incomplete explanations of electricity flow without the field concept. Why do teachers and students fall back on water circuit analogies and think of electricity as a substance? Because they do not know of an analogy that accurately addresses the way energy and electrons flow in a closed circuit. The field metaphor provides the missing explanation and is essential if scientific reasoning is to prevail.

The electric-field analogy for multiple lightbulbs in a series circuit should be in every teacher's toolkit for teaching electricity concepts. The

Figure 4.6   Depth and Pressure Analogy for Voltage in an Electric Circuit

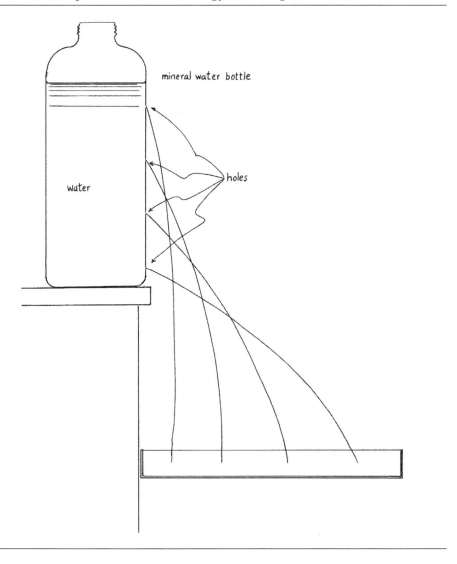

field analogy likens an electric circuit and its components to a soccer team and its members. Successful teams function as a unit—add or subtract a key player, and this affects the whole team. Everyone feels the effect of a key player's entry or exit. Players don't have to be close to the key player to feel the effect—they all know what other players can do. This is like the electric field that spreads throughout a circuit and "tells" lightbulbs or motors that there is another lightbulb or motor connected in the circuit. The field helps each lightbulb "feel" the presence of other lightbulbs. You certainly know what another team member is doing if that person scores a goal, makes a great pass, or loses the ball. Team members share the ball and know what to do, and electric components share the electrical energy because they detect the presence of other components.

Figure 4.7   The Analogy of a Number of Doors in a Hallway, for Series Versus Parallel Circuit Current Flow

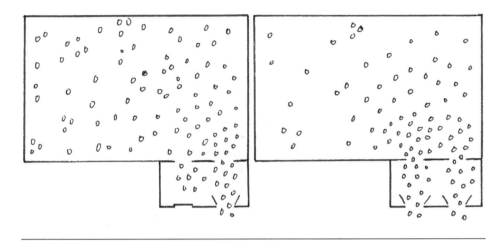

Multiple Analogies for Explaining Living Cells

In biology lessons, students look at onion, cheek, and algal cells, but the magnification and resolution of school microscopes do not allow them to explore cell organelle structure and function. In contrast, textbook diagrams show the nucleus, mitochondria, vacuoles, ribosomes, and centrioles, to name some important organelles. How can we help students bridge the gap between what they can see and what they need to know? Analogies and models again come to the rescue, and at least four popular analogies are used to explain the cell structures that students cannot see. The analogies comprise the following:

1. A cell is like a family living in a house with inputs, outputs, guidance, and rules.

2. A cell is like a factory with workers, governance, inputs, outputs, and wastes.

3. A cell is like a city and can be elaborated in similar ways as the factory and house analogies.

4. Students use their knowledge of cell structures to build a candy model cell.

The four analogies provide teaching and learning opportunities that can be varied to suit the students' background knowledge, interest, grade level, and curriculum expectations. For example, "a cell is like a family . . ." and the "confectionary cell" may be a suitable combination for Grades 7–9, while all four analogies seem better suited to Grades 9–12—especially if a more demanding modeling task is included in the learning.

The first analogy (a cell is like a family living in a house) could be taught and discussed with students. Then "a cell is like a city" could be outlined and student groups asked to complete the analysis and report their shared and unshared mappings to the class. And the "cell is like a factory" (or "a cell is like a school") could be set as an assessment task (see Tables 4.1–4.3).

The elaboration of these analogies takes account of the following cell needs and functions:

Cell inputs can be water, gases (CO_2, or O_2), foods or energy, minerals, and information.

Cell outputs can be water, gases (O_2 or CO_2), energy, wastes, specific products, toxins, minerals, and information.

Modeling a Cell Using Confectionary and Foods

Modeling a cell using candy and food items is an exciting activity for students in Grades 7–10 because the task calls for knowledge, proportional thinking, and creativity—and the students get to eat their creations when finished. Some of the materials to consider using are jelly snakes or gummy worms (membranes, chromosomes, and endoplasmic reticulum); jelly beans (mitochondria and chloroplasts); licorice strips and spaghetti (membranes); nonpareils or TicTacs (ribosomes); toffees, mints, and M&M's (Golgi bodies, plastids); rice (starch grains) and so on.

Table 4.1   A Cell Is Like a Family Living in a House

Analog—Familiar Experience	*Target—Cell Characteristics*
Parents provide the information and rules controlling family activities.	The nucleus holds all the information for cell structure and function.
House outer wall	Cell wall, cell membrane
Doors and windows, water and sewer connections	Pores in membrane allowing inputs to enter, outputs and wastes to leave
Passages and stairs	Endoplasmic reticulum
Bedrooms	Vacuoles
Kitchen for preparing foods	Ribosomes making proteins
Dining room	Mitochondria
Rubbish chute, rubbish bin	Excretory vacuoles
Telephone, Internet connection, mailbox	Nerve or hormone inputs and outputs

Table 4.2 A Cell Is Like a Factory

Analog—Familiar Experience	Target—Cell Characteristics
Manager and design department control information and plans.	The nucleus holds all the cell's information and molecular plans.
Outer fence and factory wall	Cell wall, cell membrane
Gate, deliveries, and dispatch departments	Pores in membrane that allow water, gases, foods, and minerals to enter and wastes to leave
Gatekeeper, security guards	Keeps toxins out, useful substances in
Passages, lifts or elevators, and conveyer belts	Endoplasmic reticulum
Storerooms for raw materials and products	Vacuoles
Production units	Ribosomes making proteins
Canteen	Mitochondria
Waste processing, rubbish bin	Excretory vacuoles
Telephone, Internet connection, mailbox	Nerve or hormone inputs and outputs

Table 4.3 A Cell Is Like a City

Analog—Familiar Experience	Target—Cell Characteristics
Mayor and council control information and make decisions.	The nucleus holds all the cell's information and controls most functions.
City limits	Cell wall, cell membrane
Roads, railways, and airport carry people and goods into and out of the city.	Pores in membrane allow water, gases, foods, and minerals to enter, wastes to leave.
Police and health departments	Keeps toxins out, useful substances in
Roads and trains	Endoplasmic reticulum
Warehouses, silos, storage yards	Vacuoles
Factories and businesses	Ribosomes and Golgi bodies
Power stations	Mitochondria
Garbage trucks	Excretory vacuoles
Telephone, Internet connection, mailbox	Nerve or hormone inputs and outputs

Multiple Analogies for Explaining Chemical Equilibrium

If you recall, in his 12th-grade chemistry class, Neil set out to show that many chemical reactions do not go to completion and he wanted his students to understand that at equilibrium,

1. The rate of the forward reaction equals the rate of the reverse reaction.

2. The forward and reverse reactions continue even though they are in balance.

3. The system must be closed (i.e., no reactants are added and no products are lost).

Neil told us that he planned to use a couple of analogies, and he mapped out the school dance, excess sugar in a teacup, and the busy highway analogies before each lesson. What he did not tell us was that he would end up using 10 analogies in the three lessons! The 10 analogies are described, in their order of presentation, in Table 4.4. They comprise two sets of multiple analogies: one set for the conditions for chemical equilibrium and the other set for step-by-step reaction mechanisms.

Analogies 7–10 are now summarized and their cognitive connections highlighted.

1. The School Dance Analogy: 500 boys and 500 girls wearing blindfolds pair off at the school dance. They can recognize each other because boys have stubble and girls have ponytails; they collide and pair off by feeling each other's heads. Once bonded, they go to the "commitment room" where they take off their blindfolds. The commitment room holds only 250 couples, and this limits the forward reaction. However, once they see each other, some pairs split, and as they leave the commitment room, another couple can take their place. The doors of the school hall are locked so that the system is closed. The splitting and pairing continues throughout the hours set for the dance, and the reaction is limited to 250 couples. This analogy emphasizes the simultaneous and balanced nature of forward and reverse reactions.

2. The Excess Sugar in a Teacup Analogy: Neil asked, "What happens when you put three to four lumps of sugar in a cup of tea and the tea cools down? Excess sugar settles to the bottom and lies there undissolved. But is nothing happening? No; when a molecule crystallizes and settles on the bottom, another molecule dissolves in its place." Neil knew that his students couldn't see this happening, so he linked the sugar in a teacup

Table 4.4   Multiple Analogies Used to Explain Chemical Equilibrium

Analogical models, in order of appearance in the lessons on chemical equilibrium

1. School Dance (introductory version)	Chemical reaction: reaction rate depends on rate of boys and girls colliding
2. Up and Down Skier	Activation energy: energy in before energy out
3. Air Flight, including route details	Reaction mechanism: many steps produce the overall effect
4. Assembling a Model Aircraft or Car	Reaction mechanism: many steps, some parallel, like assembling two identical wings
5. Balancing on a See-Saw	Physical equilibrium: force × distance balanced on each side
6. Being Normal or Insane	Physical equilibrium: like being mentally stable
7. School Dance (elaborated version)	Conditions for chemical equilibrium: couples committing and breaking up is continuous, rate committing equals rate breaking up, commitment room smaller than the hall (incomplete reaction), and the hall sealed
8. Excess Sugar in a Teacup (covered)	Dynamic nature of equilibrium: cup sealed, rate dissolving equals rate precipitating; process continuous, temperature dependent
9. Pot of Curry (lid in place)	Dynamic nature of equilibrium: amount of water evaporating equals amount condensing; continuous while simmering, sealed pot equals closed system
10. Busy Highway	Dynamic nature of equilibrium: rate of cars entering equals rate of cars leaving; collision rate important
Multiple equilibrium analogies: 1, 5–10	Multiple reaction mechanism analogies: 2–4

back to The School Dance Analogy and said, "An outsider won't see much happening, but all of you who know all the people at the dance will see that Jon and Sally have broken up, Josh has been dumped by Sue, and the couples are changing." For students who are accustomed to fluid teenage relationships, this analogy kept their interest.

3. Just as Neil finished the foregoing story, a student called Mal suggested the analogy of curry simmering in a pot. Mal asked if the rate of water molecules evaporating from a curry and condensing on the lid and dripping back into the pot was just like the excess sugar in the teacup. Neil agreed and capitalized on Mal's analogy. Later, Neil said that he had felt the need for another analogy so he immediately responded to Mal's suggestion.

4. The Busy Highway Analogy was then used by Neil to summarize the conditions for equilibrium. The full analogy is described in Chapter 1. In his postlesson reflection, Neil felt that the full parking lot analogy would be better because it was more structured.

Student learning outcomes were evaluated by interviewing seven students 10 weeks after the equilibrium topic (Harrison & de Jong, 2005). Five of the seven students had sound conceptions of equilibrium, and two students demonstrated a robust knowledge of equilibrium. Five students used one or two analogies to explain equilibrium conditions, and all of the analogies turned up in at least one student's explanation. Students used the available analogies to choose the explanation that best suited their background knowledge and learning needs.

Bridging Analogies

The use of one or more intermediate and easily understood analogies to bridge a wide conceptual gap is an effective teaching strategy. A classic example is the problem of a book on a table problem. A book exerts a downward force due to gravity (the weight force is obvious whenever you support a book for a long time), and the table exerts an upward force that exactly balances the book's weight. The book and the table are in dynamic equilibrium. Many students, however, think that the book's weight stops acting the moment it is placed on a strong, motionless surface, like the floor or a table.

When they saw a book sitting still on a table, "76% of a sample of 112 students indicated that a table does not push up on a book lying at rest on it. [However] . . . 96% of these students believe that a spring does push up on one's hand when the hand is pushing down on it" (Clement, 1987; see Figure 4.8). The hand on the spring is used as an "anchoring example that draws out an anchoring intuition" (p. 86). From this anchor, the student is then shown the book sitting on a board supported at each end with the book bending the board (i.e., the book is sitting on a model of a table). The book's weight can be seen bending the board. Push down with your hand on the board, and you can feel that the board is exerting an opposing force. This is the bridging analogy. It can then be reasoned that the table must exert an upward force equal to the book's downward force, even though the actual table does not visibly bend. If the students are reluctant to accept the concept of forces in equilibrium for the book on the table, a second bridging step is included: the book sitting on a foam cushion. See Figure 4.8.

While some students cannot see the analogy between the forces, they can feel them when squeezing a spring *and* when observing the forces between the book and the table. They may make the connection when the task is broken into a series of smaller conceptual steps. This is what Clement (1987) calls a *bridging analogy*. Instead of one large span, this bridge has many supports along the way—a bit like mental resting points for the learners. If students need more experience with balanced forces that they can feel and "see," I ask them to squeeze a blown-up balloon, hold a strong paper clip open for 30 seconds, and stretch elastic bands. The more experiences they have with equal and opposite forces, the more likely they are to realize that Newton's Third Law operates in every equilibrium situation.

Figure 4.8   Bridging Analogies Show the Forces That Are in Dynamic Equilibrium When a Book Sits on a Table

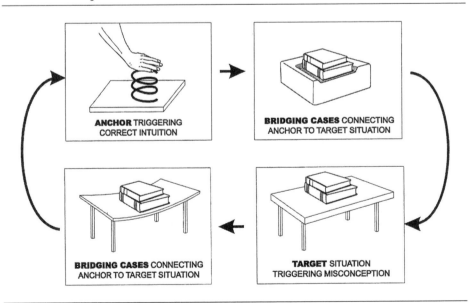

ANCHOR TRIGGERING CORRECT INTUITION

BRIDGING CASES CONNECTING ANCHOR TO TARGET SITUATION

BRIDGING CASES CONNECTING ANCHOR TO TARGET SITUATION

TARGET SITUATION TRIGGERING MISCONCEPTION

Conclusion

When you're asked to think of an example of a multiple analogy, it's often hard to think of more than one instance. As we examine the analogies we use, however, we often find that we have two or three analogies for some concepts but do not use them side-by-side. Your students may learn more and their conceptions may be richer and more scientific if you provide them with the conceptual variety that comes with multiple analogies. Remember, they do not all have the same knowledge backgrounds and interests.

Multiple analogies do not always come in sets of two or three that target the same concept. Sure, the three analogies for a cell do target the same concept—a cell is like a family, like a city, like a factory. These are parallel multiple analogies. But multiple analogies can also be sequential analogies that develop the parts of a concept one at a time—for instance, the analogies for electric current, current conservation, voltage, and complete circuits (the field metaphor). The number of electricity analogies that can be added to this list is extensive—hydraulic systems and circuits, games, garden sprinklers, and so on. These analogies all attest to the need for excellent analogies to develop electricity concepts. And multiple analogies work well with concepts like equilibrium, molecules, and forces. What would teaching be like without these sets of analogies? It would be much poorer and less interesting.

5

Inquiry-Based Teacher- and Student-Generated Analogies

Richard K. Coll

David F. Treagust

CHAPTER OVERVIEW

- Research shows that student-centered teaching and learning is very effective.
- Learners use their past knowledge to interpret current experiences and to solve problems.
- Teachers often generate analogies when they see their students struggling to understand science concepts.
- Teacher analogies developed before the lesson can be effective so long as the teacher checks that the students are familiar with the analog. Student-generated analogies are often initiated by the teacher and developed by the students.

- Students, like others, generate analogy spontaneously when they struggle to understand science concepts.
- Student-generated and teacher-generated analogies can lead to rich discussion in the classroom.

Modern science education research has been guided by a number of learning theories, and the most common—constructivism—helps explain why analogies work in some lessons but not in others. There are debates about the merits and forms of constructivism. Here we are most interested in social constructivism, a variant that acknowledges the importance of social factors in knowledge construction. However, good teachers know that learning occurs when students compare what they already know with the new ideas presented by the teacher or textbook. It is the students who decide whether or not to reconstruct their conceptions; therefore, teaching should be student centered rather than teacher centered. This means that students should be actively involved in making and interpreting analogies. If we believe that analogy use is an effective way to help students think and learn, then it makes sense to help students generate their own analogies or reconstruct the teacher's analogies to fit in with their own experiences.

It is an interesting observation that most people spontaneously generate analogies when they have trouble explaining difficult concepts. The next time you see someone presenting to a group, just watch how quickly the speaker resorts to analogy use when he or she sees people struggling to understand a concept. In a research exercise, Allan G. Harrison was sitting in a biology teacher's class as the teacher explained homeostasis. At the lesson's end, the teacher said, "What did you think of my analogy?" Allan answered, "Which one?" The teacher replied, "The person walking up the down escalator, of course." Allan then asked, "What about the other eight?" The teacher was amazed, but when Allan listed the analogies he had written down, the teacher just said, "That's just how I teach!" So how do teachers and students generate and interpret science analogies?

Inquiry, Constructivism, and Student-Centered Learning

In traditional teaching, students are seen as knowing little about the topic or topics under instruction. This seems logical when teaching about modern science concepts, such as atoms. For example, if we wanted to teach students about atomic structure, it seemed reasonable to assume they knew virtually nothing about the Bohr model or other more complex models. Based on this assumption, teachers simply told students about the model for the atom and expected that the students would, by and large, understand the topic, provided they concentrated and worked hard. Many researchers and teachers also assumed that when students struggled to learn science, it was because of inattention, lack of ability, or laziness or perhaps that they found the subject irrelevant or boring. This sort of teaching is highly teacher centered and involved direct instruction, such as reading textbooks, continuous lecturing, and the use of recipe book experiments.

Many education researchers now argue that individuals actively construct their own knowledge and that this construction (or reconstruction) depends on (among other things) what the individual already knows or has experienced (Yager, 1995). So even if students did not know anything about the scientific model of atomic structure being taught, other ideas they had about atoms (for instance, that atoms are indivisible, atoms are hard spheres) may interfere with the teaching of the Bohr model. This is one reason why it is useful to have some idea of what students already think about a topic when we teach them, whether or not we are using analogies. Constructivism suggests that student failure has much to do with the teaching style, who does the thinking, and lack of attention to what the student already knows and is interested in.

Over the past 20 years, many researchers have used constructivism to better understand how students learn scientific concepts. What is especially interesting is the way this research pointed out major differences between students' and scientists' understandings of science concepts. Teachers and researchers found that there were major differences between what teachers hoped their students would learn and what students actually learned—*even for very able students* (Duit, 2004b). Not many people would be surprised to find that less scientifically knowledgeable students held misconceptions, but it was a considerable surprise (and concern) to find that even our best students held nonscientific conceptions of science topics, such as *force*. These observations called into question whether conventional teaching approaches were appropriate for the teaching of abstract science concepts.

Constructivist theory predicts that students are more likely to find a science topic interesting and worth studying if they see it as relevant and connected to familiar things. Teaching with analogies works because analogy tries to relate the unfamiliar to the familiar. Analogical explanations should, therefore, draw on familiar knowledge and experiences, and this approach is consistent with constructivist views of learning. Like any classroom learning, learning with analogies needs input and facilitation by the teacher. Teachers can facilitate learning if they know students' abilities and prior knowledge, and if they have a reasonable understanding of what is familiar to the students. So if you want to use an analogy to help your students understand an abstract concept, you need to know what analog topics will be of interest to them (experiences like riding a bicycle, driving a car or motorcycle, boy-girl relationships, sports). The connection needs to be quite specific. For most students a football stadium is an appropriate analogy, but for some, it is not. If teachers know their students well, then they can generate ever better analogies, and when students generate their own analogies, they will draw on topics guaranteed to be familiar to them.

IMPORTANT POINTS TO REMEMBER

- Be aware of what your students already know about science and everyday things.

- Analogies use familiar objects and processes to explain unfamiliar concepts.

- Analogies work best when the analog is familiar to the students.

- Sport, bicycles, cars, and boy-girl relationships are excellent sources of analogies.

- Unfamiliar or complex analogies may engender alternative conceptions.

- Students must be involved in interpreting teachers' analogies.

- Better learning occurs when students help construct the analogies.

Student-Generated Analogies

Teacher-generated analogies that use familiar student experiences and student-generated analogies are constructivist in nature because they are planned to fit the students' knowledge and experiences. Student-centered learning and student-generated analogies are illustrated in an article by Cosgrove (1995). Cosgrove describes a set of rich discussions that arose during a series of lessons about electrical circuits in a ninth-grade class. The teacher in Cosgrove's study—let's call him Robert— found that his students could not understand the topic of electrical resistance, and he was preparing his own analogy to help his students understand the topic. He was surprised to find that one of his students, also struggling to understand the topic, had made his own analogy—the coal truck analogy—in which the student related the delivery of electrical current to a coal truck delivering coal: "I asked an electrician. It's like a train carrying coal. It drops it off, then goes back to get some more coal" (Cosgrove, 1995, p. 299).

There are two fascinating features to this student's analogy. First, the student later confessed that he had not in fact consulted an electrician but used the electrician to raise his own analogy's credibility. As we said earlier, the teacher was surprised that the student generated an analogy in the first place, and the student's comment offers some insights into why student analogy generation is not very common. Perhaps many analogies are racing through our students' minds as we discuss science ideas with them and try to help them understand science, but they are reluctant to tell their own analogies in front of the class. Second, we can see how important the teacher is in this example. In Cosgrove's (1995) scenario, once the teacher realized what was happening in his classroom, he worked with the student and encouraged other students in the class to build on this analogy and generate their own analogies. This resulted in numerous extensions, such as resistance as distance and resistance as consumption and, finally, consumption of electricity as people trying to do hard work when going without food. The teacher exercised considerable skill in scaffolding student learning, building the analogies, and pointing out problems and differences between the analogies and the target. The significance of Cosgrove's research lies in the richness of the discussions and evident enthusiasm of the students in the analogy generation process.

Wong (1993) found something similar in his study of student-generated analogies for explaining the compression and decompression of air as a plunger was pushed into a syringe (with the nozzle covered by a finger). In explaining these phenomena, preservice teachers created a variety of analogies to explain how a vacuum was created and what the air molecules were doing in terms of the compression and decompression of the air in the sealed syringe. What was evident in Wong's study was that each individual's unique knowledge base directly influenced the conceptual problems he or she faced, the analogies generated and what was finally understood. In the studies by Cosgrove (1995) and Wong (1993), student-generated analogies arose as a result of teacher initiation. It sometimes takes a little while for students to propose an analogy, but once they do and the others in the class start to understand how this might work, exciting discussions often develop.

Strategies for Generating Student Analogies

In Cosgrove's (1995) study, the ninth-grade students spent more than a week developing their analogies to explain their simple circuits. There was time to think, time to ask and answer questions, time to test each analogy's predictions, and a teacher who valued creative thinking. The teacher was able to provide needed information, give hints and help his students develop their ideas. Student-generated analogies will arise, but they need to be nurtured, and this is where a constructivist thinking environment is important. What can teachers do to foster student-generated analogies? They can be patient, know exactly what they want their students to understand, and they can suspend judgment on their students' ideas and avoid saying, "this is right" and "that is wrong." Last of all, we need to realize that not all students can generate their own analogies. Still, some students who cannot generate their own analogies can develop them in peer groups.

Teacher-Generated Analogies

Two themes about how teachers use analogies in the classroom show up in the literature: how often analogies appear in curriculum materials, such as textbooks, and how common they are in classroom practice. Dagher (1995a) classified the studies she examined into one of two categories according to whether the analogies were included in text or were presented by a teacher or researcher. She found that the level of guidance provided to readers, the degree of interaction permitted, and the way an analogy is presented in a textbook are the main factors that determine the effectiveness of learning from textbook analogies. For example, five-year-old and seven-year-old children were able to see the similarity between analog and target domains (i.e., they were able to see how the analogy and target concept were similar in a simple one-to-one correspondence), but their ability to make these links effectively was limited unless they received guidance. When it comes to the classroom, research into analogy use has focused on how teachers use analogy in the classroom, and this apparently depends greatly on the classroom environment. Dagher (1995b) observed that teachers use analogies that are based on things such as actual life experience, observed life experience, science fiction, personalized stories, and common objects.

Teacher-Generated Analogies
Developed During the Lesson

We now look at some episodes of teacher-generated analogy. The first example comes from Ritchie, Bellocchi, Poltl, and Wearmouth's (2006) study of beginning science teachers. The examples in this report are mostly about teaching metaphors, but during this process, some nice exemplars of teachers trying to use analogy in the classroom come to the surface. In the example presented here, the beginning teacher—we'll call him Joseph— felt that analogies were not likely to be helpful in his classroom. This thought arose when he observed another teacher's classroom in which he felt that analogies were overused, and he thought that the teaching became "a bit of a mess." However, look at what unfolds as he, a novice teacher, runs into some problems when teaching atomic structure:

> In my first year of teaching I was allocated two chemistry classes. Concerned that students did not understand the concepts adequately, I turned to analogies in frustration. My first reference to a

common textbook analogy was successful. This encouraged me to go further.

I *invented* [italics added] an analogical model to help explain the structure of atoms following the "Rutherford gold leaf experiment." I first questioned the students about what they remembered about the structure of the atom. From these interactions, the question, "How do we know this?" begged an answer. I continued: Imagine that we throw a sheet over our overhead projector. Now suppose we stand at the back of the room and fire an air rifle at the covered projector. If the air rifle pellet pierces the sheet and encounters empty space, it will pass straight through to the other side and leave a hole in the wall. If the pellet hits the solid form of the projector behind the sheet, it bounces straight back without hitting the wall. We fire many pellets at the sheet. In the end we have a series of holes where the pellets encountered little resistance and a pattern shape of the projector on the wall where the pellets did not penetrate. At this point the students were silent. I was concerned that I had confused them. I asked: "What will we see on the wall after we finish shooting?" "The shape of the projector, its outline," some replied. I asked, "Will this shape be an exact copy of the projector?" "No," they replied. "How is it different?" I retorted. "It's the outline only, it's not 3D," they answered. More questions and answers followed: "What information about the projector doesn't it give us?" "Color, what's it made of." "So how is this information helpful?" "It gives us an idea of what it looks like." Now that I was convinced that the class recognized the limitations of this model, I discussed the Rutherford experiment in more detail. (pp. 146–147)

It is interesting that the teacher turned to analogy use because of frustration and that despite some misgivings found that it enhanced the richness of discussion and student learning.

Teacher-Generated Analogies Developed Before the Lesson

Here are two different scenarios where, prior to the lesson, the teachers carefully considered which analogies to use to teach certain physics concepts (Treagust et al., 1992). Two high school science teachers were observed using teacher-generated enriched analogies in 12th-grade physics. When discussing the concept of half-life in radioactive decay, one teacher drew the analogy between half-life and probability-controlled games, such as a lottery or dice throwing. The teacher explained that every nucleus has the same chance of decaying into a nucleus of another element in much the same way as every lottery player has the same chance of selecting the correct number. Not only was this particular analogy a good example illustrating the two analogical domains (the radioactive nuclear decay process and the selection of number in a lottery draw), but it also was taught in an effective manner by emphasizing the similar probability of events occurring in the two domains. The teacher discussed the limitations of the analogy with the students, showing that in nuclear decay, chance happens over a certain period of time, but in a lottery it does not. The teacher also briefly mentioned the aspect of luck in winning a lottery. In another analogy, the teacher used a coin-tossing analogy to explain that after two half-lives, not all nuclei have changed but 25% are still left. This is an advantage of teacher-generated analogy—the analogy was carefully thought through, the teacher was certain that the students knew the analogy, and the limitations were clearly discussed.

A second analogy arose when a teacher compared three different types of fields—electric, magnetic, and gravitational—with much attention given to the analogies between the electric and the gravitational fields. In each case, the teacher described how the size of the force in both fields is proportional to the product of the two electric charges or two masses divided by the square of their distance apart. An interesting switch between the fields was observed in that the teacher changed the roles of analog and target several times: the electric field was used to work out features of the gravitational field and vice versa. During this discussion, the teacher described some of the limitations of the field lines in that they "are not real things; there is a field also between the field lines" and suggestions were sought from students about how the evidence for the fields could be identified.

IMPORTANT POINT TO REMEMBER

In these lessons, the teacher carefully considered the instructional purpose of the analogies, did not introduce additional ideas, the students understood the analogy, and the instructional purpose was very clear.

Students are often unfamiliar with an analog, especially if it is drawn from the adult world where they have limited experience. When an unfamiliar analogy is used to explain an unfamiliar concept, it may increase the confusion and misunderstanding because students cannot map the relationship in the expected manner (Zook & Di Vesta, 1991). Teachers should always try to choose analogs that are familiar to students or explain the features of the analog to the students in sufficient detail to help remediate this problem. It is as simple as asking students what they think the features of an analog are and how it works. If they don't know and the analog cannot be easily explained or demonstrated, don't use the analogy!

To finish this section we need to return to a feature of constructivist-based learning. We mentioned that it is important for teachers to have an idea of where their students are at, cognitively speaking. Quite some time ago, the renowned educational psychologist Jean Piaget proposed that a student's (or indeed any individual's) cognitive ability to deal with abstract thought increases progressively. According to Piaget, we all begin with limited reasoning ability and progress spontaneously with age from sensory-motor operational thought (in which we can respond only to sensory experiences), to concrete operational thought (where we can relate to physical or concrete items), to formal abstract operational thought (where we are able to perform mental modeling and relate to highly abstract mental images). While many researchers now have reservations about aspects of Piaget's ideas (e.g., we now believe that the age range for which students are, for example, concrete thinkers as proposed by Piaget is too limited), research suggests that some students are at the concrete stage when teachers assume they are capable of abstract thought. Recent research suggests that certain analogies may be useful in assisting students who function primarily at the concrete operational level. However, if students lack visual imagery, analogical reasoning, or correlational reasoning, then the value of analogies may be limited. To illustrate what we mean, some students need to physically see an analogy rather than just having it described to them.

Student-Generated Analogies

As we pointed out earlier, students sometimes spontaneously generate analogies; other times, student analogies arise from analogies proposed by the teacher. We start our description of student-generated analogies by recounting some details of student-generated analogy, and use this to see how students work to try and understand science.

Verbal Student-Generated Analogies

Harrison and de Jong (2005) report an episode in which a student-generated analogy arose during discussion about chemical equilibrium. In the prelesson discussion, the teacher (let's call him Neil) developed some verbal analogies to help his students understand equilibrium, particularly the dynamic aspect. The interplay between Neil's instruction and students' questions activated what the authors call a *formative assessment feedback loop* that encouraged knowledge construction. The link to constructivism shows up here: the teacher used his planned analogies to probe his students' understanding in a formative manner and then built on this to scaffold their learning.

In the episode, a student called Mal (a pseudonym) offered a variation on an analogy introduced by the teacher. The teacher's analogy related the dynamic nature of equilibrium to sugar in a tea cup dissolving and then solidifying.

Neil: In England at 4 o'clock . . . everybody stops, and they offer you one lump or two . . . and we've put in 5 lumps, stirred very, very nicely . . . of course, that tea is hot, but what happens is that the tea becomes cold. What happens to the sugar? You've all experienced this if you've oversugared your tea.

Mal: Lumpy at the bottom . . . sweet.

Neil: Sweet and, syrupy, isn't it? That's all the sugar at the bottom of your tea. . . . We put sugar in our tea, the tea cools and sugar falls out, so what does it say about the solubility of sugar in that tea? What sort of solution is that?

Mal: Saturated.

Neil: Meaning we can't add any more sugar without it dissolving . . . Let's say that you dissolved . . . a million sugar molecules, right? If I add a million and one molecules, is that one molecule going to dissolve?

Mal: No.

Neil: What does this have to do with equilibrium? Let's have a look at the characteristics of equilibrium. Is that cup of tea, in terms of sugar, a closed system? If I put the sugar bowl away, they can't get at it anymore.

Mal: We can assume so.

Neil: It's not quite [closed] at the moment, but what could I do to make it one?

Mal: Put a lid on it.

Neil: Put a lid on it, or seal it up. . . . So we can't get any more sugar in, the tea cannot evaporate. . . . Now, rate of forward process versus rate of reverse process. What is the process we're talking about here?

Mal: Sugar dissolving.

Neil: Sugar dissolving . . . if one molecule out of the million that I have there comes to rest, how many particles will now be here? A million minus one, which is 999,999: does that mean that one molecule [will] be able to dissolve?

Mal: Yep.

Neil: So what we've got is a situation where for every one molecule that actually comes out of solution and forms a solid, another molecule can dissolve . . . what can we say about the rates of those processes?

Mal: They're the same.

Neil: They're the same, looks . . . that's looking . . . like an equilibrium . . . Jon asked before, the point about why is this dynamic, and I think this is the hardest point to get across to you . . . imagine you can see the sugar on the bottom. You can see through the cup. . . . Now, I can sit and look at that, and after about two minutes nothing appears to be happening. But you as a chemist are well aware that for every molecule that solidifies, another one dissolves, and another molecule from up here may find its way down and another one may find its way up and so on . . . a kid will tell you nothing's going on there, but the process is dynamic, in terms of you've got solidifying occurring, you've got dissolving occurring, all at the same time, so it's dynamic on a molecular level.

It soon became evident that the students had not understood the dynamic concept in the way the teacher desired. The students knew they didn't get it but were engaged in the learning process because they could relate to some features of the concepts being discussed. But look what happens next: One student asked a question in which he showed that he had built on the teacher-generated analogy and developed his own. The teacher worked on this analogy and helped the student scaffold his learning:

Mal: Is that happening when you've got like food in a pot and you've got a lid on, and when some evaporates at the same time some is condensing and dropping down at the same time?

Neil: Ok, very good. . . . Now for all intents and purposes is that a closed system if I've got the lid on pretty tight?

Mal: Yeah.

Neil: Not completely closed, but it will do. . . . Now, you do a recipe and they tell you add this and that, simmer for 20 minutes with lid on. Why are they telling you to do that? Why leave the lid on?

Mal: Liquid stays in the pot.

Neil: And the liquid's got to stay in the pot, why?

Mal: 'Cause otherwise it'll all evaporate and everything will like go dry.

Neil: Exactly; we end up with some sort of curry that's just bits of dried up chicken with bits of dried out veggies, and little lumps of curry sticking to it. . . . I put it on the stove. What's happening to the water?

Mal: Evaporates.

Neil: Evaporates; what happens when it hits the lid?

Mal: Condenses.

Neil: It cools and condenses . . . it drops back into the solution, so you pretty well know you're going to get the consistency you want for the curry. . . . [It] is an equilibrium if we've got a closed system . . . and the level remains constant . . . the rate of evaporation equals the rate of . . .

Mal: Condensation.

This vignette shows that the curry simmering in a pot analogy, developed spontaneously by Mal, was more relevant to his own daily experiences and so he tried to relate the teacher-generated analogy (that he basically understood but didn't quite get) to something more real to him. This is interesting, because it reaffirms the main purpose of analogy, to help an individual relate the unknown (i.e., the target; in this case chemical equilibrium) to something known (i.e., the analog; in this case, a pot of curry).

Student-Generated Role-Play Analogy

Aubusson and Fogwill (2006) describe a student-generated role-play analogy. As they point out, reports of role-play by students are rare enough, let alone those that are student generated. In this case, the role-play was teacher initiated, and developed subsequently by the students. The group was an 11th-grade class who were trying to make sense of some of the chemical reactions involved in electrolysis. The teaching unit was fairly involved and looked at copper carbonate reacting with sulfuric acid, dissolution of copper sulfate, and electrolysis of copper sulfate.

The students made the copper carbonate molecules with five students. They put labels on themselves; for example, the copper ion students wore a Cu^{2+} label. Four students represented the carbonate ion (CO_3^{2-}): one was carbon and three others were oxygen atoms. They represented the covalent bonds between carbon and oxygen by linking arms. One oxygen student linked both arms with the carbon student, representing a double covalent bond. The other two oxygen students formed a single covalent bond by linking one arm with the carbon student. These two also held a book in their other hands, representing an extra electron. The students explained that they were trying to show not only that the carbonate group was negative but also the location of the extra electrons. The students decided to model the copper with a student who held her arms by her sides (representing a lack of valence electrons to share). The two oxygen students with the extra electrons (book), held their books (electrons) resting on the shoulders of the copper ion to represent the ionic bonding. Here the students were showing how they thought the copper ion was held in the copper sulfate molecule.

When the clump of students representing the copper carbonate role-played entering water, the carbonate group of four students separated slightly from the copper ion student. The oxygen students in the carbonate group retained the electron books, leaving the ion negative and in solution. The copper student with arms by her sides was now a dissolved positive ion. The idea that the students wanted to convey in the role-play was that the copper ion was stuck to the carbonate because the copper ion was positive and was attracted to the negative oxygen atoms on the carbonate ion. But when they were in the water, the water somehow separated them. This was all revealed as they were talking about and designing and modifying their role-play (Aubusson & Fogwill, 2006).

Aubusson and Fogwill (2006) point out that the teacher found this process helpful, the students enjoyed the activity, and the teacher felt that the students had learned something about the concepts under instruction. In addition, the teacher felt the role-play had provided a diagnostic function and indicated what needed to be considered in future lessons. For example, the teacher was able to use the drama of the role-play to ask some probing questions, such as, "How did water contribute to the dissolving of ionic substances?"

A Young Teacher's Response to Student-Generated Analogy

In the next example, we again draw upon work by Ritchie et al. (2006), who report on beginning science teachers' experiences. One of their case studies included a new teacher who was exposed to a student-generated analogy:

A student generated one successful analogy following my whole-class discussion of the function of a neuron. The student had not started the diagram I had requested to be drawn and when prompted, he explained he had been thinking and that a neuron was a lot like a power cord. He suggested that the axon was like the wire inside and the myelin was like the insulation on a power cord. Other students listening agreed and started expanding the analogy further by including axons, dendrites and synapses. This developed into a class discussion on the analogy and how far you could take it. Students took the core idea and applied it while also realizing its limits—namely, there was no corresponding cell body in a power cord, so they started discussing computer networks and cabling. The discussion did require me to guide it back when ideas were getting confused or ridiculous and also to field questions, including, "If myelin breaks down, is it dangerous like if insulation is damaged on a power cord?" leading to discussion on diseases. In the end the class had a good understanding of the parts and function of the neuron and demonstrated this on their overall achievement for this section of the exam. (p. 149)

What we find interesting about this example is that the other students in the classroom could also relate better to the analogy generated by one of their peers. This arguably is the greatest advantage of student-generated analogy. You can be much more confident that the analog will be relevant and accessible to all of your students when it comes from them.

Analogies and the Use of Teacher-Generated and Student-Generated Analogies

You should be able to see some common themes emerging: how analogies can help stimulate student interest and how they aid understanding by relating complex and abstract scientific concepts to students' worlds and thus are consistent with student-centered, constructivist learning. No matter how skillful, hardworking, and prepared you are as a teacher, you are always going to encounter some surprises in the classroom. Think of the teacher, Robert, in Cosgrove's (1995) example: he was skillful and prepared. He knew his students would probably find the topic difficult, and he had some analogies already prepared to help their understanding. But he did not get the chance to use them; a student preempted the situation by generating his own analogy. This teacher used this learning opportunity and used analogies skillfully, essentially following the FAR Guide.

One final point: While student-generated analogy can provide wonderfully rich discussion and motivation, this motivation typically arises because the students have the opportunity to relate the scientific concept to their own world. However, it can also easily lead to complicated discourse if too many extraneous ideas and notions are introduced in too short a time. As we keep pointing out, the uncritical use of analogy can result in students developing alternative conceptions, and if you are bombarded with numerous student analogies, it can all get out of hand rather quickly. Some moderation of the process is thus essential.

PART II

Analogies for Teaching Science

6

Effective Biology Analogies

Grady J. Venville

I n his famous book, *The Origin of Species,* Darwin (1967) included a passage that eloquently, almost poetically, represented his ideas about evolution in the form of an extended analogy using a branching tree.

> The green and budding twigs may represent existing species; and those produced during former years may represent the long succession of extinct species. . . . Of the many twigs which flourished when the tree was a mere bush, only two or three now grow into great branches, yet survive and bear the other branches; so with the species which lived during long-past geological periods, very few have left living and modified descendants. From the first growth of the tree, many a limb and branch has decayed and dropped off; and these fallen branches of various sizes may represent those whole orders, families, and genera which have now no living representatives, and which are known to us only in a fossil state. (p. 126)

The rich imagery evident in Darwin's analogy creates a concrete picture of the abstract and dynamic process of evolution. The use of analogies in biology has a strong history, not only as a way of representing ideas but also as a source of knowledge. Konrad Lorenz (1974) delivered a lecture titled *Analogy as a Source of Knowledge* in 1973 when he received the Nobel Prize in Physiology or Medicine (Lorenz's speech can be downloaded from the official Nobel Prize Web site: http://nobelprize.org). By analogy, Lorenz refers to the similarities between species caused by parallel adaptation. For example, he refers to the analogy of structure between a bird and a shark for streamlining and the analogy between the eye of a vertebrate and a cephalopod. His own work focused on an analogy between the behavior of human beings and of geese, particularly when they fall in love and are jealous, and how the analogy demonstrates the survival value of such behaviors. Lorenz claimed that the use of analogy has been an enormous source of knowledge for evolutionists and embryologists.

Students and teachers of biology can use analogies as a means of representation and as a source of knowledge in a way similar to the explanations of biologists Darwin and Lorenz. Biological concepts, such as those related to genetics, homeostasis, and ecological interdependence, require a considerable degree of abstract reasoning, and analogies can be useful for the purpose of providing an alternative, more accessible representation. The problem with analogies often used in biology textbooks and by biology teachers, however, is that they tend to be used in a nonelaborated way (Thiele, Venville, & Treagust, 1995). Biology is replete with terms such as *shovel-like feet*, *pouch-like bill*, *file-like radula*, and *whip-like flagella*. These particular phrases convey important structural and functional attributes, but they generally are not worth developing into more extended instructional analogies. Other analogies that are used in a nonelaborated form, however, may have considerable worth if developed into extended instructional tools. Examples of such analogies include these: mitochondria are the powerhouse of the cell, ribosomes are protein factories, and enzymes interact with substrates like a lock and key. The problem with these analogies is that they have become mechanical clichés that biologists, including teachers and textbook authors, use without thinking about the message being conveyed. Such analogies might be very useful to students if they were explained in a more detailed manner.

The 12 biology analogies presented on the following pages may be very familiar to biology teachers as frequently cited, unelaborated metaphors. Once biology teachers recognize how often they use analogies, they may begin to appreciate the potential value of extending more of them into a repertoire of fun, engaging, and creative models; role-plays; activities, and stories that can be used in the classroom.

The 12 biology analogies are now described and summarized in the FAR Guide format:

1. The City Analogy for a Cell
2. The Supermarket Analogy of a Classification System

3. The Rechargeable Battery Analogy for ATP

4. The Lock and Key Analogy for Enzyme Action

5. The Fluid-Mosaic Analogy for Cell Membranes

6. The Geography Analogy for the Human Genome

7. The Building a House Analogy for Protein Synthesis

8. The Buckets and Pumps Analogy for the Heart

9. The Clothespin Analogy for the Structure of DNA

10. An Earth Analogy for Cell Components

11. A Web Analogy for the Interdependence of Organisms

12. The Analogy of Homeostasis Being Like a Student Walking Up the Down Escalator

The City Analogy for a Cell

Students in all high school grades and some older elementary school children learn about cells. Cells are the basic building blocks of all organisms, and they comprise a central concept that is related to all aspects of biology.

Most cells, however, are visible only with a microscope. Students can become very excited when participating in laboratory activities in which they prepare and stain slides and view cells under the microscope, and these activities are highly recommended. Unfortunately, school microscopes usually do not highlight the internal structure of the cell very well and do not enable the students to understand its compartmentalized nature. Students also find it difficult to understand that organelles have specific functions while at the same time being interactive and interdependent on each other.

An analogy with a city can be used to explain the internal structure of a cell and the functions of each of the organelles. Most important, the analogy can also be extended to consider the interdependence between the various aspects of a cell. Most students are familiar with a city and, with some help, will be able to transfer important concepts, such as government and control, construction, transportation, energy production, waste management, and interdependence from their understandings of a city to their developing understandings of a cell.

This activity works quite well in small groups as a way to consolidate ideas learned about the cell. Teachers can give each group a list of organelles and their functions and ask the students to collaboratively develop their own analogy based on their knowledge of a city. Each group is given a large piece of paper on which to develop their analogy (see Figure 2.3, the example for the cell city analogy in Chapter 2). Groups share their ideas at the end of the lesson so the teacher can monitor the similarities that they have discussed to ensure that no misconceptions have developed. For example, one group of Grade 8 students decided that the nucleus of the cell was like the city council. Initially this seemed to be a good idea to the teacher, but when she asked one of the students more probing questions, she discovered that in the student's experience, the city council was primarily responsible for garbage disposal. The student transferred this functional understanding to the cell, developing the misconception that the primary function of the nucleus was waste disposal. Dissimilarities between the City Analogy and the cell target concept also can be discussed as a whole-class group, and this process is also likely to reveal any misunderstandings that need attention from the teacher.

The City Analogy for a Cell		
Focus	**Concept**	The functions of cell organelles and their interrelationships are abstract and difficult for students to understand and communicate. Interest in the human genome and the increasing need to understand basic organelle functions increases the focus on cellular biology. Students also have many questions about cells. No cell is an island nor is it an independent entity.
	Students	Young students attribute multicellular function and activity to cells (e.g., cells can think); others confuse cellular and molecular characteristics. Junior high school students see the protoplasm as undifferentiated goo. Some students think proteins, fats, and carbohydrates are made of cells.
	Analog	Comparing a cell to a city helps students understand that cells have activity sites that perform citylike functions—importers of raw materials, factories, distribution (transportation), and waste handling facilities. Cities and cells have control centers, communication systems, and storage areas.

	The City Analogy for a Cell (Continued)	
Action	**Likes—Mapping the Analog to the Target**	
	Analog—City with inputs and outputs	**Target—Cell with inputs and outputs**
	City council governs and controls city.	Nucleus controls all the cell's activities.
	A power station provides electricity.	Mitochondia provide chemical energy (adenosine triphosphate [ATP]).
	Construction companies build houses.	Ribosomes construct proteins.
	Roads, cars, buses and trucks provide transportation.	Endoplasmic reticulum is a transportation system.
	Warehouses store food, clothes and hardware.	Plastids store substances like starch.
	Factories make things for export (e.g., shoes and cosmetics).	Golgi bodies produce substances exported to other cells (e.g., hormones, skin oils).
	Food processors prepare foods like bread.	Chloroplasts make the cell's sugars.
	Unlikes—Where the Analogy Breaks Down	
	• Chloroplasts trap sunlight energy, but a bakery uses wheat and electricity. • City government changes direction after elections and is very adaptable; cell control from the nucleus is fixed.	
Reflection	**Conclusion** Did the students make the planned connections between the city and cell functions? Did they realize that the functions are integrated and interdependent? Do I need to clarify some of these points in the next lesson? Would a further analogy comparing a cell with a house be useful to extend or consolidate the students' understandings?	
	Improvements Should students make group cell-city models? Will SimCity help?	

The City Analogy for a Cell (Continued)	
Science Content Standard C, Life Science, Grades 5–8: "Structure and function of living systems" (National Academy of Sciences [NAC], 1996, p. 156). Living systems are organized at the cellular level. Grades 9–12: "The cell," cells are differentiated for specialized functions (p. 184). Using evidence to build analogical models makes prediction and communication part of inquiry. Science Content Standard A, Inquiry for Grades 5–8: "Abilities necessary to do inquiry . . . predictions and models using evidence" (pp. 145) and Grades 9–12 (p. 175).	
Suggested strategies	In groups of two to four, students can map the cell-city similarities and make analogical models of a city and a cell as a project. This could be used for formative or summative assessment.
Resources	Model-mapping worksheets, a stylized diagram of a city (e.g., SimCity), model-making equipment (paper, glue, matches, plastic straws, beads, cellophane, etc.).
Applications	Depending on the level of structure and function, this model (especially when coupled with hands-on model making) could be used from Grades 4–12. It is very adaptable and interesting.

The Supermarket Analogy of a Classification System

Young children often think that ants and flies aren't animals, because they are insects, and a carrot isn't a plant because it's a vegetable. The problem for these children is that they don't understand that a fly can be an insect and an animal at the same time and a carrot can be a vegetable and a plant at the same time. In science, we use a hierarchical (box within box) classification system that is difficult for students of many ages to understand. A more familiar scenario of a hierarchical classification system is the local supermarket. The very visual classification system within a supermarket can be used as an analogy for a biological classification system. If the students can understand that feta can be a cheese and a dairy product at the same time, they may be able to transfer this understanding to the way they think about the living world. Diagrams and photographs like Figures 6.1 and 6.2 are very helpful when using this analogy.

Figure 6.1   The Box-Within-Box Classification System for Organisms

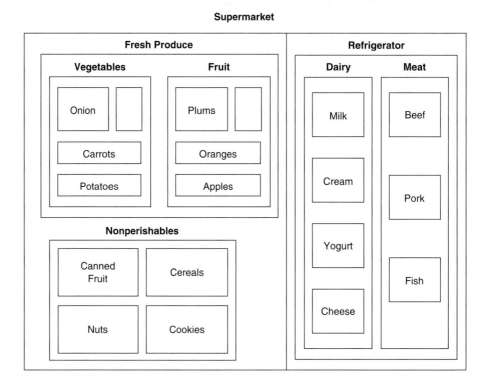

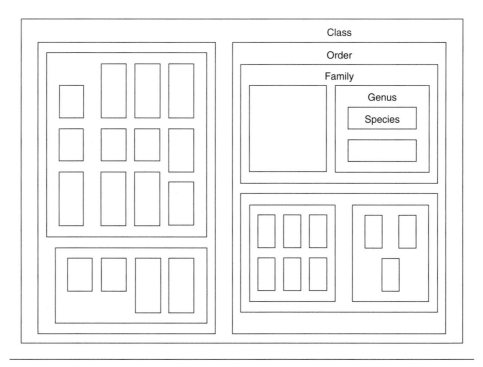

Figure 6.2   Photographs of the Classification System in Supermarkets

The Supermarket Analogy for a Classification System		
Focus	Concept	Biologists have named 2 million species of plants and animals, and the number of different species may reach 20 million or more. How can we investigate, understand, and communicate this vast array of information? Biologists classify organisms into groups and study the groups. For example, in the classical kingdom system of classification, each species is first placed in a kingdom, then a phylum, class, order, family, genus, and species. Molecular biology has led to an alternative domain system based on ribosomal RNA, but this alternative system is still hierarchical and can be explained with the box-within-box model.

The Supermarket Analogy for a Classification System (Continued)

	Students	Hierarchical classification systems challenge students; they have difficulty understanding how one species can belong to a number of levels—phylum, class, order, family, genus, and species at the same time. Young children can classify vertebrates but are inconsistent in the way they deal with simpler animals and most plants. Most nonvertebrates are "bugs."
	Analog	The way organisms are classified is like the way retail items are arranged in a supermarket. Items for sale are divided into departments, then aisles, shelves, and positions on each shelf. A small supermarket can be likened to the plants and animals in and around your area. Food and nonfood items are systematically organized so that celery, Coca-Cola, matches, and baked beans all have their special places. Staff and customers know where each item is.

Action	Likes—Mapping the Analog to the Target	
	Analog—A supermarket	**Target—Classifying organisms**
	A supermarket is organized into regions to help customers and staff find items.	Classification brings order to the study and identification of organisms.
	It has many levels: food—nonfood; fresh, frozen, preserved foods, meat, dairy, fruit, vegetables.	It is hierarchical, from large groups with high diversity to small groups with little diversity.
	Each product has distinctive characteristics for finding or placing it on a shelf.	Each species has distinctive characteristics that place it in levels of increasing specificity.
	Some goods are hard to put into specific places (e.g., should canned tomatoes go with the pasta sauces or canned vegetables?).	Some organisms don't easily fit into groups (e.g., *Euglena* can photosynthesize like a plant and ingest food like an animal).

The Supermarket Analogy for a Classification System (Continued)

	Different supermarkets arrange their goods in different ways, but they always use a system.	Different taxonomists classify organisms differently, but they always use a system.

Unlikes—Where the Analogy Breaks Down

- The living world has far more variety than even the biggest supermarket.
- Few supermarkets sell every item, but all classification systems treat all known species.
- Supermarkets arrange goods according to buyer behavior, shelf life, and size; biologists restrict their classification system to body structure and function. Color, size and behavior are rarely used to classify organisms but are used in supermarkets.

Reflection	Conclusion	Was the comparison of a supermarket with a biological classification system useful? Could the students identify the shared and unshared attributes? Do they need to visit a local supermarket? Do they now understand box-within-box (hierarchical) classification?
	Improvements	Should I take the class to the supermarket before the lesson? Can I get a map of a local supermarket from its proprietors? Should the students be given an activity where they explain box-within-box classification in their own words?

Science Content Standard C, Life Science, Grades 5–8: "Structure and function of living systems" (NAS, 1996, p. 154); "Diversity and adaptations of organisms" p. 158). Living things are diverse and there are millions of species; phyla, classes . . . genera and species are organized according to structure and function. The Supermarket Analogy demonstrates the benefits of systematic classification.

Suggested teaching strategies	Introduce the problem of classifying, say, a snail, a grasshopper, a jellyfish, a sea star, moss, a spider, a mouse, a fern, a bee, a petunia, a frog, and so on. Collect student ideas. Use an overhead transparency (OHT) map of a local supermarket to show how a large retail shop deals with diversity. Obtain permission to visit the local supermarket. Visit the supermarket and ask students to draw a map showing placement of 30–40 items listed on a worksheet.

The Supermarket Analogy for a Classification System (Continued)	
Resources	Most biology textbooks suitable for Grades 8–12; especially Biological Sciences Curriculum Study (BSCS) texts and workbooks.
Applications	Suitable for Grade 5–10 depending on the supermarket and classification system detail.

The Rechargeable Battery Analogy for ATP

A readily available source of energy is required by cells for activities such as building complex molecules, maintaining organization, the movement of cellular organelles, cell division, the active uptake of substances from outside the cell, and the transmission of nervous impulses. Learning about adenosine triphosphate (ATP) and adenosine diphosphate (ADP) is essential for understanding how energy is stored and used in living cells. The chemical reactions that occur in a cell either produce energy (chiefly the reactions of respiration) or require energy. ATP is the chemical substance that links these reactions by providing energy when it is needed and temporarily storing it when it is generated. All living cells make and use ATP in their energy-releasing and energy-using processes.

The reversible reaction that captures and releases energy is difficult for many students to understand. ATP is a large molecule made up of adenosine and three smaller phosphate groups attached to it. Energy is released and is then available for use when the third phosphate molecule is broken from the ATP to make ADP, and energy is stored when the reverse reaction takes place. ATP is continually being made up and broken down in cells in a cycle that drives energy-requiring processes. An analogy with a rechargeable battery, commonly observed and used by students, is a useful way to represent the ATP and ADP molecules and the related chemical reaction. Word equations, such as those presented in Figure 6.3, create a symbolic analogy that is relatively easy for students to understand. The photograph in Figure 6.4 shows a commonly used battery recharger containing four AA-sized rechargeable batteries.

Figure 6.3   Word Equations Comparing ATP–ADP With a Rechargeable Battery

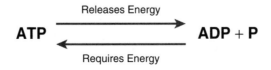

Figure 6.4   A Common Battery Recharger

The Rechargeable Battery Analogy for ATP		
Focus	Concept	The role of ATP in living cells is an important biochemical concept, but it is abstract, unobservable, and difficult for many students. ATP is the immediate source of energy for the activities of the cell. When ATP breaks down to ADP and an inorganic phosphate, a large quantity of energy is released. The ADP can then be recycled and joined with inorganic phosphate molecules to make ATP again.
	Students	The students' current understanding of ATP or energy storage in living things could be elicited by doing a group activity in which students are challenged to work out how energy gets from the mitochondria in the cell to places where energy is needed, like ribosomes.

The Rechargeable Battery Analogy for ATP (Continued)		
	Analog	Most students will have experienced rechargeable batteries used in various electronic devices, electronic games, or mobile phones. Rechargeable batteries are concrete and observable by students.
Action	Likes—Mapping the Analog to the Target	
	Analog—Rechargeable battery	Target—ATP and ADP
	A charged battery is energy sufficient.	ATP is energy sufficient.
	Batteries move energy to where it's needed to power an electronic device.	ATP is moved to where energy is needed in the cell.
	A charged battery converts into a flat battery as energy is used.	ATP converts to ADP when energy is used.
	A rechargeable battery can be used over and over again.	ATP can be used over and over again: ATP + P $\Leftrightarrow$ ATP
	A battery recharger is the site where energy is reintroduced to the flat batteries.	Mitochondria are the sites where energy is used to change ADP to ATP.
	Recharged batteries can be used in a variety of machines for a variety of energy-requiring tasks.	ATP can be used at many sites in the cell (ribosomes or cell membrane) for tasks such as protein production or active transport.
	Unlikes—Where the Analogy Breaks Down	
	• A battery's energy is released gradually, whereas a single molecule of ATP will release all the energy tied up in the terminal phosphate bond in a single instant. • A phosphate breaks away from ATP; nothing breaks away from the battery. • Usually two batteries are used in a Walkman or electronic game; many ATP molecules are used in a cell.	
Reflection	Conclusion	Were the students able to visualize the function of ATP in a cell as being similar to a rechargeable battery? Did they make

	The Rechargeable Battery Analogy for ATP (Continued)	
		connections between ATP–ADP and energy producing–energy requiring reactions in the cell? Will I need to clarify some of these points next lesson?
	Improvements	Would the use of a different or additional analogy help the students? For example, I could explain that ATP is like energy money that the cell can use to "pay for" a whole range of different processes.
Suggested strategies	Small-group discussion can be used to elicit students' ideas prior to introducing ATP. The teacher should demonstrate a rechargeable battery and recharger to the whole class.	
Science Content Standard C, Life Science, Grades 9–12: "The cell; cells contain "molecules . . . that carry out such cell functions as energy production, transport . . . waste disposal, synthesis of new molecules" (NAS, 1996, p. 184). The Rechargeable Battery Analogy explains the ATP–ADP energy cycle in the cell.		
Resources	An overhead or slide showing the word equations for ATP and charged batteries. An actual example of batteries and a charger could also be used.	
Applications	This analogy is most useful for students in Grades 11–12 when they are studying introductory biochemistry in courses such as biology, human biology, or integrated science but also may be useful for advanced placement Grade 10 students.	

The Lock and Key Analogy for Enzyme Action

Enzymes are very important chemicals in cells that are used to speed up cellular reactions to rates that allow the cell to function properly and survive. Enzymes are very specific, which means that they can speed up only the particular reaction to which they belong. For example, the enzyme *amylase* is able to split the large starch molecule into smaller molecules of maltose. The enzyme *phosphorylase* is able to take small molecules of glucose-1-phosphate and build them into large molecules of starch. These enzymes—amylase and phosphorylase—do not speed up other reactions in the cell; they are specific to these particular chemical reactions.

Teachers and textbooks often state, in a very simplified way, that enzymes act in a similar manner to locks and keys. The comparison between a lock and key and enzyme action is of much greater value if it is developed into a more extended analogy. Enzymes are made of very large protein molecules that are folded in a way that creates a particular pocket-like shape on the surface that exactly fits the shape of the chemicals it reacts with. This pocket is like the hole in a lock that fits exactly the shape of one key and no other keys; in cells, this is called an *active site*. The enzyme is able to hold the chemical reactants in a way that enables the desired chemical reaction to occur much quicker than it would if the enzyme wasn't there. When the chemical reaction has taken place, the products are set free from the enzyme in a similar way to a key that is set free from a lock once it has been opened. The enzyme, like the key, can be reused. Figure 6.5 shows a diagrammatic representation of the comparisons that can be made between a lock and key and the action of an enzyme. This diagram could be used on an overhead or a slide as a tool for developing this comparison into an extended analogy.

Figure 6.5   A Diagrammatic Representation of the Analogy of a Lock and Key for Enzyme Action

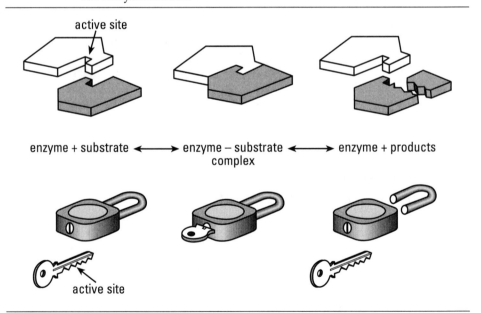

SOURCE: Redrawn from Otto and Towle (1969, p. 47).

The Lock and Key Analogy for Enzyme Action

Focus	Concept	Enzymes are an abstract concept, and the notion of active sites that react only with specific substrates is a difficult idea for students to understand. The idea of enzymes is particularly difficult for students who do not study chemistry and do not understand catalysts.
	Students	Students often think that enzymes eat things up. This idea may come from popular washing powder advertisements that claim to contain enzymes that help to remove dirt from clothing. Enzymes are represented as "munching bugs" in such commercials, which is likely to create alternative conceptions about the function of enzymes.
	Analog	The familiar lock and key analogy is a concrete way to model substrate interaction with enzymes. The analogy is of much greater value if it is explained in detail.

Action	Likes—Mapping the Analog to the Target	
	Analog—Lock and key	Target—Enzymes and substrates
	Key	Enzyme molecule
	Lock (padlock)	Substrate molecule
	Notched part of key (has unique shape)	Active site (has unique chemical makeup)
	Keys unlock only specific locks.	Enzymes react only with specific substrates.
	Key breaks apart (unlocks) a padlock.	Enzyme action breaks apart substrate molecules.
	The key comes out of the lock unchanged and can be reused.	The enzyme comes out of the reaction unchanged and can be reused.

The Lock and Key Analogy for Enzyme Action (Continued)

	Unlikes—Where the Analogy Breaks Down	
	• Locks are usually bigger than keys; substrate molecules are usually smaller than the enzymes they react with. • The lock and key relationship is based on physical shape; the enzyme and substrate fit is based on chemical bonding patterns. • Padlocks don't usually break completely apart to form different products as some substrate molecules do. • A key can lock or unlock a padlock; an enzyme speeds up a chemical reaction.	
Reflection	**Conclusion**	Did the students understand the specific nature of enzymes as a result of this analogy? Did they understand how the enzymes speed up chemical reactions in the cell?
	Improvements	What improvements can I make next time I use this analogy? Could I use a role-play, with some students acting as enzymes and some acting as substrate and product?
Science Content Standard C, Life Science, Grades 9–12: "The cell" (NAS, 1996, p. 184); cells contain "molecules . . . that carry out such cell functions as energy production...synthesis of new molecules" (p. 184). The processes are regulated by enzymes that are specific to each reaction (NAS, 1996, pp. 184, 186). The Lock and Key Analogy explains enzyme specificity in the cell.		
Suggested teaching strategies	As an attention-grabbing activity, the teacher can ask students to take out all the keys they have in their pockets and bags, put them on the table, and ask them to guess which one will open a padlock you have put on the table. (You can ask a student to work with you before the lesson and plant the specific key in a bag or pocket before the lesson.) Compare the shape of all the keys, and talk about how the shape is related to whether it will open a lock or not. Introduce the terminology of *specific* in this familiar context before starting to use it in the context of cells and enzymes.	
Resources	An overhead of an enzyme-substrate complex and lock and key as demonstrated in Figure 6.5 is a very useful resource while developing the extended analogy.	
Applications	This analogy is mostly suitable for students studying Grade 11 and Grade 12 biology and human biology or integrated science, but it could also be used for advanced placement Grade 10 students.	

The Fluid-Mosaic Analogy for Cell Membranes

Many explanations and analogies used to describe cell membranes emphasize their static barrier properties. For example, membranes are often described as being like string bags. This analogy may be useful when explaining to students in a very simple way that membranes allow some substances, such as water, to move freely from one side of the membrane to the other. This is called *high permeability*. The same membrane may not allow the free movement of other substances, such as proteins, from one side of the membrane to the other. This is called *low permeability*. Using the string bag analogy, the water molecules are small enough to fit through the pores of membranes, just like the holes of a string bag, but protein molecules are too big. Membranes are most permeable to water and some small, uncharged organic molecules. They are least permeable to large organic molecules and inorganic molecules and inorganic ions with an electrostatic charge.

However, this model does not account for other properties of cell membranes. At certain times the cell must select and concentrate certain substances that are needed for particular functions. For example, plant root cells sometimes need to concentrate mineral ions from the soil. Membranes can alter their permeability to some substances at particular times to allow for this concentration, depending on the presence of chemical or electrical triggers. The process is called *active transport*. Membranes are very flexible, dynamic structures. The fluid-mosaic model of cell membranes helps account for these properties when elaborated in an appropriate manner.

This model can actually be divided into two analogies, that of the mosaic and that of the fluid. Examples of mosaic art (Figure 6.6) can be brought into class in case the students are unfamiliar with that style of art. The mosaic idea can be used to explain that proteins are embedded within two layers of lipids, and the fluid idea can be used to explain the mobility of proteins within the lipid bilayer. The proteins can move about in the fluid layer to make channels through which specific substances can move across the cell membrane. That is, when electrical and chemical triggers cause the proteins to make these channels, substances can be transported across the cell membrane. When the triggers are removed, the proteins move back, and the channel no longer exists. This movement of the proteins in the two layers of lipids enables active transport of substances needed by the cell.

The purpose of this model is to draw students' understanding of cell membranes away from the *structural* attributes, such as the idea that a cell membranes is a barrier with holes in it, and to emphasize the *process* attributes, such as the fluid nature of cell membranes and the associated functions, such as the ability of proteins to move about and create channels through which polar molecules and ions can pass.

Figure 6.6   An Example of a Piece of Mosaic Artwork

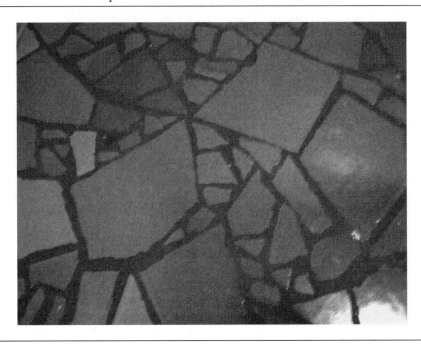

The Fluid-Mosaic Analogy for Cell Membranes		
Focus	**Concept**	This analogy is used to explain the structure of cell membranes as proteins embedded in a bilayer of lipids. The focus is on the dynamic nature of cell membranes that enables active transport by the movement of the proteins in the lipid bilayer to make channels through which certain substances required by the cell can move.
	Students	Students often prefer to focus on static models of cell membranes, such as the string bag model, because they are easier to understand and explain high and low permeability of membranes.
	Analog	The fluid-mosaic model can be broken into two parts, the mosaic and the fluid. A real example or a photograph of a mosaic may be useful to ensure that the students are familiar with the analog.

The Fluid-Mosaic Analogy for Cell Membranes (Continued)

Action	Likes—Mapping the Analog to the Target	
	Analog—Fluid-mosaic	**Target—Cell membrane**
	Mosaic tiles	Membrane proteins
	Fluidlike grout around tiles	Membrane lipid bilayer around proteins
	Tiles can move around in the fluidlike grout.	Proteins can move about in the lipid bilayer.
	The tiles can sometimes be seen above and below the fluidlike grout, creating a tile channel or bridge from one side to the other.	Proteins can act as channels for substances to be transported by diffusion and active transport.
	The tiles can be made of different substances and are often of different colors.	Proteins in the membrane can have different functions (i.e., they transport different substances across the membrane).
	The tiles can sometimes be completely embedded in the fluidlike grout.	Proteins can be moved so that the transport of some substances is blocked by the membrane. Moving the proteins around allows some substances to move across the membrane while others are blocked.
	Unlikes—Where the Analogy Breaks Down	
	• The tiles in a mosaic can't actually move around the way that proteins can in a membrane, but the idea that the grout can be seen as a fluid enables this comparison to be made. • Nothing is transported through the tiles of a mosaic, whereas the proteins are important channels for substances moving in and out of the cell. • The grout has a continuous look to it, whereas the lipid parts of a membrane are in two distinct layers.	
Reflection	**Conclusion** — Were the students able to relate the microscopic explanation of cell membrane structure to macroscopic, observable phenomena, such as osmosis?	

The Fluid-Mosaic Analogy for Cell Membranes (Continued)		
	Improvements	It may be necessary to make more explicit links between the microscopic explanations, such as the fluid-mosaic model, with more concrete, macroscopic examples of active transport and its relationship to the survival of plants and animals.
Science Content Standard C, Life Science, Grades 9–12: "The cells" (NAS, 1996, p. 184). "Every cell is surrounded by a membrane that separates it from the outside world" (p. 184) and controls movement of materials in and out of the cell. The Fluid-Mosaic Analogy explains cell membrane action by focusing on the dynamic features of membranes.		
Suggested teaching strategies	A good overhead or slide of pictorial representations of bilipid–protein membranes together with a real example of a mosaic picture enable a great comparison between the analog and target. A role-play may be useful (students act as moving molecules through a "furniture membrane").	
Resources	Many biology textbooks have pictures of bilipid protein membranes. Check the art department for an real example of a mosaic art piece or a picture of one.	
Applications	This analogy is mostly suitable for students studying Grade 11 and Grade 12 biology and human biology or integrated science.	

The Geography Analogy
for the Human Genome

Chromosomes are often described as being made up of genes like beads on a string. The difficulty with this analogy is one of scale. There are about 100,000 working genes in the genome of a human being, and three million DNA "letters." Most genes use only the information coded in a few thousand DNA bases to actually make a protein. This means that there is much more DNA than is needed for the production of proteins. In fact, only about five percent of the DNA in human beings is part of functioning genes. The extraordinary structure of genes in the DNA of chromosomes is, in actual fact, nothing like a string of beads. Steve Jones (1993) suggests that a geographical analogy, like a road map, might be a more fruitful alternative way for us to think about the whole of our own DNA:

Imagine the journey along the whole of your DNA as being equivalent to one from Land's End to John O'Groat's via London. This is about a thousand miles altogether (which means that its American equal would be roughly equivalent to a trip from New York to Chicago). To fit in all the DNA letters into a road map on this scale, there have to be fifty DNA bases per inch, or about three million per mile. The journey passes through twenty-three counties of different sizes. These administrative divisions, conveniently enough, are the same in number as the twenty-three chromosomes into which human DNA is packaged. . . . The scenery for most of the trip is very tedious. Like much of modern Britain it seems to be totally unproductive. About a third of the whole distance is covered by repeats of the same message. Fifty miles, more or less, is filled with words of five, six or more letters, repeated endlessly next to each other. Many are palindromes. They read the same backwards as forwards. . . . Some of these "tandem repeats" are scattered in blocks all over the genome. The position and length of each block varies from person to person. The famous 'genetic fingerprints,' the unique inherited signature used in forensic work, depend on variation in the number and position of tandem repeats. . . . Much of the inherited landscape is littered with the corpses of abandoned genes, sometimes the same one again and again. The DNA sequences of these "pseudogenes" look rather like that of their working relatives, but they are riddled with decay and no longer produce anything. . . . After many miles of dull and repetitive DNA terrain, we begin to see places where something is being made. These are the working genes. . . . Many functioning genes are arranged in groups making related products. There are about a thousand of these "gene families" altogether. . . . Another surprising aspect of the map of ourselves is that genes are of very different size, from about five hundred letters long to more than two million. Nearly all the working segments are interrupted by lengths of noncoding DNA. In very large genes (such as the one which goes wrong in muscular dystrophy) the great majority of the DNA codes for nothing. (pp. 68–71)

Since Jones (1993) constructed this analogy, much more has been discovered about the sections of repetitive DNA found in between the productive sites of DNA that are responsible for the coding of proteins. For example, these sections that were once referred to as *junk DNA* are now known to play a major role in the regulation of the DNA that encodes for the proteins. The analogy remains an evocative and useful way for students to imagine the human genome but, as with all good teaching strategies, it must be adapted to accommodate new scientific information.

The Geography Analogy for the Human Genome

Focus	Concept	Chromosomes are made up of a lot of repetitive DNA that is not part of the direct code for proteins but that is important in the regulation of the genes. Genes, or the parts of the chromosomes that do make up the direct code for producing a protein, make up only about five percent of the human genome.
	Students	Students are often taught that genes are like beads on a string, homogenous in size and lined up one after another. Students often do not understand the relationship between genes, DNA, and chromosomes. Some students think that genes and DNA are very different things with different functions.
	Analog	A map, or geography analogy, is concrete and can be visualized. Most students have been on long train or car journeys and understand that there are very monotonous, repetitive regions, such as forests, deserts, or agricultural land, as well as more active regions like towns and cities. They can understand that while the monotonous regions look inactive, they play an important role for the towns and cities. It is best to create the analogy from the geography with which the students are most familiar.

Action	Likes—Mapping the Analog to the Target	
	Analog—Geographical map	**Target—Human genome**
	1,000 mile (1600km) road journey from Sydney to Brisbane (John O'Grotes to Lands End in UK or New York to Chicago)	Length of the human genome
	Regions along the journey (e.g., counties or states)	Chromosomes
	Monotonous sections of the journey such as forests or deserts, fields, or prairies	Repetitive DNA with regulation functions
	Busy cities and towns	Genes—areas of DNA that code for proteins

The Geography Analogy for the Human Genome (Continued)

		Some cities are very large and other towns are small.	Genes vary in size, with some being many DNA letters long and others relatively short.
		Some cities and towns are grouped together.	Families of genes producing similar things are grouped together.

Unlikes—Where the Analogy Breaks Down

- Monotonous sections along a road journey are often very productive (e.g., agricultural and forest regions), but repetitive sections of the genome do not code for proteins.
- Cities and towns manufacture goods on site, whereas genes are a code for proteins that are manufactured at different sites (ribosomes).

Reflection	Conclusion	Do the students now have a better understanding of the relationship between genes, chromosomes, DNA, and the humane genome? Can they visualize the map analogy and transfer that visual image to the notion of a genome?
	Improvements	Can I use this analogy for formative or summative assessment? For example, the students could be given, or asked to find, a map of a trip they may have taken. They are then required to use genes on a specific chromosome to build up a picture based on explicit analogical links with the things that they saw when they took their journey.

Science Content Standard C, Life Science, Grades 9–12: "The molecular basis of heredity" (NAS, 1996, p. 185) is a substantial part of the biology syllabus. Genomics is a rapidly expanding part of cell and molecular biology, and The Geography Analogy is an excellent explanation and basis for student modeling activities.

Suggested teaching strategies	Students could work in groups to construct their own 1,000-mile journey based on their knowledge of local geography.
Resources	Maps and atlases may be helpful and should be borrowed from social studies teachers or libraries. Details of the genome from textbooks and the Internet allow students to develop their understanding and make as many links as possible between the target and analog.
Applications	This analogy is mostly suitable for students studying biology in Grades 10–12.

The Building a House
Analogy for Protein Synthesis

Research has shown that the majority of students complete introductory genetics courses with an understanding that a gene is something that is passed from parents to offspring and that genes influence characteristics (Lewis & Kattmann, 2004; Venville & Treagust, 1998). However, students often don't know how genes influence characteristics, even when they have studied the structure of DNA and protein synthesis. This is mainly because students fail to connect these ideas with their understanding of a gene (Venville & Treagust, 1998). Some students see genes as trait bearing or they do not differentiate genes from characteristics (Lewis & Kattmann, 2004). This is how geneticists viewed genes more than 50 years ago, before the discovery of the structure of DNA.

If, in students' minds, a gene is equivalent to a physical trait, or they have no knowledge about the involvement of genes in the biochemical production of proteins, then there can be no understanding of the hierarchy of biological processes through which the environment or social interaction can influence the physical or behavioral development of an organism. This lack of knowledge is likely to be a formidable barrier to students' understanding the potential social and technological benefits and consequences of advances in biotechnology.

Curriculum documents, teaching manuals, and teachers themselves often reflect the opinion that it is acceptable not to teach protein synthesis to students in introductory genetics courses because it is too difficult or too abstract. A better approach may be to introduce protein synthesis through a concrete analogy, such as building a house, that will enable students to understand the functioning of genes and give them insight into the mechanism through which genes influence phenotype. Some students may not be familiar with the house-building process, and pictures, such as the one in Figure 6.7, may be useful.

Figure 6.7   A Building Site for a House

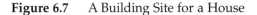

The Building a House Analogy for Protein Synthesis

Focus	Concept	To understand how genes determine phenotype, students must understand protein synthesis. Protein synthesis is a complicated process involving many components and sites of activity, which all occur in the unfamiliar and abstract context of cellular biology. It is difficult for students to get a big picture of the process and, at the same time, understand the functions of each of the individual components.
	Students	It is necessary that before they attempt to learn protein synthesis, students understand that proteins are made of chains of amino acids and that proteins directly or indirectly determine the phenotype of individuals. Students also should understand the structure of DNA.
	Analog	It is possible to compare building a protein with building a house. The house analog is concrete, and the processes are more familiar to students.

Action	Likes—Mapping the Analog to the Target	
	Analog—Building a house	**Target—Protein synthesis**
	Master plan	DNA
	Architect's office (safe place for master plan)	Nucleus
	Copying of master plan and transfer to building site	Transcription
	Master plan copy	mRNA
	Tradesmen bringing bricks and other materials	tRNA
	Bricks	Amino acids
	Mortar to bond bricks together	Energy, to bond amino acids to form a protein
	Following the plan to organize bricks and build a house as planned	Translation of DNA code into mRNA

The Building a House Analogy for Protein Synthesis (Continued)

	Following the plan to organize bricks and build a house as planned	Translation of DNA code into mRNA
	The same kinds of brick arranged differently can build lots of different houses.	The same kinds of amino acids can be arranged to build lots of different proteins.
	Mistakes made by bricklayers, carpenters	Mutations

Unlikes—Where the Analogy Breaks Down

- Protein synthesis is submicroscopic; houses are not.
- Bricks can be cut up to fit; amino acids are always used in their entirety.
- In building a house, intentional change can be made by the architect; in protein synthesis, no intentional changes are made.

Reflection	**Conclusion**	Did the students understand the connection between the DNA code and phenotype as a result of this analogy?
	Improvements	When concepts like DNA structure, proteins, and protein synthesis are taught in different lessons, it is difficult for students to join these ideas and create a big picture. Teachers can explore ways to improve the connections they make between related ideas. Diagrams, class discussions, and concept maps are very helpful for making these links.

Science Content Standard C, Life Science, Grades 9–12: "The molecular basis of heredity" (NAS, 1996, p. 185). Genomics and phenomics now central to the biology syllabus. The Building a House Analogy is an excellent activity for consolidating DNA, RNA, protein synthesis and enzyme action, and cellular reactions (NAS, 1996, pp. 195–196).

Suggested teaching strategies	This analogy can be used as a consolidation activity. Teach protein synthesis the normal way (diagrams and discussion). In a later lesson have students work in groups and use the knowledge they gained on protein synthesis to develop the analogy with building a house. This will give the students the opportunity to work out what they do

The Building a House Analogy for Protein Synthesis (Continued)	
	and don't understand about protein synthesis and to use the correct terminology. In a plenary session, different groups can compare their ideas.
Resources	A similar analogy for protein synthesis with the manufacture of a product in a factory is presented in the textbook, *Biology Two* (Evans, Ladigess, & McKenzie, 1995, p. 234).
Applications	This analogy is suitable for students studying Grades 11–12 biology and integrated science.

The Buckets and Pumps Analogy for the Heart

Technical language can be confusing and threatening for students. When learning about the circulation of the heart, young students have to grapple with words like *valves, ventricle, atrium, vena cava,* and *aorta.* Moreover, students often are overwhelmed by complicated diagrams of the heart presented in textbooks. This analogy represents these parts of the heart with familiar, analogical terms like *faucets (taps), buckets,* and *pumps* in a simple box-shaped model. Using the comparison with buckets and pumps gives the students insight into the function of these chambers of the heart.

We encourage teachers to use this analogy to motivate their students and promote the idea that it is possible to learn seemingly complicated scientific ideas by using analogies and models. This analogy was first described by Wilkes (1991) and later by Venville and Treagust (1996). A sequence of overhead transparencies or PowerPoint slides, such as those presented in Figure 6.8, can be overlaid one on top of the other so that the functions of the different aspects of the heart can be added to the model step by step. The chambers of the heart are presented as four simple boxes in Slide 1. For students, this is a much easier structure to visualize than diagrams that are drawn to more accurately represent the shape of the heart. Slide 2 can be placed on top of Slide 1 to show that the right atrium can be compared with a bucket that collects blood from the body, which is represented as a factory in this slide. The right ventricle can be compared with a pump that pumps the blood to the lung, which is represented as a place where oxygen is introduced into the blood in Figure 8. This process continues until all three slides are superimposed as shown in Figure 6.8.

Figure 6.8   Examples of Slides or Overhead Transparencies That Can be Used to Help Students Understand the Structure and Function of the Heart

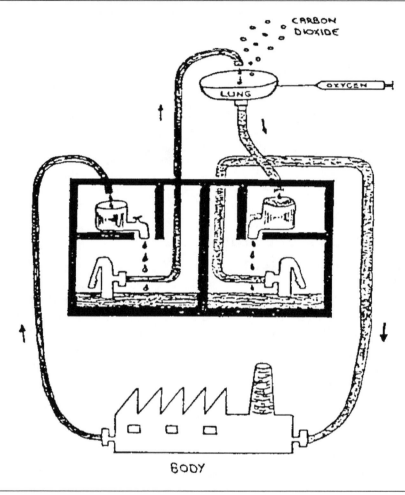

SOURCE: From Wilkes, W. (1991). A model to illustrate the structure and function of the heart. *SCIOS, The Journal of the Science Teachers' Association of Western Australia, 26*(4), 33–38.

The Buckets and Pumps Analogy for the Heart

Focus	Concept	The simplified demonstration of the flow of oxygenated and deoxygenated blood through the four chambers of the heart, the lungs, the body, and eventually back to the heart
	Students	Students find the dual system of pumps in the heart confusing and cannot distinguish between the pathways of the oxygenated and deoxygenated blood.
	Analog	Buckets are quite familiar to most students. Most students also are familiar with the idea of a pump as they may have seen one in their home fish tank, swimming pool, or garden well.

Action	Likes—Mapping the Analog to the Target	
	Analog—Buckets and pumps	Target—Chambers of the heart
	Buckets collect water.	The right and left atria collect the blood as it returns from the body and lungs, respectively.
	Pumps actively pump water to places where it is wanted.	The right and left ventricles actively pump blood from the heart to the lungs and body, respectively.
	Faucets (taps) can be closed to prevent water from flowing backwards.	Heart valves prevent blood from flowing in the wrong direction.
	Needles can inject substances into places.	The lungs put oxygen into the blood coming from the right ventricle.
	Factories use up materials.	The body is like a factory that uses up the oxygen in the blood.
	Unlikes—Where the Analogy Breaks Down	
	• Buckets have an open top where water overflows, whereas the atria have valves that allow the movement of blood to the ventricles. • The movement of gases into and out of the blood in the lungs is by diffusion, not by an active, injectionlike process.	

The Buckets and Pumps Analogy for the Heart (Continued)

		• The heart is made of organic substances, whereas buckets and pumps are made from inorganic materials. • The atria actively pump the blood to the ventricles; this is not a passive process like the dripping of water from a bucket.
Reflection	**Conclusion**	Did the students understand the flow of the blood through the heart and the functions of the various aspects of the heart as a result of this analogy? Even though students can use the analogy to help them understand the functions of the chambers of the heart, they often have difficulty remembering the technical terminology that goes with their newly developed understandings.
	Improvements	Activities such as fun games or drawing diagrams can be used to help the students remember the terminology associated with the flow of blood through the heart and body. This will consolidate the connection between the new knowledge formed with the analogy and the scientific language required.

Science Content Standard C, Life Science, Grades 5–8: "Structure and function in living systems" (NAS, 1996, p. 156). "The human organism has systems for . . . circulation, etc." (p. 167). Living things are organized and large animals have a central heart: The analogy of buckets and pumps is a practical way to show how the mammalian heart works.

Suggested teaching strategies	Four transparencies or slides such as those in Figure 6.8 can be used to build up the complexity of the heart using simplified steps. Students can be encouraged to make an educated guess about what might happen to the blood at each stage. This model can be used in conjunction with a model of the heart and a dissection of a real heart so that students can make the connections between the analogy and the real thing.
Resources	This analogy was originally presented by (Wilkes, 1991) and later evaluated by Venville and Treagust (1993, 1996).
Applications	This model is suitable for all students in Grades 5–8 when learning about the heart.

The Clothespin Analogy
for the Structure of DNA

Building models has played an important part in breakthroughs of think-ing about many scientific concepts. The building of a model was a critical aspect of the process that James Watson and Francis Crick went through to interpret critical empirical information provided by Rosalind Franklin and other scientists to determine the structure of DNA. Watson's (1968) famous book, *The Double Helix*, is a fascinating account of this model-building process and its importance to the history of science.

Students also can be involved in the model-building process and with the use of a few simple materials can create a concrete and easily manip-ulated model to help them think about and understand submicroscopic aspects of our world, such as the structure and function of DNA. A model of DNA constructed from (clothespins) first appeared in the BSCS students' manuals, the *Web of Life* (Australian Academy of Science, 1981), and later in *The Common Threads* manuals (Australian Academy of Science, 1991). While our understanding of molecular biology has pro-gressed in many ways since this model was first used in schools, the understanding of basic genetics concepts is fundamental to understand-ing biotechnological advances. This model helps students visualize the basic structure of DNA.

The model is constructed from lengths of plastic tubing (or pipe clean-ers) and color-coded clothespins. Four different colors are used to repre-sent adenine, thymine, cytosine, and guanine. If you plan to use uracil for mRNA, use a white pin for thymine and a white pin with a colored tag for uracil. Students can be challenged to work out appropriate details of the model from their knowledge and understanding of DNA. The model also can be used for simulating DNA replication, translation, and transcription. Figure 6.9 shows a photograph of a completed clothespin model for the structure of DNA.

Figure 6.9   A Completed Clothespin Model of the Structure of DNA

The Clothespin Analogy for the Structure of DNA		
Focus	**Concept**	The double helix structure of DNA is made up of two molecular strands twisted into a helix, like a twisted ladder. The sides of the ladder are made of alternating deoxyribose and phosphate molecules and the rungs are made of two bonded nitrogen bases. There are four nitrogen bases—cytosine always bonds with guanine and adenine always bonds with thymine. This structure is the key to the code for the sequence of amino acids in proteins that will be constructed by the cell.

The Clothespin Analogy for the Structure of DNA (Continued)

	Students	Students have difficulty understanding how genes influence the characteristics of the organism through protein synthesis. If they have a clear understanding that DNA is the chemical makeup of genes and that DNA holds the code for the production of proteins, they are more likely to understand the causal mechanisms of genetics.
	Analog	While a twisted ladder analogy creates an immediate image of the double helix structure, a model built from plastic tubing or pipe cleaners and colored clothespins is concrete, enables manipulation by the students, and can be extended to help students understand DNA replication, translation, and transcription.

Action	**Likes—Mapping the Analog to the Target**	
	Analog—Clothespin model	**Target—Structure of DNA**
	6–10 clothespins (Color 1)	Cytosine nitrogen base
	6–10 clothespins (Color 2)	Guanine nitrogen base
	6–10 clothespins (Color 3)	Thymine nitrogen base
	6–10 clothespins (Color 4)	Adenine nitrogen base
	Plastic tubing or pipe cleaners	Deoxyribose and phosphate molecules
	Clothespins clipped together	Weak hydrogen bonds between base pairs

Unlikes—Where the Analogy Breaks Down

- Clothespins clipped together are physical bonds, whereas hydrogen bonds are chemical.
- Any of the colored clothespins will clip together, whereas cytosine will bond only with guanine and thymine will bond only with adenine.
- The plastic tubing doesn't indicate the different deoxyribose and phosphate molecules or the opposing directions of the two strands of the DNA molecule.
- DNA molecules are typically very long, made up of thousands of base pairs, whereas this model is relatively short: only six base pairs of clothespins.

The Clothespin Analogy for the Structure of DNA (Continued)		
	Conclusion	Were the students able to build the model of DNA from the clothespins and plastic tubing? Did they demonstrate that they understood the specific nature of the base pairs? Were they able to replicate their DNA?
	Improvements	The model can be extended to test students' understanding by asking them to use the model to demonstrate DNA replication, transcription, or translation. Students will feel empowered if they can keep going back to their own models to see if they can be used to represent more complicated concepts.
Science Content Standard C, Life Science, Grades 5–8: "Reproduction and heredity" (NAS, 1996, p. 157) and "The molecular basis of heredity," Grades 9–12 (p. 185). The Clothespin Analogy for DNA can be used in its simplest form for Grades 5–8 and in more sophisticated versions (replication, transcription, etc.) for Grades 9–12. Visualizing DNA is central to modern life science, and modeling DNA and its translation into proteins involves inquiry.		
Suggested teaching strategies	This activity is best used to consolidate and apply students' knowledge of the structure of DNA. This model can be extended for modeling activities such as the replication of DNA and translation and transcription.	
Resources	BSCS students' manuals and many other modern textbooks use this analogical model.	
Applications	This model is most suitable for students in Grades 7–12 biology and integrated science, provided you choose the level of sophistication to suit the students' needs.	

An Earth Analogy for Cell Components

Teachers and students of biology often look at cells through light microscopes, but they rarely have the opportunity to actually look at DNA or genes. It is therefore difficult to visualize the size of genes. An analogy first presented by Cook-Deegan (1994) compares the cell with the earth to describe the relative sizes of the subcellular entities involved with genetics. The advantage of this analogy is that it gives a rough notion of the very small sizes of codons and base pairs because most people are better able to visualize the difference in size between the earth and a street address than between a cell and a codon. The comparative diagrams in Figure 6.10 give a useful pictorial representation of the analogy.

Figure 6.10   A Comparison Between the Earth and a Cell and the Relative Sizes of Aspects of the Earth and Subcellular Entities

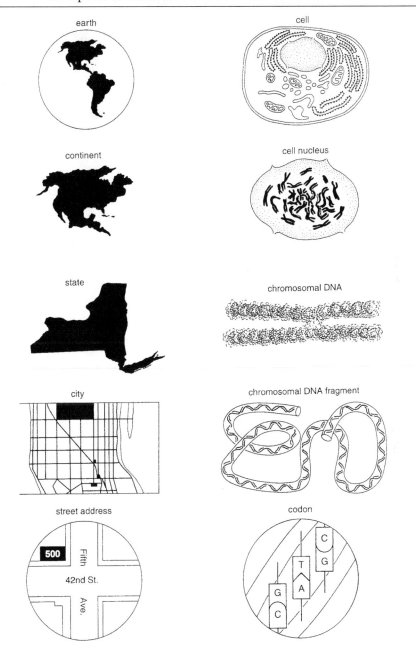

SOURCE: From *The Gene Wars: Science, Politics, and the Human Genome* by Robert Cook-Deegan. Copyright © 1994 by Robert Cook-Deegan. Used by permission of W. W. Norton & Company, Inc.

An Earth Analogy for Cell Components		
Focus	**Concept**	Chromosomal DNA exists within the cell, inside the cell nucleus. DNA is a code for protein synthesis. DNA is made up of a series of base pairs; three pairs make a codon that determines the next amino acid in the sequence that makes up a protein.
	Students	Students have great difficulty visualizing the very small nature of cells and subcellular entities. Young students sometimes confuse cells with atoms.
	Analog	The earth can be used to give a rough sense of the relative sizes of the subcellular entities related to genetics. The earth is more concrete than a cell and with frequent travel and satellite images, students often have a better idea about the size of the earth.

Action	Likes—Mapping the Analog to the Target	
	Analog—The earth to a street address	**Target—The cell to a codon**
	The earth	A cell
	A continent (e.g., North America or Australia)	The cell nucleus
	A state (Texas or New South Wales)	A chromosome
	A city (Dallas or Sydney)	Chromosomal DNA fragment
	Street address (25 Fifth Avenue)	Codon

Unlikes—Where the Analogy Breaks Down
• Because it is the relative sizes that are being compared in this analogy and not structure and function, the unlike features are minimal. • It is important, however, that students understand this is a rough comparison of size and that the analogy does not imply similar structural or functional similarities.

An Earth Analogy for Cell Components (Continued)		
Reflection	**Conclusion**	Did the students get the impression of the relative sizes of the components of the cell and understand that each component is a subcomponent of the previous structure?
	Improvements	It may be necessary to build a model of the components of a cell so that students understand that a codon is part of the DNA chemical structure, that chromosomes are inside the nucleus, and that all cells have a nucleus. Students who do not have a great deal of worldly experience may need some extra help understanding the relative sizes of the analog. Maps, globes, and pictures of the earth from the Internet may be useful for the purpose of ensuring analog familiarity.

Science Content Standard C, Life Science: Grades 9–12: "The molecular basis of heredity" and genomics is a key part of the biology syllabus (NAS, 1996, p. 185). The Earth and Street Address Analogy helps explain relative sizes of cell components. If the students build their own models, this can encourage inquiry and raise fruitful questions; "Abilities necessary to do scientific inquiry" (p. 175), and "raise alternative questions and models."

Suggested teaching strategies	This analogy can be used as an advance organizer and then referred to at any time throughout a genetics course to remind the students of the relative sizes of the components of the cell. In this example we have focused on genetics aspects of the cell, but other organelles could also be added to the analogy to build up a more complete picture of cell.
Resources	Cook-Deegan (1994), *The Gene Wars: Science, Politics and the Human Genome*, p. 24. Satellite photographs of the Earth might be useful in a PowerPoint presentation.
Applications	This analogy could be used with a wide spectrum of students from Grades 8–12 and even with students in college.

A Web Analogy for the Interdependence of Organisms

There are so many references to the web of life in biology that we rarely stop to consider what this actually means. This phrase has certainly become one of the mechanical clichés referred to at the beginning of this chapter that has inherent meaning but is far more useful if extended into an elaborated analogy. It is possible to develop this analogy into a role-play where students in the class represent different species in an ecosystem (see Figure 6.11). Each species is linked to others with string to represent some kind of relationship, such as a feeding relationship. Be warned that the classroom is likely to end up a dense web of string. The teacher can pull on pieces of string to represent disturbances in the ecosystem, such as the extinction of a species, so that the students can see how this impacts on many other species. This is a fun and simple role-play analogy that conveys the complex notion of the interdependence of organisms.

The image in Figure 6.11 shows a class of Grade 6 students on an excursion to a local ecosystem that included a parkland and a lake. The students studied various species in the ecosystem, such as the beautiful and ancient

Figure 6.11   Students From Grade 6 Studying a Local Ecosystem

Zamia palm that can be seen in the photograph. They also spent some time investigating the relationships between other species. As a conclusion to the unit, the teacher used the web of life role-play, and the students represented each of the species they studied. The links between the species were made with string. The teacher reported that the students had considerable fun creating their classroom web of life.

A Web Analogy for the Interdependence of Organisms			
Focus	**Concept**	The interdependence of organisms is an overarching idea that impacts on many aspects of students' understanding of biology	
	Students	Students have great difficulty understanding that even though one organism may not be directly linked with another in a food chain, all species in an ecosystem are interdependent in some way.	
	Analog	Using a web analogy, students can understand that when something hits the web, there is a ripple effect that impacts on all parts of the web. A string web can be role-played in the classroom for a bit of fun and students can feel that when one part of the web is pulled out of shape, they can all feel the difference it makes to their part of the web.	
Action	**Likes—Mapping the Analog to the Target**		
	Analog—The web of string connecting all the students in the classroom		**Target—The interconnection of all living things in an ecosystem (feeding, selecting, etc.)**
	Students at the nodes of the web		Each species
	Movement or disturbance of the web		Disturbance of the balance within the ecosystem
	Many string connections		Interactions of one species with many others

A Web Analogy for the Interdependence of Organisms (Continued)

	Unlikes—Where the Analogy Breaks Down	
	• There are lots of differences between this role-play analogy and the interdependence of organisms. For example, real ecosystems are generally much more complex than a web that can be constructed in the classroom. They also include the nonliving aspects of the environment as well as the living. The point of this role-play analogy is to create an effective image in the students' minds that helps them to understand interdependence.	
Reflection	Conclusion	Did the students understand that when one species is seriously affected in some way, all other species in the ecosystem are affected because they are interdependent?
	Improvements	Do the students need to do more research about the roles of specific species in a particular ecosystem to be able to understand relationships beyond feeding?
Science Content Standard C, Life Science, Grades 5–8: "Populations and ecosystems . . . Diversity and adaptations of organisms" (NAS, 1996, pp. 157, 158). Interdependence is central to ecosystem vitality and cycling by producers, consumers, and decomposers. The Web Analogy models knowledge students collect in the field. Modeling adds an inquiry element by asking what-if questions.		
Suggested teaching strategies	This analogy can be used as part of the conclusion of a unit on ecology where students are learning about food chains and food webs. It will reinforce the notion of interdependence. It can be adapted to fit in with any real-world examination of a particular local environment, such as a lake, bushland, or national park. Students can research a species and then represent that species in the web that they construct in the classroom. They can be responsible for suggesting string links to other species and justify why these links should be made.	
Resources	Lots of string is needed to create the links between species in the classroom web. Example of food webs and other relationships between species in a specific ecosystem may be helpful to make direct links with a real-world situation.	
Applications	This role-play analogy is a fun learning activity best used with younger students from Grades 5–8.	

The Analogy of Homeostasis Being Like a Student Walking Up the Down Escalator

Homeostasis is a key concept in biology and resembles equilibrium situations in chemistry and physics. Many animals and plants maintain a constant internal environment by balancing inputs and outputs of materials like water, glucose, oxygen, carbon dioxide, wastes, and essential minerals. A constant internal environment is beneficial because biochemical reactions like photosynthesis, respiration, and protein synthesis are controlled by enzymes that work best at certain temperatures, pH, and water concentrations.

Take, for example, a mammal; mammals function best at a constant temperature of about 37°C. If mammals overheat by more than 2–3°C, they can die. If they cool by more than 2–3°C, they slow down and cannot catch prey or escape predators. Mammals are very efficient at 37°C, and they maintain this temperature by shivering when cold to generate heat (muscle contraction) and sweating or panting to cool down when they overheat. Homeostasis is a dynamic process; mammals (and birds) generate heat in just the needed amounts when cold and lose heat in just the right amounts when hot. A mammal's surroundings are rarely at the optimal temperature, so all mammals are either gaining or losing heat to maintain their body temperature.

An excellent analogy for the dynamic gain or loss of heat is the student walking up the down escalator in a department store. If the student walks up the escalator at the same speed as the escalator is descending, the student stays still at the same level. This is like maintaining a constant temperature. If the student walks faster upward than the escalator is descending and rises, this is like overheating during work or sport. If too hot, the person will become exhausted and will need to rest (a compensating response because resting cools a person down). If, on the other hand, the student walks up slower than the escalator descends and moves downward, this is like getting cold due to inactivity or losing heat too rapidly to the environment, like swimming in cold water or standing in a cold wind. Activity must increase if the optimum temperature (or level on the escalator) is to be maintained. This analogy is illustrated in Figure 6.12.

Figure 6.12   A Student Walking Up the Down Escalator Is Like Homeostatic Control of Body Temperature

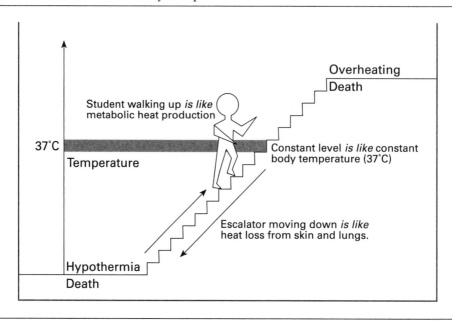

The Analogy of Homeostasis Being Like a Student Walking Up the Down Escalator		
Focus	Concept	Homeostasis is a key biology concept. It explains how many animals and plants maintain a constant internal environment by regulating input and output of things like heat, water, O_2, CO_2, nutrients, and minerals.
	Students	Students think that constant internal environments in plants and animals occur because the plant or animal body is sealed. They do not visualize homeostasis as a dynamic process in which materials and heat flow in and out of the body in a balanced way. When students see homeostasis as a dynamic process, they better understand how animals and plants respond to changing conditions.
	Analog	A student walking up the down escalator at the same rate as the escalator is descending understands the need to match the escalator's speed in order to stay at the same level (like maintaining constant temperature). Many students have done this.

The Analogy of Homeostasis Being Like a Student Walking Up the Down Escalator (Continued)

Action	Likes—Mapping the Analog to the Target	
	Analog—Walking up the down escalator	**Target—Balancing heat input and output**
	The escalator is constantly descending.	Heat is constantly lost through lungs and skin.
	The student is walking upward.	Human body generates heat by exercise.
	The student walks up as fast as the escalator descends.	Heat loss and heat production are balanced, so temperature remains constant.
	The escalator descends faster than the student walks up; the student's level drops.	When heat loss is faster than heat is generated, a person gets cold.
	The student walks up faster than the escalator descends; the student's level rises.	When heat is generated faster than heat is lost, a person gets hot.
	Unlikes—Where the Analogy Breaks Down	
	• The escalator runs at a constant rate, but heat loss (output) varies with environmental temperature—it can be low or high and can change. The student can walk up the escalator as fast as the escalator descends at any point along the escalator; heat gain and heat loss balance at one temperature (like just one position on the escalator), namely, 37°C.	
Reflection	Conclusion	Were the students convinced that heat loss versus heat gain is a dynamic relationship and that mammals and birds have a fixed internal temperature (about 37°C and 38°C, respectively)? Could they transfer the application to heat loss and gain to other inputs and outputs?
	Improvements	A video of a student walking up the down escalator is useful as is discussion ensuring that students know how an escalator works.

The Analogy of Homeostasis Being Like a Student Walking Up the Down Escalator (Continued)

Science Content Standard C, Life Science, Grades 9–12: "The cell" and "Matter, energy and organization in living systems" (NAS, 1996, pp. 184, 186–187). Homeostatic equilibrium applies to cells, organisms, and the behavior of organisms. The analogy of a student walking up the down escalator demonstrates the dynamic nature of balanced inputs and outputs at the level of single cells, individual organisms, and ecosystems.

Suggested teaching strategies	This analogy can be explained as balanced heat loss and heat gain producing a constant internal temperature, and then it can be applied to water balance, blood glucose levels, O_2 and CO_2 levels. Students could, in groups, devise an explanation for these other homeostatic levels and present the analogy again to the class. This is formative assessment.
Resources	Stories of students walking up the down escalator (or down the up escalator); a video of someone doing this, sets of plant and animal materials and properties that are internally regulated by balancing input and output. The complete analogy is published in Harrison and Treagust (1994b, pp. 40–42).
Applications	Homeostasis (equilibrium) is a universal concept and applies to properties and substances and also occurs at a macro scale in ecosystems and communities. Suits Grades 9–12.

7

Effective Chemistry Analogies

Richard K. Coll

What is the structure of the hydrocarbon benzene like? At the start of the eighteenth century this was unknown. It was known that benzene contained equal numbers of hydrogen and carbon atoms and had the molecular formula C_6H_6, but how were the atoms arranged? The famous organic chemist Kekulé pondered this question and in a dream thought of snakes biting their tails. This led him to propose a model for the structure of benzene like that shown in Figure 7.1.

Kekulé's model of the structure for benzene shows how scientists use ideas from another domain or area to help them understand scientific problems or concepts. So according to Kekulé, the structure of benzene is *like* snakes biting their tails. Of course Kekulé didn't take this literally, but he *mapped* or used some attributes from his dream to help him compose a model for the structure of benzene. Kekulé's model soon ran into problems; in fact, this scenario is very common in science and in chemistry. It was found that Kekulé's model explained some aspects of the structure of benzene but failed to explain others (e.g., benzene was much less reactive than Kekulé's model predicted). But scientists didn't immediately discard this model; rather, they used the model and improved on it, modifying it so that it could explain aspects of the structure and reactivity for which Kekulé's model failed.

Figure 7.1   The Kekulé Model for the Structure of Benzene

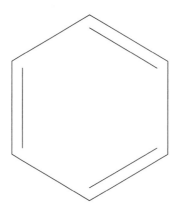

Chemistry is a fundamental science concerned with the nature of substances and changes to those substances. The understanding of chemistry is developed on two broad levels—the macroscopic level and the microscopic level. Kekulé's model shows one of the biggest problems facing chemists. The macroscopic study of chemistry is concerned with things like the observation of physical and chemical properties of substances: color, melting points, boiling points, why some elements exist in their free state whereas others occur only in combination with other elements, and so on. However, in order to explain chemical and physical properties of substances, scientists need to develop theories of what chemicals are like at the microscopic level. Herein lies the problem of understanding chemistry, both for scientists involved in the practice and for students seeking to understand it. In order to explain macroscopic phenomena, we need to use analogical models of microscopic materials and events, things beyond the limit of our senses—materials and events that we are destined to never see (although some text books talk about scientists "seeing" atoms with machines like tunneling electron microscopes). It is this interplay between the macroscopic and microscopic that leads to chemistry being dominated by the use of models, including analogical models. These models vary tremendously, both in complexity and in explanatory power. Scientists—in typically pragmatic fashion—use both simple and complex models to understand or explain the same events or phenomena, routinely interchanging models as their needs dictate. Research into the use of models, however, has shown major differences between experts and novices in their use and understanding of models. Experts remain conscious at all times that all models possess limitations and understand fully the limitations of the particular model they are using for the situation at hand. So an expert chemist might use an octet-rule-based model for the chemical bonding in dichlorine (Cl_2) because it is convenient and works, and invoke a more complex model—perhaps based on quantum theory—when and if it proves necessary to describe the bonding in dioxygen (O_2), for example, when the simple octet rule model breaks down or lacks explanatory power.

Research has identified a large variety of models used by chemists and other scientists, some of which you may not have thought of as models. It is easy enough to see that the ubiquitous ball-and-stick graphic used to illustrate structural chemistry is a model. But chemical formulas also are models used by chemists to summarize or depict the stoichiometry and aspects of chemical structure for substances in a convenient shorthand manner. Scientists' use of models also has a very human dimension, and they use models—particularly analogies—to help generate ideas or theories as well as to understand chemical phenomena. There are two particularly well-known reports of the use of analogy to generate chemistry theories: the Kekulé model and Neils Bohr's solar system model for the structure of the atom (Holyoak & Thagard, 1996). There are many more analogies used formally in chemistry teaching and others generated informally by teachers (and students) as they strive to understand chemical concepts (Coll, 2006; Coll, France, & Taylor, 2005).

The Use of Analogies in Teaching Chemistry

Scientists use models to provide explanations of chemical substances and chemical phenomena; some of these models are analogical models, and others are physical models or structural formulas, and so on. Chemistry teachers use models in subtly different ways from scientists. First, they need to teach students about current scientific models, which represent the practice of chemistry. So secondary students are taught about certain models for the atomic nature of matter or for the structure of the atom itself. Second, teachers may use models like that of the ball and stick (or analogies) to guide students to understand particular chemical concepts, such as aspects of structural chemistry.

The chemical education literature provides many examples of analogies, and many authors strongly recommend their use in the classroom (e.g., Pogliani & Berberan-Santos, 1996). Research suggests we can draw upon students' worldviews and use common ideas to illustrate chemical concepts (Coll, 2006). For example, we can talk about currency inflation or the devaluation of motor vehicles and use these ideas to aid the understanding of difficult aspects of topics like chemical kinetics. Other examples of analogy use include illustrating basic chemical concepts like solubility and kinetic theory (Coffman & Tanis, 1990), modeling physical properties and molecular structure (Crane & Liu, 1986), chemical reactivity and equilibrium (Reingold, 1995), and stereochemistry (Mezl, 1996). It is important to note that the descriptions of analogies and recommendations for their use is for classroom use only.

It is interesting that there are some highly abstract chemical theories for which there are few reports of the use of analogies. A good example is that of chemical bonding. The literature consists primarily of examples of appropriate analogies as described earlier. For example, Licata (1988) provides an analogy for covalent bonding related to eating one's lunch: Sharing one's lunch is a nonpolar covalent bond, unequal sharing of lunch is a polar covalent bond, and stealing someone's lunch is a coordinate covalent bond! As mentioned earlier in the book, the use of amusing or highly relevant analogies like this can do a lot to stimulate students' interest as well as to provide vivid mental images that aid recall.

Difficulties in Using Analogies in Teaching and Learning Chemistry

Because so many chemistry concepts lie outside the world experience of students, analogies possess considerable potential to aid students' understanding (Justi & Gilbert, 2006; Thagard, 1992; Vosniadou, 1989). However, inappropriate use of analogies can prove detrimental to students' understanding, and this is a particular danger in chemistry teaching because of the widespread use of models and analogies. Even if teachers try to use analogies that involve things they think are familiar to students, failures can arise because students' knowledge is not organized the same way as teachers' or experts' (Thagard, 1992). Let's look at an example. Which sports are your students most interested in? Probably baseball, or basketball, or maybe soccer; but you probably will agree that the actual sport students are passionate about will vary depending on the country. There is a nice example in the literature of how unfamiliarity with students' sporting interests might adversely impact how a teacher tried to use an analogy. When a pea on the cricket pitch of the Melbourne Cricket Ground (MCG; called "the MCG analogy," Bucat, 1984) was used as an analog for the nucleus of a hydrogen atom in one Australian school (the stadium represented the extent of the lone electron) students asked, "What's the MCG?" They were basketball fanatics and did not have a mental image of the MCG's size, so the analogy did not work for them. In another example, it is common for students to hold major misconceptions in areas where teachers and textbooks assume familiarity: Students might think the spheres used to illustrate an ionic lattice are copies of real atoms or ions, or they may mistake sticks in ball-and-stick models of ionic lattices for individual chemical bonds (Butts & Smith, 1987; Duit, 1991).

Research thus indicates that the use of analogies does not always aid conceptual understanding. For example, a study of first-year college chemistry students found no improvement in their understanding of the conservation of matter when using real-world analogies. It seems that in this case at least, other factors, like the students' mathematical anxiety, spatial visualization skill, and proportional reasoning ability, were more important (Friedel, Gabel, & Samuel, 1990). The main danger is that students may develop and retain views of physical or analog models, seeing them as scale models of reality (Ingham & Gilbert, 1991) and thus believing that chlorine atoms are green, for instance. So teaching with analogies, like any chemistry teaching, requires an understanding of, and careful use of, appropriate pedagogy, including things such as developing an understanding of your students' prior knowledge that might impact their understanding of the analog model (Coll et al., 2005; Justi & Gilbert, 2006).

In summary, the use of analogies is not a panacea for learning difficulties in chemistry; nevertheless, analogy use is a potent tool for chemistry teachers and an important part of effective teaching. The research evidence indicates that the use of analogy can enhance the learning of chemistry in particular, if for no other reason than chemistry itself is dominated by the use of models. I must mention once again that is crucial that teachers make students aware of the limitations of each analogy used (e.g., in what ways the target and analog are similar, and in what ways they are not). Analogy can also be used as a vehicle to introduce students into the appropriate use of other models and help guide students to understand how chemists (and other scientists) use models in the most pragmatic ways, remaining aware at all times that any model possesses limitations.

Chemistry Analogies

Here are 13 useful analogies you can use in the teaching of a variety of abstract chemical conceptions:

1. The Sports Stadium Analogy for the Hydrogen Atom

2. The Balloons Analogy for Molecular Shapes

3. The School Dance Analogy for Chemical Equilibrium

4. The Solar System Analogy for Atomic Structure

5. The Tunnel Analogy for Catalysis

6. The Rice Grains Analogy for Avogadro's Number

7. The Role-Play Analogy for Chemical Reactions

8. The Ham Sandwich Analogy for Stoichiometry

9. The Coconut Shy Analogy for Effective Molecular Collisions

10. The Soccer Analogy for Weak and Strong Acids and Bases

11. The Fan Analogy for Electron Clouds

The Sports Stadium Analogy for the Hydrogen Atom

The analogy between a large sports ground and a simple atom (e.g., hydrogen) goes like this: If a hydrogen atom was the size of the MCG (or similar local ground), the nucleus (one proton) would be as large as a grain of rice on the cricket pitch, and the electron cloud would fill the entire stadium.

In a hydrogen atom, the ratio between the diameter of the nucleus and the electron cloud is approx. $1 : 10^5$.

Thus, if the rice grain is 3–5mm in dimension and the electron cloud will be 300–500m in diameter. In fact, the stadium model doesn't exaggerate the cloud's size; it isn't even big enough.

This model is an excellent way to show why chemists and physicists say that matter is almost all space. Watch out for the alternative conception that says the space between the nucleus and the electron is filled with air. It's actually a vacuum (despite Aristotle saying that nature abhors a vacuum).

Figure 7.2   The Sports Stadium Analogy for the Hydrogen Atom

SOURCE: www.clipart.com.

The Sports Stadium Analogy for the Hydrogen Atom

Focus	Concept	A hydrogen atom contains one proton in the nucleus and is surrounded by one electron. The atomic nucleus is minute, and the atom is mostly space. The ratio of the nucleus diameter : atomic diameter = approx 1 : 100,000.
	Students	Students visualize the atom as a solid sphere (from molecular models) and have great difficulty conceptualizing that the atom is mostly space and that the nucleus is so tiny and so dense. Most students have seen or been in a large sports stadium and have some idea of its size.
	Analog	If a grain of rice is placed in the center of the playing area in a football or baseball stadium, then the outer row of seats is the limit of the electron's influence. The rest of the atom is empty space. The electron seems to be everywhere at once like the seats surrounding the playing area.

Action	Likes—Mapping the Analog to the Target	
	Analog—sports stadium	**Target—hydrogen atom**
	Grain of rice (about 2mm thick)	Hydrogen atom nucleus (one proton)
	Playing area and seats out to the last row	Region where the electron might be found
	Ratio of grain of rice : whole stadium	Ratio of nucleus : electron cloud

Unlikes—Where the Analogy Breaks Down

- This is a two-dimensional representation of a three-dimensional atom.
- Different elements have bigger nuclei and more electrons, and the ratio is a bit smaller than 1 : 100 000 for large atoms, but it is still huge and all atoms are mostly space.
- It is the proportion that is important, not the size.
- The atom is filled with empty space, but the stadium is filled with air.
- Take care: in some classes there will be students unfamiliar with a large sport stadium—check!

The Sports Stadium Analogy for the Hydrogen Atom (Continued)		
Reflection	Conclusion	Were the students familiar with a large stadium and could they make the connection? Can they use this concept to build a similar analogy using an appropriately sized ball as the nucleus and the distance of their home from school as the limit of the electron cloud?
	Improvements	Do I need to explain this again? Do I need another model? Will I need an overheard transparency of a large stadium next time I use the analogy? A visit to a stadium would have a powerful impact, especially if you hold a rice grain in your hand
Content Standard B, Physical Science, Grades 9–12: "Structure of Atoms" (NAS, 1996, p. 176). The Sports Stadium Analogy shows that the structure of the atom is mostly empty space, with an enormous difference in size between the nucleus and outer shell.		
Suggested teaching strategies	Challenge the students to describe a popular stadium. Ask students to choose a suitably sized ball for the nucleus if the distance from their classroom to their home is the range of the electron cloud. Use a series of balls—golf ball up to a basketball—and predict how far the electron cloud would extend.	
Resources	Overhead transparency (OHT) of a popular stadium, a golf ball, baseball, basketball, ruler, and a local map. Bucat (1984): Melbourne Cricket Ground analogy Pimentel (1963, p. 88): Yankee Stadium analogy	
Applications	Useful in high school advanced chemistry.	

The Balloons Analogy for Molecular Shapes

Chemistry teachers and textbooks often talk about molecular shapes. In school chemistry, teachers mostly use the valence shell electron pair repulsion (VSEPR) theory to explain molecular shapes. This is an abstract idea, and some students find it hard to visualize the fact that electron orbitals repel each other. A concrete way to help these students see the concept is to use balloons to model the electron orbitals.

Balloon air pressure is used to model an electron orbital's negative electric field. When you press one balloon into another, the pressures produce reaction forces. The balloons bounce apart when released. This model helps students visualize the way invisible orbitals push each other apart. It is useful to blow up balloons and let the students feel the pressure in them.

The target of this explanation is the shape differences between ethane (C_2H_6), which is tetrahedral; ethene (C_2H_4), which is planar; and ethyne (C_2H_2), which is linear.

Ethane's tetrahedral structure is modeled by trying together four tightly inflated balloons. The balloons assume a tetrahedral shape, and you can discuss why the pressure forces produce this orientation. The analogy is that four sp^3-orbitals will do the same thing (four sp^3 hybrid bonds in an alkane are like four similar balloons).

If you burst one balloon, the three remaining balloons pop into a planar shape (the analogy being the $H_2C =$ unit in ethene). Popping a further balloon produces a roughly linear structure, though it tends to sag at each end. This models ethyne with its HC-triple bond.

Figure 7.3   The Balloons Analogy for Molecular Shapes

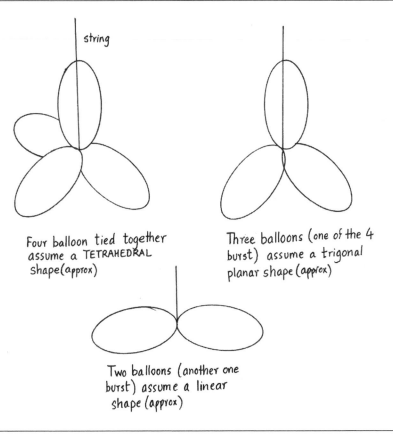

Four balloon tied together assume a TETRAHEDRAL shape (approx)

Three balloons (one of the 4 burst) assume a trigonal planar shape (approx)

Two balloons (another one burst) assume a linear shape (approx)

The Balloons Analogy for Molecular Shapes

Focus	Concept	Electrostatic attractions and repulsions between atoms and electrons produce covalent bonds. The VSEPR theory is a useful way to explain the shapes that result when atoms in molecules share electrons. The valence shell electron pairs repel each other and take positions that maximize the distance and minimize the force of repulsion between bonds. This accounts for tetrahedra and other shapes.
	Students	Students have difficulty visualizing invisible forces like electrostatic repulsion. They are familiar with pressure forces in inflated balloons.
	Analog	A simple way to demonstrate the repulsion between adjacent electron pairs is to model the covalent bonds using inflated balloons. Four balloons inflated to the maximum have their necks tied tightly together. The air pressure—elasticity—pushes each of the balloons equally apart. They assume a tetrahedral shape. This is like methane (CH_4). While talking about these forces and what they represent, pop one balloon with a pin, and the remaining three will assume a planar form. When a second balloon is popped, the two remaining take a linear shape.

Action	Likes—Mapping the Analog to the Target	
	Analog—balloons	**Target—covalent molecules**
	Maximum inflated balloon	Electron pair of a covalent bond
	Four balloon necks tied together	Four sigma bonds around one carbon atom
	Balloons repel each other—air pressure	Bonds repel each other—electrostatic force
	One balloon is burst.	Two bonds unite as a double bond.
	Two balloons burst.	Three bonds unite as a triple bond.

The Balloons Analogy for Molecular Shapes (Continued)

	Unlikes—Where the Analogy Breaks Down	
	• There are 2, 4, or 6 electrons per bond, but each balloon contains millions of particles. • The electron density in the bond is not uniform, but the air pressure in the balloon is. • The shape of the electron-rich bond region is not the same shape as the balloon. • Electrostatic repulsion is force-at-a-distance, but balloon pressure is a contact force. • Students can think that the balloons represent atoms; in fact they represent bonds.	
Reflection	**Conclusion**	Was the analogy visually convincing? Did the balloons behave as expected? Have a repeat set of balloons available as students may miss the point, because things happen very quickly.
	Improvements	Are other models needed alongside the balloon model? Is more preparatory discussion about VSEPR needed? Were the students satisfied with the identified shared and unshared mappings?
Content Standard B, Physical Science, Grades 9–12: "Structure and Properties of Matter" (NAS, 1996, p. 176). The Balloons Analogy for Molecular Shapes shows that the electron cloud around the core of the atom is arranged to minimize repulsion, information required to determine the shape of the molecule using VSEPR.		
Suggested teaching strategies	The model can be used as an advance organizer; however, once the VSEPR theory has been elaborated, you may need to use the model again. It seems to work best as an embedded explanation once the theory of VSEPR has been explained. As with most models, using this demonstration alongside space-filling and ball-and-stick models is recommended. The balloons model adds a dynamic twist, and students like it.	
Resources	Hunter, Simpson, & Stranks, (1976, p. 361). Lots of balloons and thread.	
Applications	Organic chemistry and VSEPR in high school.	

The School Dance Analogy for Chemical Equilibrium

Most students are familiar with school dances, and this provides an exciting analogy for one of chemistry's more tricky conceptions, chemical equilibrium. Like other chemistry topics, there is a significant body of literature pointing to student alternative conceptions about chemical equilibrium. In particular, some students struggle with the dynamic nature of equilibrium situations, thinking that once a chemical system has reached equilibrium, then chemical reactions stop.

In contrast, a dance held in the school gym, in which students find partners, is a pretty dynamic situation. The school dance analogy thus potentially provides a potent reminder of this important feature of equilibrium. See Figure 7.4. A fuller account of the story is provided in Chapter 3.

Figure 7.4   The School Dance Analogy for Chemical Equilibrium

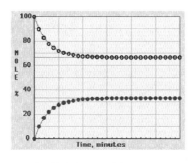

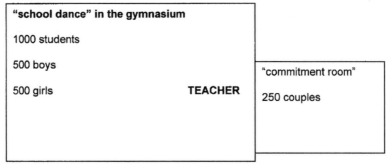

"school dance" in the gymnasium

1000 students

500 boys

500 girls   **TEACHER**

"commitment room"

250 couples

The School Dance Analogy for Chemical Equilibrium

Focus	Concept	Almost all chemical reactions ultimately reach a state of equilibrium. When a reaction begins, there are reactants and no products. As the reaction proceeds, products are formed and reactants consumed. At the same time, some products interact to produce the original reactants in a reverse reaction. Chemical equilibrium is reached when the rates of the forward and reverse reactions are the same. At equilibrium, no further change in reactant or product concentrations occurs although the forward and reverse reactions are still occurring.
	Students	Students have difficulty visualizing the dynamic nature of equilibrium. They assume that when equilibrium has been reached, the reactions have stopped.
	Analog	The analog concept is the school dance and the commitment room (Figure 7.4). There are 1,000 students at the school dance, half boys and half girls. Everyone has to walk around until they find a partner; then they can go into the commitment room, up to a maximum of 500 students or 250 couples, with the teacher as gatekeeper. If more want to go to the room, some have to leave.

Action	Likes—Mapping the Analog to the Target	
	Analog—school dance	**Target—equilibrium**
	Dancing students in the gym (reactants)	Moving and colliding particles
	Commitment between students	Formation of a chemical bond (and products)
	Number of students in the gym	Concentration effect on reaction rate
	Changing size of gym (for same number of students)	Concentration effect on reaction rate
	Speed of dancing students	Temperature effect on reaction rate

The School Dance Analogy for Chemical Equilibrium (Continued)

	Couples going in and out of commitment room	Simultaneous forward and reverse reactions
	Couples going in and out at same time	Forward and reverse rates same
	Gym doors sealed	Reaction system closed

Unlikes—Where the Analogy Breaks Down

- There are 1,000 students in the gym, but millions of particles in chemical reactions.
- The particles move much faster than the students.
- The particles are much smaller than the students.
- There are big gaps between gaseous particles compared with gaps between students.

Reflection	Conclusion	Was the analogy convincing? Do I need to recapitulate the school dance story?
	Improvements	There is an unshared attribute that needs explanation. The closed-system concept is easy to understand with respect to the commitment room, but is not a logical conclusion for the gym. Any number of students could be in the gym so long as there are more than 250 couples. In chemical equilibrium the relative reaction concentrations in both the gym and commitment room are important.

Content Standard B, Physical Science, Grades 9–12: "Chemical Reactions" (NAS, 1996, p. 176). The School Dance Analogy shows that chemical reactions are dynamic in nature and that reversible reactions all eventually reach a state of dynamic equilibrium.

Suggested teaching strategies	This analogy will need an illustration.
Resources	Harrison and de Jong (2004). See also Rayner-Canham (1994).
Applications	Physical and general chemistry in high school.

The Solar System Analogy for Atomic Structure

Atomic structure is a key scientific theory, and research has shown that students hold many alternative conceptions. For example, they may see models of atomic structure as miniature copies of reality—such ideas are often reinforced by images produced by recent techniques such as tunneling electron microscopy (see Harrison & Treagust, 1996). One thing to emphasize here is that we are dealing with a *model* and that even the best scientific theory for atomic structure is still an approximation. One advantage of using what is clearly an analog for the structure of atoms (i.e., the solar system) is that it may be easier for students to grasp the model aspect for atomic structure.

The classical Bohr model for the atom used here is not the currently accepted scientific one, but the more advanced models for atomic structure (e.g., quantum mechanical models) are typically too complex and mathematical for school-level science. The Bohr model, despite its limitations, is commonly taught in high school. The approach described here allows you to point out some of its deficiencies during the teaching process.

The Solar System Analogy also helps overcome any alternative conception that atoms are indivisible (as is commonly stated in textbook definitions and on many Web sites) since it makes it plain that atoms are composed of other more fundamental particles.

Figure 7.5   The Solar System Analogy for Atomic Structure

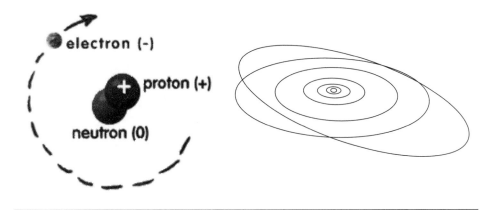

The Solar System Analogy for an Atom

Focus	Concept	Atoms are made up of elementary particles: a central nucleus consisting of two heavier types of particles, protons (positively charged) and neutrons (not charged); and lighter particles, electrons (about 1800 times less heavy and negatively charged), which are arranged around the nucleus. The arrangement of these particles in space determines many properties of atoms and elements and dictates chemical reactivity.
	Students	Students have difficulty visualizing tiny, submicroscopic particles like atoms and elementary particles like electrons and protons. They are more familiar with planets and the solar system and find visualization of planets and planetary motion easier as a consequence of exposure to pictures and representations in resources like encyclopedias and on the Internet.
	Analog	Our solar system, consisting of the planets orbiting the sun, provides a simple analogy for students to grasp the essentials of the Bohr model for the atom. The greater size of the planets and sightings of the sun make them seem more real to students than things that cannot be seen.

Action	Likes—Mapping the Analog to the Target	
	Analog—Solar System	**Target—Atomic Structure**
	Sun	Nucleus
	Planets	Electrons
	Planetary orbits	Electron orbits
	Planetary rotation	Electron spin
	Spherical shape of sun and planets	Spherical shape of nucleus and electrons
	Planets at fixed distances from the sun	Electrons at fixed distances from the nucleus
	Nucleus containing two elementary particles: neutrons and protons	Sun composed of hydrogen and helium

The Solar System Analogy for an Atom (Continued)		
	Gravitational attraction between sun and planets	Electrical attraction between the electrons and the nucleus
	Unlikes—Where the Analogy Breaks Down	
	<ul><li>The sun is hot, whereas the nucleus is not.</li><li>The shape of orbits for electrons is circular; orbits for planets are elliptical.</li><li>The electrons can change their orbits if they gain energy; planets remain in stable orbits.</li><li>Real electrons occupy clouds of space around the nucleus rather than following a strict orbital pathway.</li><li>Protons are positive and electrons are negative. Planets and sun have no charges.</li><li>Some planets have moons, whereas the electrons are alone in their orbits.</li><li>Planets are different sizes; electrons are the same size.</li></ul>	
Reflection	**Conclusion**	It is interesting that students relate so well to this analogy given their limited exposure to real planets. It probably works because the earth and sun seem very real to them. Were the students aware of this analogy from previous experience?
	Improvements	As with most models, using this demonstration alongside other models is recommended. It is tricky for the students to get a feel for the space between the particles and the planets and sun. This analogy would work well with the sports stadium model.
Content Standard B, Physical Science, Grades 9–12: "Structure of Atoms" (NAS, 1996, p. 176). The Solar System Analogy shows that the structure of the atom is mostly empty space, with a core nucleus containing most of the mass and the electrons arranged in shells around the nucleus.		
Suggested teaching strategies	This model may be best used with pictures from textbooks or the Internet or with a computer simulation. The more impressive the image, the more likely it is to be retained. It also may be possible to use an existing planetary model from physics or astronomy classes to illustrate the solar system.	
Resources	Zumdahl (1989)	
Applications	Physical and general chemistry in high school.	

The Tunnel Analogy for Catalysis

Catalysis is a process of major industrial importance. The general principal is quite straightforward. However, students seem to struggle to understand it, particularly the way catalysts actually work. This is probably because of the rather abstract nature of reaction chemistry itself and the concepts related to activation energy barriers.

The general idea is that a catalyst speeds up a chemical reaction (sometimes by a factor of many millions) and remains unchanged itself. Teachers often say it is not used up or not consumed during the process. In fact, such a situation applies only to the so-called ideal catalyst. In truth, most catalysts have a life span or go through a number of catalytic cycles and gradually lose their catalytic activity. Catalysts are important because they speed reactions up and also because they allow certain reactions to occur when they would not otherwise (e.g., the breaking of very strong bonds, like in N_2). This obviously has major implications for the commercial viability of some processes (a classic example is the Haber process for the manufacture of ammonia, NH_3).

The analogy is that of a car or other vehicle attempting to drive over a very steep and very high hill, demanding a great deal of energy, and the use of a tunnel to avoid the high hill and reach the destination. The students can see the relationship between the barrier and hill and come to understand that the energy barrier is avoided by using the tunnel—and in the same way, a reaction is made easier if we use a catalyst.

Figure 7.6   The Tunnel Analogy for Catalysis

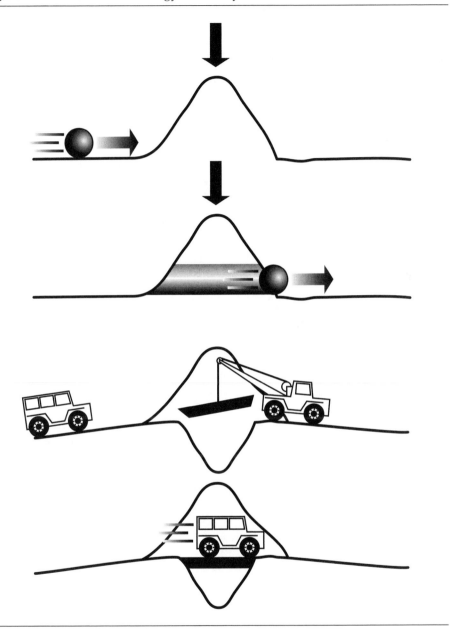

The Tunnel Analogy for Catalysis

Focus	Concept	In order for any reaction to occur, reactants have to form an activated complex (a complex species in which bond breaking and making occur—often at the same time) and thus overcome the activation barrier. For some reactions this barrier is very high and so the reactions are slow. Catalysts speed up reactions by providing an alternative pathway with a much lower energy barrier. Because the reactants do not require so much energy input to reach an activated complex, the reaction proceeds more rapidly.
	Students	Students are confused about the rather esoteric idea of an activated complex and the energy barrier, but they will be familiar with hills and tunnels.
	Analog	The analog consists of the idea of a car or similar vehicle trying to make it up and over a steep and high hill. This is something students can easily relate to, especially if they drive an older car. The steep hill is replaced by an alternative pathway, a tunnel, which is the analog of the catalyst's alternative reaction pathway.

Action	Likes—Mapping the Analog to the Target	
	Analog—tunnel through hill	Target—energy barrier
	Height of hill	Height of energy barrier
	Car	Reactants
	Driving over hill	Reactants overcoming energy barrier
	Tunnel	Alternative pathway provided by catalyst
	Ease of alternative travel through tunnel	Speed of reaction
	The tunnel can be rebuilt again and again.	Reactants can overcome energy barrier again and again.

The Tunnel Analogy for Catalysis (Continued)

		Unlikes—Where the Analogy Breaks Down
		• There is only one car, and but there are many, many reactant particles. • The car and hill are large, but atoms and particles are very small. • Cars move fairly slowly; atoms and particles move rapidly. • Many atoms and particle are charged; cars are not.
Reflection	Conclusion	The idea of an activated complex is a very abstract one. Have the students understood this? This analogy makes the idea much more real to students, especially if coupled with the activity detailed in Suggested Teaching Strategies.
	Improvements	This analogy could be enhanced by a physical activity—for example, getting students to climb a hill and comparing the effort and time with walking around it. You can also use a tunnel if there is one.

Content Standard B, Physical Science, Grades 9–12: "Chemical Reactions" (NAS, 1996, p. 176). The Tunnel Analogy for catalysis shows why some chemical reactions are slow and how catalysts can accelerate chemical reactions.

Suggested teaching strategies	The analogy can be introduced in conjunction with a dramatic demonstration of a catalyst speeding up a chemical reaction. There are many reactions that use a catalyst, and they can take different forms. The catalyzed decomposition of hydrogen peroxide works very well. Take a large (e.g., 3L) measuring cylinder and add about 200mL of fresh H_2O_2 and a generous squirt of dishwashing liquid and some bright dye. Shake the cylinder and place it inside the sink or large tray. Point out that the peroxide is undergoing a decomposition reaction but that it is too slow to be observed. Then get one of the students to add a generous spatula full of the catalyst, solid potassium iodide. A huge brightly colored column of foam is produced (the demonstration is best done in a sink or on a big tray to contain the foam that spills over).
Resources	Hunter et al. (1976, p. 257). Catalysis.
Applications	High school.

The Rice Grains Analogy
for Avogadro's Number

Atoms are very, very small; in fact, too small to work with conveniently or efficiently. Chemists need to deal with reasonably sized physical quantities of matter (e.g., grams), and these quantities contain many, many atoms. To illustrate, a very accurate laboratory balance is capable of weighing to 0.001g of a substance. Even though this is a very small amount and in some cases barely visible, it still contains something like 10^{20} atoms (or other particles like ions). *Avogadro's number* is an extremely useful construct enabling teachers and chemists to deal with reasonable quantities of matter and to perform calculations when conducting chemical reactions.

One feature of Avogadro's number is its sheer size. Students may well be able to recite the number mantralike (often in singsong mode) but have little appreciation of just how big it is. There are two issues here: one is students' inability to really understand scientific notation and orders of magnitude (e.g., a difference that is 10^3 is 1,000 times the difference); the other is students' inability to fully appreciate how small atoms and other particles like ions and molecules really are.

The analogy used here employs the visualization of rice grains covering a large country like the United States, or the use of fruit or some other familiar object compared to the size of the earth, to give students an appreciation of how big Avogadro's number is and how many atoms are present in even a small amount of matter. This is very helpful to advance their understanding of this crucial concept.

Figure 7.7   The Rice Grains Analogy for Avogadro's Number

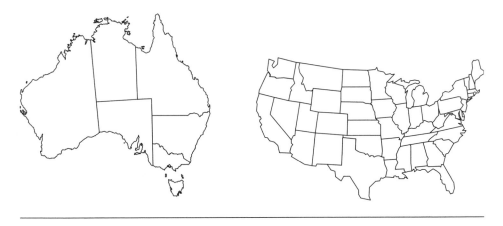

The Rice Grains Analogy for Avogadro's Number

Focus	Concept	Matter is made up of atoms, which are very, very small. Even a *tiny* amount of matter contains an enormous number of atoms. The *mole* concept and Avogadro's number are used so that chemists can deal with these numbers more easily. One mole of a substance contains Avogadro's number of that substance (i.e., 6.023×10^{23}).
	Students	Students have difficulty visualizing just how tiny submicroscopic particles like atoms and elementary particles like electrons and protons are. As a consequence they find it hard to understand just how many such particles are present in an observable amount of matter. They are more familiar with the size of their own country, and size dimensions are more obvious (e.g., if it takes many hours of constant driving to go from one part of a big country to another). This plus dealing with more familiar measurements (like miles or kilometers) makes it easier for students to appreciate the size of Avogadro's number.
	Analog	A simple way to demonstrate the size of Avogadro's number is to relate it to the size of a large country like the United States. This is something more familiar and thus easier to relate to. The analog is the relationship between a familiar object of familiar size and the dimension of the country or the earth, with the object like rice or oranges representing atoms or other particles and the vastness of the country showing how many are needed to get to Avogadro's number.

Action	Likes—Mapping the Analog to the Target	
	Analog—rice and country	**Target—Avogadro's Number**
	Rice grain	Atom or ion
	United States or other large country covered with rice grains to depth of 1 km	Avogadro's number of rice grains
	Oranges	Atom or ion

The Rice Grains Analogy for Avogadro's Number (Continued)		
	Earth	Avogadro's number of oranges would fill a sphere the same size as the earth
	Unlikes—Where the Analogy Breaks Down	
	<ul><li>Rice grains or oranges are much, much larger than atoms or ions.</li><li>Atoms and ions contain charged particles, but rice grains and oranges do not.</li></ul>	
Reflection	**Conclusion**	Was the analogy visually convincing? How close were the student's predictions compared with the values you used in the analogy? Were they surprised at how many atoms were present?
	Improvements	You should either use your own country and make appropriate conversions (land areas are easily available from a variety of Web sites, such as http://www.odci .gov/cia/publications/factbook/index.ht ml) or you can use countries like China or Russia that are well known and that you feel sure your students will think are very big. You could reduce the amount of substance by 1,000 and redo the calculations: this will emphasize idea of the orders of magnitude.
Content Standard B, Physical Science, Grades 9–12: "Structure of Atoms" (NAS, 1996, p. 176). The Rice Grains Analogy shows just how minute the atom is and how large Avogadro's number is.		
Suggested teaching strategies	This could be started by presenting students with one mole of a familiar substance. A good strategy is to then ask students in advance how big they think Avogadro's number is. For example, ask them how big a pile of oranges or rice grains would have to be to contain an Avogadro's number of these items (i.e., the same number as present in one mole of the substance). You also could get the students to walk one mile or kilometer to show how deep the rice particles would need to be (either before or after). This again emphasizes the sheer number of particles present in a mole of substance.	
Resources	Feynman (1994); Hunter et al. (1976).	
Applications	General chemistry in high school.	

A Role-Play Analogy for Chemical Reactions

Electrolysis is sometimes a difficult topic for students. Research suggests that students find a number of features hard to understand. For example, they are often confused about which electrode is positive and which is negative; they subsequently become confused about which species is attracted to which electrode and what happens when they get there. Some underlying alternative conceptions include confusion about the nature of complex ions like sulfate (SO_4^{2-}), and these alternative views can interfere with their understanding of electrolysis.

Based on a research project, a teacher and a science education researcher, Peter Aubusson and Steve Fogwill (2006), worked together on a role-play analogy for the extraction of copper metal from copper carbonate involving the electrolysis of copper sulfate ($CuSO_4$). In the extraction process, copper carbonate is first reacted with dilute sulfuric acid to form copper sulfate. Copper electrodes are placed into this copper sulfate solution, and metallic copper is collected at the negative terminal; the solution remains blue throughout. If the copper electrodes are replaced with carbon electrodes, the solution becomes colorless. There are visible bubbles produced at the positive electrode as oxygen (O_2) is produced, and hydrogen ions (H^+) go into solution to replace the copper ions (Cu^{2+}).

The aim of using role-play is to portray the ideas of science in a fun way, and you need to do it in the three steps of the extraction process: dissolution of copper carbonate, formation of copper sulfate, and electrolysis of copper

Figure 7.8   A Role-Play Analogy for the Extraction of Copper Metal and Electrolysis

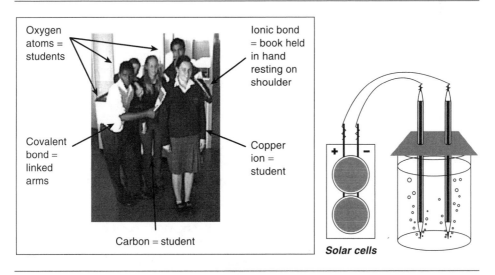

SOURCE: Aubusson, P. J., & Fogwill, S. (2006). Role-play as analogical modeling in science. In P. J. Aubusson, A. G. Harrison, & S. M. Ritchie, *Metaphor and analogy in science education* (pp. 93–104). With kind permission of Springer Science and Business Media.

sulfate. The students assume the role of atoms or ions and electrodes and are labeled accordingly (e.g., copper ion students are labeled with Cu^{2+} labels). The model described here also helps students find out more about intermolecular and intramolecular forces, which is an added benefit.

$$Cu^{2+} + 2e^- \rightarrow Cu(s)$$
$$2H_2O \rightarrow 4H^+ + O_{2(g)} + 4e^-$$

A Role-Play Analogy for Extraction of Copper Metal and Electrolysis		
Focus	**Concept**	Copper carbonate is dissolved in dilute sulfuric acid to produce copper sulfate ($CuSO_4$). The copper ions (Cu^{2+}) present in aqueous copper sulfate ($CuSO_4$) are reduced to metallic copper (Cu) during electrolysis. At the other electrode, water is oxidized to produce oxygen gas (O_2) and hydrogen ions (H^+). Metallic copper is plated out onto the negative electrode, and the oxygen gas is evident as bubbles at the positive electrode.
	Students	Students are easily confused about what happens at which electrode and about the oxidation–reduction processes generally. Other alternative conceptions about the nature of ions and stoichiometry of ions can lead to additional confusion about the electrolysis process itself.
	Analog	Students are individually assigned roles as atoms or ions and are labeled as such. Some students are copper ions, others are oxygen atoms. To begin with, five students make up copper carbonate ($CuCO_3$), with four students representing the carbonate ion (CO_3^{2-}), three labeled as oxygen atoms, one as carbon, and one the copper ion (Cu^{2+}). Linking of arms represents covalent bonds within the complex ion, and an ionic bond between copper ions and the electrons are represented by two books held on the shoulder. Thus before dissolution in water, we have a group of four students linked together by their arms, two of whom are holding books (i.e., the CO_3^{2-} ion) and the books are on the shoulder of a

A Role-Play Analogy for Extraction of Copper Metal and Electrolysis (Continued)

fifth student (i.e., the Cu^{2+} ion). When dissolution occurs, the group of four separates from the fifth and retains the books (i.e., the electrons showing that the CO_3^{2-} is charged). In the second scenario, the formation of copper sulfate is enacted. In this case six students are needed, five representing the sulfate ion and one the copper, and two books representing electrons. Finally, for the electrolysis reactions, three more students are needed to represent water (see the foregoing equations) and two chairs are needed to represent the electrodes. The copper ion students go to one chair and accept the two books (i.e., electrons) and sit on the chair, showing that they are attached to the electrode (i.e., they have become metallic copper). The water students go to the other chair and give the chair two books (i.e., electrons). Two students then link both arms to represent a double-bonded oxygen molecule and wander off (i.e., a gas disappearing from the system). The sulfate students meander around aimlessly being spectator ions.

Action	Likes—Mapping the Analog to the Target	
	Analog—role-play	**Target—electrolysis**
	Individual labeled student	Oxygen and carbon atoms
	Four students linking arms	Carbonate ion
	Individual labeled student	Copper ion
	Book resting on student's shoulder	Electron
	Students separating	Dissolution
	Water	Air
	Linking with one arm	Single bond
	Two-arm links	Double bond
	Chair	Positive electrode
	Chair with books on it	Negative electrode

A Role-Play Analogy for Extraction of Copper Metal and Electrolysis (Continued)

	Unlikes—Where the Analogy Breaks Down	
	• Students and books are much, much larger than atoms, ions, or electrons. • The shapes of ions and electrons are different from student arrangements. • The forces bonding atoms together are much stronger than the linking of arms. • There are many more atoms, ions, and electrons present in these solutions than students in the classroom.	
Reflection	**Conclusion**	Did the students enjoy the role playing? Some may need encouragement to begin with. A key feature is to encourage interactive dialogue as the students attempt to play out their roles. They need to explain their actions in terms of the science.
	Improvements	You could omit the copper carbonate being converted into copper sulfate if this seems too complicated. If you think it is not too complicated, you can also show the hydration effect of water in the dissolution process.
Content Standard B, Physical Science, Grades 9–12: "Chemical Reactions" (NAS, 1996, p. 176). The Role-Play Analogy for the extraction of metals shows that chemical reactions involves transfer of electrons between reacting ions, molecules, or atoms and the role of electrolysis in reaction chemistry, including preparation of metals.		
Suggested teaching strategies	It is probably best to represent the process in three separate role-play scenarios, one being dissolution of copper carbonate, a second being formation of copper sulfate, and the third being the electrolysis of copper sulfate. The role of water in hydration can be added later.	
Resources	Aubusson & Fogwill (2006, pp. 93–104)	
Applications	High School	

The Ham Sandwich
Analogy for Stoichiometry

The science education research literature suggests that stoichiometry is a difficult concept to grasp, with students often confusing the combinations of elements when figuring out molecular and ionic formulae (Dahsah & Coll, 2007; Gabel & Samuel, 1986). It is pretty difficult for students to do any calculations and design chemical reactions if they cannot get basic stoichiometry right. It is one of the core topics students need before they can do much chemistry.

Students might not be that familiar with combination and valency rules, but most students love to eat and are very familiar with sandwiches. The Ham Sandwich Analogy is used to explain the notion of limiting reagents. This analogy involves representing a recipe for a ham sandwich, consisting of two slices of bread and one of ham, in terms approximating those used in chemistry: where H represents a slice of ham, B represents bread slices, and HB_2 the ham sandwich:

$$H + 2B \rightarrow HB_2$$

In stoichiometry it is often necessary to know the molar mass of a compound in order to perform mass/mole calculations. The molar mass of a compound has the unit, grams per mole, abbreviated g/mol. For this purpose you can introduce the notion of grams per slice (g/slice) in the analogy. In this case, slices are analogous to moles and g/slice analogous to g/mol. Rather than talk about the unit of *sandwich* in the ham sandwich equation, it is best to refer to the complete sandwich in slices (i.e., two slices of bread and one slice of ham makes one sandwich).

As students gain confidence with ideas about g/slice and demonstrate ability in problem solving using these terms, replace the word *slice* with *mole* and *g/slice* with *g/mol*. You can progress further by replacing the sandwich equation with actual chemical equations. After practicing stoichiometry problems using chemical equations, students can write their own analogies and their own questions using chemical equations.

The developers of this analogy suggest that students are able to demonstrate the ability to perform stoichiometric calculations using the analogy. They recommend that emphasis be placed on showing how the ham sandwich equation relates to a chemical equation of the same ratio and then extending the analogy to include more complex ratios. The reason for this is that students may find the analogy useful in understanding the concept initially but not be clear how the analog and target are related if you do not use ratios other than 1:2 in the analogy.

Figure 7.9   The Ham Sandwich Analogy for Stoichiometry

The Ham Sandwich Analogy for Stoichiometry		
Focus	**Concept**	Reaction stoichiometry involves fixed ratios of chemicals reacting according to a balanced chemical equation. Understanding the concept of stoichiometry and using it to determine reacting quantities in a chemical reaction involves manipulating ratios.
	Students	Students may already be familiar with balancing equations and chemical symbols for reactants and products. But they may find it difficult to visualize what is happening when reaction stoichiometry is modeled with chemical symbols, equations, and mathematics. Students are familiar with recipes and making sandwiches.
	Analog	Making a ham sandwich and representing the recipe using symbols can be used to model the stoichiometry of a chemical reaction and the ratios involved as well as the limiting reagent concept. When a sandwich is made with two slices of bread and one slice of ham, the ratio of ham and bread that go together is 1:2. By using the masses of ham and bread per slice it is possible to model mass-mass and mass-mole/mole-mass calculations.

The Ham Sandwich Analogy for Stoichiometry (Continued)

Action	Likes—Mapping the Analog to the Target	
	Analog—The ratio of ham to bread in a ham sandwich	**Target—The ratios involved in stoichiometric calculations**
	Symbols H and B for ham and bread and HB_2 for sandwich	Symbols for reactants and products in a chemical equation (e.g., H_2, O_2, and H_2O)
	Sandwich equation $H + 2B \rightarrow HB_2$	Chemical equation (e.g., $2H_2 + O_2 \rightarrow 2H_2O$)
	Ham and bread make a sandwich in a ratio of 1:2	H_2 and O_2 react in a ratio of 2:1 (for instance)
	Slices of ham and bread and complete sandwich	Moles of reactants and products
	Mass per slice of ham and bread	Molar mass of compounds
	Slice-slice calculations, slice-mass/mass-slice calculations	Mole-mole, mole-mass/mass-slice calculations
	Unlikes—Where the Analogy Breaks Down	
	<ul><li>Ham and bread don't react.</li><li>Making the sandwich involves physical processes that are easily reversed. Not all chemical reactions are reversible by physical means.</li><li>The symbols H and B may represent the reacting parts in the sandwich equation, but in a chemical equation molecules are often involved, such as H_2 and O_2, and these may involve more than one atom.</li></ul>	
Reflection	**Conclusion**	Could the students perform the slice-slice, slice-mass calculations? Did they see the connection between the ham sandwich equation and quantities and the chemical equation?
	Improvements	Making a real ham sandwich can help students visualize the sandwich "reactants" and the amounts involved in making one sandwich. By giving students the opportunity to choose the symbols for the components of the sandwich, they have some ownership of the pseudo equation and may gain appreciation for what symbols in an equation represent.

The Ham Sandwich Analogy for Stoichiometry (Continued)	
Content Standard B, Physical Science, Grades 9–12: "Structure and Properties" of Matter (NAS, 1996, p. 176). The Ham Sandwich Analogy shows how a compound is formed when two or more kinds of atoms bind together chemically to from compounds with fixed ratios of atoms.	
Suggested teaching strategies	Use real ham and bread and make the sandwich (or use other ingredients for a sandwich the students like or are more familiar with and to make more complex ratios). Ask students to answer questions such as, "If I have 3 slices of ham, how much bread is needed to make complete sandwiches?" Do all the stoichiometric types of manipulations with the analogy and then repeat them with an equation with a similar ratio of reactants and products. Get the students to write their own analogies using either food or other things that they like for the equations. Students can write questions based on their equations and ask others to answer them. Ask students to explain the stoichiometry concept to the class using their analogy. Have students write their own stoichiometry problems using chemical symbols.
Resources	Materials for making sandwiches. Whitten, Gailey, and Davis (1992, pp. 92–93).
Applications	High school students reacting quantities, stoichiometry, limiting reagents

The Coconut Shy Analogy for Effective Molecular Collisions

The rate of chemical reactions according to the scientific model is dependent on the number of effective collisions. One consequence of this is that the higher the concentration (and some other variables too, like temperature) the more likely we are to see effective collisions, and thus an increase in the reaction rate.

The notion of effective molecular collisions seems a reasonably intuitive concept, yet reaction rate chemistry is, like other aspects of kinetic theory, seldom well understood by students. Most students are familiar with fairground competitions like the coconut shy, where you have to try to knock an object off a stand. Clearly, as with any analogy, you need to tailor this one to something you are sure your students are familiar with (think of appropriate activities from your local festivals and fairs). Alternatively, this is a model you could actually act out, making it an exciting and fun activity, but you will need a fair bit of room to allow for inaccurate shots. There also are quite a few cartoon or pictorial representations of the coconut shy notion on the Internet, in which you knock unusual objects off the stand (e.g., http://www.cartoonstock.com/directory/c/coconut_shy.asp). The difficulty students face when trying to knock a coconut off the stand shows how infrequent effective collisions are.

Figure 7.10   The Coconut Shy Analogy for Reaction Rates

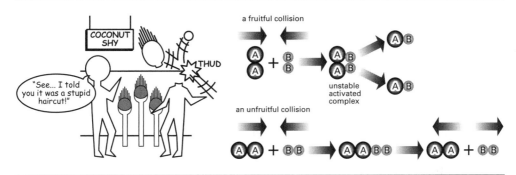

SOURCE: Adapted from Otto and Towle (1969).

The Coconut Shy Analogy for Reaction Rates		
Focus	**Concept**	Chemical substances are made up of tiny charged or uncharged particles. Chemical reactions proceed when bonds are broken and new bonds formed. Kinetic theory models reactions as effective collisions. Effective collisions result in bond breaking, and the resultant particles can form new molecules by forming new bonds. In order to break a bond, sufficient energy is needed to produce an effective collision. The likelihood of effective collisions can be increased by increasing the number of particles in a given space (i.e., increasing concentration) and by increasing temperature (which increases the velocity and thus the energy of the particles).
	Students	Students have difficulty visualizing tiny, submicroscopic particles like atoms, ions, and molecules. It is also hard for them to visualize collisions and effective collisions. They are more familiar with fun activities like the coconut shy seen in many fairs and festivals.

The Coconut Shy Analogy for Reaction Rates (Continued)

	Analog	We can visualize an effective collision as knocking a coconut off the stand at the fair (a competitive activity). The greater the number of attempts we are able to make, the more likely we are to knock the coconut off the stand and thus the greater the likelihood of an effective collision. We can also throw the ball at the coconut harder (i.e., supply more energy), in which case it goes faster; if it hits, it is then more likely to actually knock the coconut off the stand.

Action — **Likes—Mapping the Analog to the Target**

Analog—coconut shy	Target—effective collisions
Ball and coconut	Reacting particles
Number of attempts	Number of collisions
Hitting coconut with ball	Effective collision
Likelihood of hitting coconut	Likelihood of effective collisions
Speed of throw of ball	Kinetic energy of reacting particle
Increasing the closeness to the coconut	Concentration increase

Unlikes—Where the Analogy Breaks Down

- A ball will travel much, much slower than colliding particles.
- There are many, many more particles present in even a tiny amount of reacting substances than there are coconuts or balls.
- In the coconut shy, one object is still (the coconut) and the other moving (the ball); in kinetic theory, both reactants are moving rapidly.
- Reactants are often confined to a reacting vessel; in principle you could throw a ball at the coconut from almost anywhere.

Reflection	**Conclusion**	Were the students able to hit the coconut? You will need to have plenty of balls on hand as the students may get frustrated if they keep missing the coconut.

The Coconut Shy Analogy for Reaction Rates (Continued)		
		Also the ball will need to be heavy enough to actually dislodge the coconut from the stand. Did students understand the connection to chemical collisions?
	Improvement	If you act out this activity, you can have many students all firing their balls at the coconut. This is much more likely to result in an effective collision. If they cannot hit the coconut, have them stand closer. This could then be related to the size of the container (i.e., concentration as particles per unit volume).

Content Standard B, Physical Science, Grades 9–12: "Chemical Reactions" (NAS, 1996, p. 176). The Coconut Shy Analogy shows how reaction rates depend on how often the reacting atoms and molecules encounter one another.

Suggested teaching strategies	This analogy probably needs a diagram. Be sure that the students are familiar with the activity, as the nature of this will vary from place to place (e.g., in your town or city, it may best be some other item). If the students are not familiar with the activity, it is best to act it out with balls and hittable objects.
Resources	Thiele & Treagust (1994).
Applications	General chemistry in high school.

The Soccer Analogy for Weak and Strong Acids and Bases

Acids and bases are very common and very useful substances. Their chemistry is very interesting and rather more complex than it might first appear. One of the reasons students find difficulty in dealing with acids and bases is that they often encounter several definitions of these familiar terms. Chemists began with some fairly simple ideas for defining acids and bases, often describing the evidence for their presence (e.g., sour taste, slippery feel, turns blue litmus red) and progressed to more general and useful ideas that related to the actual chemical nature of these substances (e.g., the Brønsted-Lowry notion of an acid as a proton donor and a base as a proton acceptor). Students can relate pretty well to the physical manifestations of properties of acids and bases, but they may struggle with some of the chemical features. One concept that is well established in the literature as being difficult is that of weak and strong acids and bases. The literature further suggests that students struggle to understand the notion of dissociation and typically confuse a strong acid with a concentrated acid (and similarly for bases). Questions such as, "Which is the stronger acid, 1.0 molar CH_3COOH or 0.10M HCl?" reveal such confusion—and are useful probes of student understanding. It seems the notion of partial ionization is the underlying problem. It is not obvious to students why there should be partial or incomplete ionization for weak acids and bases, and they assume that full ionization occurs every time when they see equations like the one that follows:

$$HB_{(aq)} \rightleftharpoons H^+_{(aq)} + B^-_{(aq)}$$

Soccer is a keen interest for many students. We can model the notion of partial ionization by comparing proton donation and acceptance with passing a soccer ball, either by hand or foot. In this analogy an acid is like a soccer player with the ball in his or her possession. The soccer player's job it is to deliver the ball to a receiver. A good soccer player delivers the ball efficiently. The player gets rid of the ball quickly and easily, just as a strong acid gets rid of, or donates, a proton. A similar relationship exists with the receiver and the base. A soccer receiver is a player whose job it is to catch or capture the ball, just as a base is a proton acceptor. A good receiver catches or captures the ball every time; a bad one misses: likewise a strong base accepts the proton every time, a weak one much less often.

$$H^+_{(aq)} + B^-_{(aq)} \rightleftharpoons HB_{(aq)}$$

Figure 7.11   The Soccer Analogy for Weak and Strong Acids and Bases

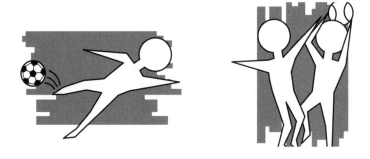

The Soccer Analogy for Weak and Strong Acids and Bases

Focus	Concept	Strong acids are those that are fully ionized in water. Weak acids are only partially ionized. Strong bases are bases that are fully protonated, whereas weak bases are only partially protonated.
	Students	Students are confused by the use of the term *strong*, which they commonly interpret to be the same as *concentrated*. Likewise they consider weak acids and bases to be the same as acid and base solutions that are low in concentration. They cannot see the link between the extent of ionization and the resultant strength or weakness.
	Analog	A strong acid is like a soccer player who is an excellent distributor of the ball. The passes are always accurate and go straight to the receiver. A weak acid is like a poor distributor of the ball. The ball is seldom sent accurately to the receiver. A strong base is like an excellent receiver of the ball, capturing every ball sent. Conversely, a weak base is a poor receiver, always out of position, constantly fumbling the ball or missing the pass.

Action	Likes—Mapping the Analog to the Target	
	Analog—soccer players	**Target—acids and bases**
	Soccer ball	Proton
	Soccer player with ball	Protonated acid or base
	Soccer player after having passed the ball	Deprotonated acid or base
	Good passer of ball	Strong acid
	Poor passer of ball	Weak acid
	Good receiver of ball	Strong base
	Poor receiver of ball	Weak base

The Soccer Analogy for Weak and Strong Acids and Bases (Continued)		
	Unlikes—Where the Analogy Breaks Down	
	• The soccer player is large, whereas an acid or base particle is very, very small. • A soccer ball is large, whereas a proton is very, very small. • The electron is negatively charged, whereas the soccer ball is not. • The soccer player after passing the ball has no charge, whereas an acid after donating a proton is negatively charged. • Even the fastest of soccer players moves very much slower than protons or acid and base particles. • There are only a few individuals and soccer balls; there are many millions of acid and base particles and electrons in even a tiny amount of acid or base solution.	
Reflection	**Conclusion**	Did the students relate to the analogy? Maybe you need to make sure you are using a sport they can relate to. Did you ask them first which ball sports they liked most?
	Improvements	This would be a good analogy to do as an activity or to talk about after a recess in which students may have been playing ball games. You also could use a video presentation of a recent and dramatic game.
Content Standard B, Physical Science, Grades 9–12: Chemical Reactions (NAS, 1996, p. 176). The Soccer Analogy shows that some chemical reactions involve loss and gain of hydrogen ions (acid-base reactions) and how this varies with the acid or base.		
Suggested teaching strategies	This model works quite well even as a pictorial demonstration, or you could use a video clip of a recent exciting game (e.g., Euro 2006, the Rugby or Netball World Cup). It is important to tailor the analogy to your audience, especially with respect to gender.	
Resources	Silverstein (2000).	
Applications	Physical chemistry in high school.	

The Fan Analogy for Electron Clouds

Over the years scientists have come up with many models for the structure of the atom. Simple notions are of atoms as indivisible species that are the smallest particles that make up matter. More sophisticated models contain many different elementary particles. The rather esoteric details of the structure of the atom and the nucleus are very interesting, but most chemists are more concerned with the arrangement of elementary particles that affect chemical reactions and the arrangement of the electrons, neutrons, and protons. Rutherford and Bohr (as cited in Zumdahl, 1989) devised the notion of the nuclear atom—with the bulk of the atom's mass, consisting of the massive particles of the neutron and the neutron concentrated in a very small space (see the Sport Stadium and Solar System Analogies)—and the electrons organized around this nucleus.

The solar system is one of the easiest models of atomic structure to understand, but scientists use more sophisticated models and see the electrons as a cloud of electron density surrounding a nucleus. This is tricky and a nonintuitive concept, and science education research shows that even advanced-level tertiary students struggle to understand what this model is like. The hardest thing to understand is how the electron can be a cloud of negative charge. It is not a cloud like those you see in the sky. Instead, it is just the place where electrons are likely to be found.

This simple Fan Analogy goes some way to helping students understand how an electron can appear to be in many places at once. It works best if you just focus on a simple system, like the hydrogen atom with one electron and one proton.

Figure 7.12   The Fan Analogy for Electron Clouds

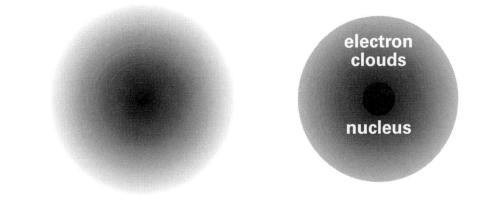

The Fan Analogy for Electron Clouds

Focus	Concept	The electrons are tiny, negatively charged particles that move very rapidly around the nucleus. They move so fast we cannot state with certainty where exactly they are at any point in time. We say they are like a cloud of electron density around the nucleus, with the average distance depending on the electron (e.g., s, p).
	Students	The notion of an electron cloud is confusing when students are used to thinking of electrons as individual particles. Students are familiar with fans when switched on and off.
	Analog	The electron cloud is related to a space-filling model similar to the motion of a high speed fan (see Figure 7.12). When the fan is stationery we can see where the blades are; when it is moving at very high speed we see a blur of the vanes and we know it is occupying the space even though we are not certain where it is at a particular time.

Action	Likes—Mapping the Analog to the Target	
	Analog—fan	Target—electron cloud
	Fan center	Nucleus
	Fan blade	Electron
	Fan rotation	Electron movement
	Fan blurring	Electron cloud
	Number of fan blades	Number of electrons in orbital
	Tips of fan blades	Outermost part of electron cloud

Unlikes—Where the Analogy Breaks Down

- Electrons move much faster than the fan can rotate.
- Electrons are much, much smaller than fan blades.

		• Electrons and protons are charged, but the fan center and blades are not. • The blades of the fan are fixed to the fan center, but the electron is not fixed to the nucleus. • In most atoms there are multiple electrons at different distances from the nucleus. • The fan is two dimensional; electron clouds are three dimensional.
Reflection	**Conclusion**	This works best with an actual fan rather than a diagram. Were the students able to get the idea and to extend the analogy to multielectron atoms?
	Improvements	A faster fan probably is more impressive and helps to emphasize the speed of the electron. You could use a multispeed fan and crank up the speed to illustrate this point, or a multiblade fan to represent multiple electrons. This shows more intense blurring, emphasizing the increased electron density in multielectron atoms. You could also use different sized fans to illustrate different orbital radii. You can throw a crunched up ball of paper to show the effect more dramatically.

Content Standard B, Physical Science, Grades 9–12: Structure of Atoms (NAS, 1996, p. 176). The Fan Analogy shows that each atom has a nucleus that is surrounded by negatively charged electrons.

Suggested teaching strategies	It would be good to demonstrate the analogy by showing students an actual high speed fan, although you should avoid sticking anything into the pathway of the fan blades for obvious reasons.
Resources	Bucat (1984).
Applications	Physical chemistry for high school.

The Bookshelf Analogy for Atomic Energy Levels in the Atom

Some students confuse the order or ranking of electrons in the atom in terms of energy level and distance from the nucleus. According to modern atomic theory there is some relationship between distance and energy level, but the distances get a bit mixed up due to things like inner shell screening and so on. Students should understand the notion of quantization of energy levels in the atom and the processes associated with shifting from one energy level to another. The analogy used here of a bookshelf helps work through these ideas, or that of a building works, too.

According to quantum theory, each electron in an atom is permitted to be at only certain fixed energy levels. Electrons can gain energy and shift up one or more levels; electrons at higher energy levels can fall down and upon doing so, emit the difference in energy between the two levels. The analogy with books in a bookshelf is nice and obvious. We have a large bookshelf with shelves at different heights. A book (i.e., an electron) may reside only on the shelves: if it is placed elsewhere, it falls onto a shelf. We have to use energy (e.g., lifting) to move a book from one shelf to another. Only a certain number of books will fit on one shelf in the same way that only a certain number of electrons may reside at one energy level.

Figure 7.13   The Bookshelf Analogy for Atomic Energy Levels in the Atom

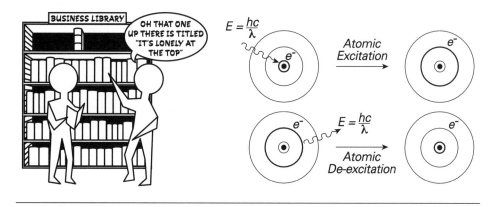

The Bookshelf Analogy for Atomic Energy Levels in the Atom

Focus	Concept	Electrons are arranged around a nucleus. Electrons can reside at only certain fixed energy levels. An electron can gain energy and shift from a lower to a higher energy level. Electrons at higher energy levels may fall to vacant lower energy levels and in doing so emit energy in the form of radiation or light, if the energy gap is such that the wavelength of the radiation is in the visible portion of the electromagnetic spectrum.
	Students	Many students cannot understand why electrons cannot be just anywhere and why they must be in fixed energy levels. They find it hard to understand why electrons need fixed energy (or emit fixed amounts of energy) when moving from one level to another.
	Analog	A large bookshelf with many levels of shelves provides the analogy. Each shelf is at a different height, corresponding to different energy levels. Each shelf can contain only a certain number of books. To shift a book from a lower shelf, energy is needed to lift it.

Action	Likes—Mapping the Analog to the Target	
	Analog—bookshelf	**Target—energy levels**
	Bookshelf	Energy levels in an atom
	Shelves	Specific energy levels
	Books	Electrons
	Capacity of shelves	Capacity of energy levels
	Number of books on a shelf	Number of electrons in an energy level
	Lifting a book to a higher shelf	Raising electron to higher energy level
	Shifting a book from a higher level to a lower level	Electron dropping from higher energy level to lower energy level

The Bookshelf Analogy for Atomic Energy Levels in the Atom (Continued)

	Unlikes—Where the Analogy Breaks Down	
	• Electrons are tiny in comparison with books. • The bookshelf is much, much larger than an atom. • When a book is lifted down, there is no obvious emission of energy; when an electron drops down a level, it emits radiation. • Books come in different sizes; electrons are the same size. • Electrons are moving rapidly; books are stationary. • Electrons are charged; books are not.	
Reflection	**Conclusion**	Did the students pick up on the important differences between the analogy and the target? You can use a bookshelf in the classroom to illustrate the concept.
	Improvements	You could use very heavy books to make the idea of energy input more evident when shifting books up a level in the bookshelf.
Content B, Physical Science, Grades 9–12: Structure of Atoms (NAS, 1996, p. 176). The Bookshelf Analogy shows that matter is made up of minute particles called atoms, and atoms are composed of even smaller components: a positively charged nucleus surrounded by negatively charged electrons arranged in shells.		
Suggested teaching strategies	This would be a good analogy to use after a library visit or using a classroom bookshelf. It is probably a good idea to use same-sized books as you demonstrate, but be sure to point out that this is deliberate.	
Resources	Hunter et al. (1976).	
Applications	Physical or general chemistry in high school.	

Students in School and States of Matter

The kinetic theory about states of matter is an important scientific concept that is used to explain physical properties and changes of state. It is actually a remarkable theory as it is fairly simple in principle and description, but there are some important, fine details that students often overlook, and these result in numerous misconceptions. This is quite surprising as it is not particularly abstract in nature. Because of its importance, it is crucial that students understand this theory. One common misunderstanding relates to spacing between particles of matter; it is common for pictures and diagrams in textbooks to imply that there are quiet large gaps between particles in the liquid state. In fact according to kinetic theory, this is not so; remember that water is essentially incompressible. The gist of the theory is that particles of matter in the *solid* state have relatively low energy and high order, being packed close together in regular arrays with essentially fixed positions. They thus have fixed shapes. The particles can vibrate around these fixed positions, but don't move away from them. In the *liquid* state, the forces of attraction between the particles of matter are broken down, and while the spacing remains much the same as in a solid, the particles can move as well as vibrate. So the particles now have less order, more energy, and take the shape of their container. In the *gaseous* state, the particles are very far apart indeed and move randomly around with high energy. They are so far apart, any interaction between particles can be ignored; they move in straight lines and collide elastically with each other and the walls of any container.

Developed by Harrison and Treagust (1994b), the school analogy for states of matter is obviously going to be relevant to all students. The analogy works well in class because each state of matter is related to various classroom practices: first about students at their desks (the *solid* state), then to what happens in, say, a practical class or classroom activity (the *liquid* state), and finally the end of class, when students can move almost anywhere in the school (the *gaseous* state). We need to be conscious here of the anthropomorphic nature of the analogy. There is the possibility students may start to think of particles of matter as being like humans—for example, being purposeful in their actions.

Figure 7.14   Students in School and States of Matter

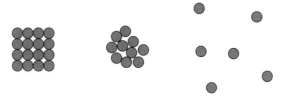

Students in School and States of Matter

Focus	Concept	Matter is composed of three states, solid liquid, and gas. In solids the particles are in fixed positions and do not move but can vibrate around these positions. They are low in energy. In the liquid state, the particles are still as close together as in the solid state, but can move around and take the shape of their container; they have more energy. In the gaseous state the particles are very far apart and move with high speed, only colliding elastically with other particles and the walls of any container. They have high energy.
	Students	Many students think that there are gaps between the particles in liquids. Textbook diagrams that try to show the relatively freer movement of particles in the liquid state may develop or reinforce this misconception.
	Analog	School students represent the particles. When sitting at their desks the students represent the solid state. Moving around in the classroom or laboratory represents the liquid state. Moving around the school represents the gaseous state.

Action	Likes—Mapping the Analog to the Target	
	Analog—students in school	**Target—states of matter**
	Students	Particles of matter
	Students sitting at desk	Fixed positions of solid state
	Students breathing, moving arms or legs while at desk	Vibration of solid particles around fixed positions
	Students moving around laboratory or classroom	Movement of particles in liquid state
	Classroom boundaries	Walls of vessel containing liquid
	Students moving around school at recess	Particles in gaseous state moving around randomly
	School boundaries	Walls of vessel containing gas

Students in School and States of Matter (Continued)		
	Unlikes—Where the Analogy Breaks Down	
	<ul><li>Particles of matter are tiny in comparison with students.</li><li>The school and classroom are larger than containers.</li><li>Students come in different sizes; particles of a given substance are the same size.</li><li>Particles, especially in the gaseous state, are moving rapidly; students move much more slowly.</li><li>Particles in solids and liquids are closely packed; even when at their desks, students are not.</li><li>Solid particles vibrate continuously; students do not move continuously.</li><li>Particles are inanimate and do not move or act purposively; students *may* act purposively.</li><li>In the gaseous state, particles move very rapidly and continuously; at recess students may not move much (e.g., at lunchtime).</li><li>In the gaseous state, particles move *independently,* continuously; at recess students may sit around with their friends in groups.</li></ul>	
Reflection	**Conclusion**	It is impossible to observe the behavior of particles in the solid, liquid, and gaseous states. The analogy of atoms and molecules with a classroom of students helps students understand that solid particles vibrate around fixed positions; liquids have fixed volume, variable shape, and the particles are mobile within the liquid; and in gases, the particles are independent and the gas lacks fixed volume or shape.
	Improvements	You also can add to this analogy by an extra illustration: A student takes a message from you to the school principal—leaving his or her desk and classroom and moving around the school—and returns. This is like a particle that evaporates and then condenses again.

Content Standard B, Physical Science, Grades 9–12: "Structure and Properties of Matter" (NAS, 1996, p. 176). The Students in School Analogy shows that the physical properties of compounds reflect the nature of the interactions among its molecules; solids have fixed volume and shape, liquids have fixed volume and variable shape, and gases variable volume and shape.

Students in School and States of Matter (Continued)	
Suggested teaching strategies	This might be a good analogy to use around lunchtime or recess. Some humor might help; for example, you might say in an *ideal* world, students *on some occasions at least*, stay at their desks. You can also use this analogy while demonstrating changes of state, for instance, beginning with a block of ice that you heat: work through the analogy as students observe the changes to the ice into water and eventually water vapor.
Resources	Harrison & Treagust (1994b).
Applications	Physical or general chemistry at high school.

8

Effective Physics Analogies

Allan G. Harrison

The abstract nature of physics concepts particularly challenges teachers and students. For instance, how do we describe forces, in particular, forces that act at a distance, like gravity, magnetism, and electric force? How can we explain refraction? A ray of light bends toward the normal as it passes from air to water because it slows down, but why does it slow down and how does this slowing down change the direction of a photon? And how do we easily explain nuclear decay and radioactivity? Sophisticated quantum explanations are available to physicists, but where are the everyday explanations that school teachers can use with elementary and middle school students?

The answer, of course, is to use analogies and models.

In *A Brief History of Time* (Hawking, 1988) at least 74 everyday analogies were used to explain astrophysics and quantum ideas; in *Six Easy Pieces,* Richard Feynman (1994) employed 12 analogies to explain "Atoms in Motion" (his first chapter); and history shows that Robert Boyle, Christian Huygens, Johannes Kepler, and James Clerk Maxwell all used analogies to solve conceptual problems. So remember, whenever you invent or modify an analogy to help your students' learning, you're in excellent company.

Here follow three particularly valuable groups of analogies as they apply to high school physics classes:

1. Analogies for Light

A ray of light changes direction when it passes from air into water because it slows down. Refraction of light rays is commonly compared to the way water waves change direction. This analogy works because students can see water waves slowing down and changing direction as the waves move from deep water into a shallower region. Of course, this phenomenon has to be demonstrated before the analogy between water waves and light waves can be made. Ripples in a pond or tank are an excellent way to demonstrate refraction of water waves. The analogy between water waves and light waves is productive because it also explains the diffraction of light. Student understanding is advanced even further when the water wave analogy is augmented by the analogy of the pair of wheels rolling from a smooth to a rough surface, featured later in this chapter and in Treagust, Harrison, Venville and Dagher (1996).

2. Field Metaphors and Analogies

Forces that act at a distance are best explained by talking about gravity and magnetic and electric fields. The field concept is a metaphoric analogy based on agricultural, battle, and sport fields, areas in which crops, battles, or games are confined. In agriculture, plants, animals, and soil are intimately related, and each is affected by what happens in other parts of the field. There are specific rules and relationships that apply inside it. For instance, on a sports field or battlefield, the addition or loss of a star player or the introduction or destruction of a major weapon affects all parts of the field. Players and soldiers know to some degree what each other is doing and respond to overall changes in the ebb and flow of power. The Field Analogy explains how a magnet affects every magnetic substance in its field of influence. A magnetic field models the way that magnetism works within and around a magnet. Other than the field concept, there is no effective way to explain force at a distance. Magnetic and electric fields puzzled Faraday and occupied Maxwell for many years. Maxwell's mathematical equations emerged from the analogical models of weights, pulleys, and strings that he used to model forces acting at a distance (Nersessian, 1992).

3. Analogical Models for Electricity

More analogies and models have been used to explain electrical circuits than for any other science concept. Electricity is used everywhere, yet it is so counterintuitive. For example, in series circuits, electric energy is shared between lightbulbs like water is shared between sprinklers along a hose. This analogy suggests that as lightbulbs are added to a series circuit, more current should flow, but the reverse happens. This is a question that only The Electric Field Analogy can help solve.

But there is another paradox: Add lightbulbs to a series circuit, and they all get dimmer; add lightbulbs side by side in a parallel circuit, and all are equally bright (within limits). The analogy that works is one that shows that parallel circuits actually are independent circuits. The school hall with two or three separate sets of doors satisfies this need. People leave the hall two or three times faster when two or three doors are opened. Independent exits are like independent parallel circuits.

The other counterintuitive conception for electric circuits is the problem of why the current isn't used up. Lightbulbs grow dim after a while and batteries go flat. Something must be used up. Grayson (1994) says the problem comes from confusing *current* with *energy*—current is conserved while the battery's energy is used up. This is right, and students more readily exchange the misconception of consumed current for the understanding that energy is transferred when multiple current conservation analogies are employed. Students need the correct terminology, and they need logical explanations. Analogies provide these explanations. And multiple analogies are recommended for explaining electricity concepts.

The most popular electricity analogies are those that employ water circuits and water flow (e.g., Hewitt, 1999, p. 535). Water circuit analogies are useful for demonstrating that electricity flows, *but that's all*. The downside of these analogies is the student conclusion that electricity is a fluid and that electricity leaks out onto the carpet from electric sockets that have no plugs in them. The incorrect inference that electricity is a material fluid supports the idea of current being used up because water is rarely recycled in the students' homes; it is used up and lost. Why shouldn't they conclude that current is used up?

Science educators should use The Continuous Train, Bicycle Chain, and Student M&M's Circle Analogies to reinforce the notion that current is conserved, not consumed (Osborne & Freyberg, 1985). To teach electricity concepts effectively, I recommend a set of two or three analogies drawn from the list below, which is numbered 8–14 because these analogies are found in the second half of this chapter:

8. The Water Circuit Analogy for Electric Current

9. The Water Pressure Analogy for Voltage

10. The Shared Water Flow Analogy

11. The School Gymnasium Analogy for Parallel Circuits

12. The Continuous Train Analogy for Current Conservation in a Series Circuit

13. The M&M's Circle Analogy for Electric Current

14. The Field Analogy for Electric Circuits

As you see, these seven analogies include the Water Circuit Analogy, but *it should never be used on its own*—it engenders too many misconceptions.

First, here are seven additional physics analogies:

1. The Dominoes and Books Analogy for Conduction of Heat

2. The Gravity Warps Space-Time Analogy for Bending Starlight

3. The Supernova Cola Analogy for Exploding Stars

4. The Matches, Mousetraps, and Dominos Analogies for Nuclear Fission

5. The Eye Is Like a Camera Analogy

6. The Pair of Wheels Analogy for the Refraction of Light

7. Bridging Analogies for the Balanced Forces of a Book on a Table

The Dominoes and Books Analogy for Conduction of Heat

Heat transfer by conduction is easy to feel and demonstrate. If you simultaneously heat the ends of steel, copper, and aluminum rods, you can measure the rates that heat travels along them. Another way is to hold the ends of a wooden skewer and a piece of wire in a candle flame. You quickly drop the wire but you can hold the wooden stick even when it's on fire.

Mrs. Jones had her Grade 8 students feel the water tap, bench top, a sweater, and a pencil, asking, "What do they feel like?" Knowing that the lesson was about heat, students said, "[The] faucets feel colder than the bench top and that's cooler than the pencil and my sweater feels warm." Mrs. Jones handed out some thermometers and asked the students to try and measure the temperature of the objects they had felt. Discussion followed on how to lay the thermometer bulb on the objects and for how long to make it a fair test. Most students agreed that the objects that felt different were in fact about the same temperature. They talked about experimental error; then Mrs. Jones directed the class to a demonstration she had set up while they had used their thermometers (see Figure 8.1).

For a couple of minutes they talked about metals—iron, copper, and aluminum. "Which one conducts heat fastest . . . what's slowest?" Some students also asked, "How does a metal conduct heat and why's wood a bad conductor?" Anticipating this question, Mrs. Jones turned to her books and domino analogy.

The class had talked about kinetic theory, so the students were familiar with particle ideas. Mrs. Jones said that the books represented the atoms or molecules that make up the metals and wood. The dominoes represented electrons that are free to move around in metals but not free to move in wood or plastic.

Figure 8.1   The Dominoes and Books Analogy for Metal Conduction

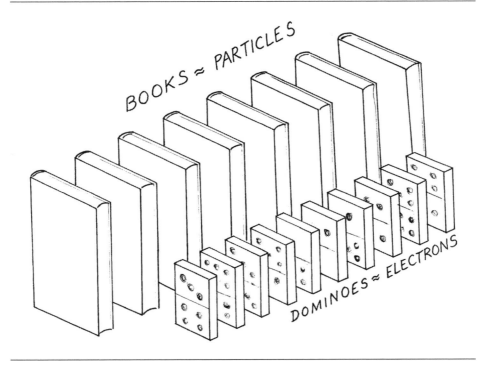

Mrs. Jones said, "If I push this end book over, what happens?" She did so, and each book fell onto the next book, pushing it over and so on for about 20 books. She stood the books up again and then asked two girls to help her. "When I say 'go,' I want Gail to push the first book over like I just did and Sal to push the first domino over at the same time." When she said "go," the girls pushed over the end book and domino. The line of books fell slowly but the dominoes fell nearly three times faster. She then used this analogy to explain conduction:

Mrs. Jones: Metals are different from other sorts of substances because their electrons are free to move. In metals there are lots of free electrons, and this is why metals are very good conductors. In metals we've got our big particles—these books are like atoms—and the dominoes, the little ones, represent free electrons. Little dominoes move lots faster than big books. Now when I heat one end of the metal, as well as making the particles vibrate, the free electrons also vibrate, so we've got a double way of passing on the vibrations. Nonconductors like wood and plastic don't have free electrons, only very big molecules, so in metals, the vibrations or heat travels much faster. . . . You saw that the books fell slowly and the dominoes fell quickly. It's the free electrons that make metals good conductors.

Mrs. Jones: What state of matter do you think would be the worst conductor?

Student: Gases

Mrs. Jones: That's right, gases. Why are gases the worst conductor?

Student: Because the particles are so far apart that they don't touch each other.

Mrs. Jones: That's good. [They are] so far apart they can't touch each other when they vibrate. Gases are like having one book here, and the next book might be right at the end of the bench. . . . So it does not matter how much I heat this gas particle, there is no way it is going to pass on its vibrations. So metals are the best, then solids, then liquids, and gases are pretty poor.

The Dominoes and Books Analogy for Conduction of Heat		
Focus	**Concept**	Conduction of heat relies on particles. Students can visualize solids as close particles that jostle each other and transmit heat energy from one particle to another; metals conduct heat quickly while wood, plastic, and cloth are poor conductors because of the difference in structure.
	Students	Students are familiar with lines of people jostling each other and that materials are good or poor conductors of heat.
	Analog	Lines of dominoes, close but not touching, will all fall over if the first domino falls onto the next one. Books stood up like dominoes also fall in a line if the first is disturbed but much less quickly.

The Dominoes and Books Analogy for Conduction of Heat (Continued)		
Action	**Likes—Mapping the Analog to the Target**	
	Analog—Dominoes and books	**Target—Enzymes and substrates**
	Dominoes standing up that can fall over	Free electrons that can move around
	Books standing up that can fall over	Atoms and molecules that vibrate
	Dominoes falling over quickly one after another, in a line	Free electrons speeding up when heat is absorbed and moving around bumping others
	Books falling over slowly, one after another, in a line	Atoms vibrating faster when heat is absorbed and jostling atoms next to them
	Fast-falling dominoes compared to slow-falling books	Good heat conductors compared to poor ones.
	Slow-falling books (no dominoes)	Nonconductors having only vibrating atoms or molecules
	Unlikes—Where the Analogy Breaks Down	
	• There are many, many more electrons and atoms than dominoes and books—remember, the analogy is a gross oversimplification. • Dominoes and books fall once, one way, and in a straight line; electrons and atoms vibrate continuously in all directions all the time. • The difference in size between electrons and atoms is much greater than the size difference between dominoes and books.	
Reflection	**Conclusion**	Metals conduct heat well because they have free electrons; wood, plastic, and cloth are poor conductors as they lack free electrons. Was this concept understood when the analogy was demonstrated once or twice?
	Improvements	Did I spend enough time building the phenomenon of conductivity? Were the students receptive to the analogy?

The Dominoes and Books Analogy for Conduction of Heat (Continued)		
		Did I carefully negotiate the shared and unshared attributes, and did we draw a suitable conclusion?
Science Content Standard B, Physical Science, Grades 5–8: "Properties and changes of properties in matter; Transfer of energy." The Dominoes and Books Analogy shows that conduction is a "change [that] involves energy transfer" and that substances have characteristic properties such as conductivity (NAS, 1996, p. 154–155).		
Suggested teaching strategies	Prepare for the analogical explanation by having students assess a variety of objects for coldness, establish that coldness is a function of conductivity, and demonstrate the analogy when students ask *how* and *why* some materials are good conductors and others are not.	
Resources	Thermometers, 20 similar sized books (e.g., encyclopedia set). Two boxes of dominoes.	
Applications	This is suitable for Grades 5–8 and is a useful and needed explanation in inquiry science on energy or heat topics.	

The Gravity Warps Space-Time Analogy for Bending Starlight

Einstein's 1915 General Theory of Relativity predicted that very large objects like the sun should curve space-time. This means that the sun's powerful gravity should change the direction of photons (light rays) that pass close by. The closer light rays are to the sun, the stronger the effect. The idea was received with skepticism; but the theory and its math were sound and the prediction was clear: light rays will change direction when they pass through intense gravitational fields that curve space-time.

Scientists argued about the prediction, and the best way to deal with the idea was to test it. Arthur Eddington (1922) planned to measure the deviation of starlight as it passed close to the sun. But he had a problem: the star's light needed to skim past the sun and still be observable on Earth and its deviation measured. But you can't normally do this. The sun is so bright that stars cannot be seen in daylight, least of all ones very close to the sun.

Eddington (1922) knew that stars almost in line with the sun can be seen during a total eclipse. So if the sun was blanked out, it would be possible to measure where a star appeared to be, compared to where astronomers knew it should be (remember, the sun moves relative to the stars). If Einstein was right, the difference between the apparent and calculated position should match the predicted relativistic deviation.

In 1919 Eddington went to West Africa where an eclipse was total, and he measured the position of a star almost in line with the sun and compared it to where it should be. Within the limits of experimental error, the deviation matched the prediction. "Einstein's theory is completely confirmed. The predicted displacement was 1".72 and the observed 1".75 ± .06" (Eddington as quoted by Bronowski, 1973, p. 254; Eddington, 1922, pp. 110–122).

We just can't demonstrate the change in direction of a ray of light as it passes a massive object like the sun. And eclipses are rare. Thus a model or analogy is important and useful. The analogy is best explained using a diagram (see Figure 8.2).

The flexible sheet is a crude analogy for space-time. The change in direction of the rolling ball is much greater than the change in direction experienced by a light ray passing a massive object like the sun.

Like most analogies, it is important to discuss with students ways in which the analog (the rubber sheet distorted by a heavy ball) is *like* the target and the ways in which it is *unlike* it. Remember that the difference in the scale of the sun and a photon is far greater than the difference between a large stationary ball and a smaller rolling ball.

Figure 8.2   A Rolling Ball Changes Direction as it Rolls Past a Heavy Ball That Distorts a Flexible Sheet

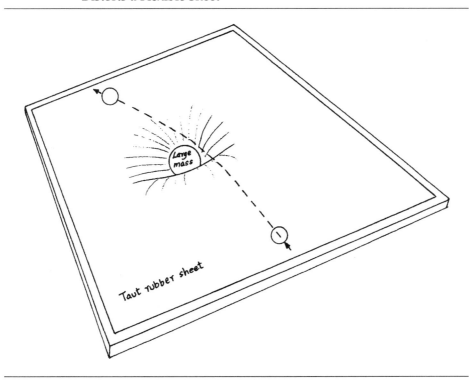

The Gravity Warps Space-Time Analogy for Bending Starlight		
Focus	**Concept**	A gravitational field is not a mysterious force of attraction between masses but is a feature of space itself. All objects modify or curve the space around them. Very large objects modify the path of nearby objects and light itself (photons).
	Students	Students will be aware that if they try to run across a downhill slope, their path will deviate down the slope. The same happens if they try to roll a ball across a slope—it bends downhill.
	Analog	This analogy should be demonstrated. A large sheet of thin plastic or rubber sheeting (up to 1m square) is stretched across a frame (Figure 8.2). A lead sinker is placed in the center of the sheet to make a depression. A small ball (marble) is rolled across the sheet so that it passes near the large mass. The students can see its path bend toward the large mass.
Action	**Likes—Mapping the Analog to the Target**	
	Analog—Heavy ball on flexible sheet	**Target—Large objects warping space**
	Flexible sheet of plastic or rubber	Space-time
	Lead sinker or heavy ball (baseball)	Sun or large star
	Depression in the plastic or rubber sheet	Curved space-time near massive object
	Curved trajectory of rolling marble	Deviation in the path of light past a massive object
	Marble rolling down slope of the depression	Gravitational field effect on space-time

	The Gravity Warps Space-Time Analogy for Bending Starlight (Continued)	
	Unlikes—Where the Analogy Breaks Down	
	• The flexible sheet is two-dimensional; space is three-dimensional. • The magnitude of the effect in the analogical model is much greater than that experienced in gravitational fields. • A marble is much larger than a photon and, unlike the photon, it has mass	
Reflection	Conclusion	Was the demonstrated analogy convincing? Could the students make the link between the two-dimensional sheet and three-dimensional space? Did they need other analogies (ball rolling across a slope) to visualize the effect of curved space-time?
	Improvements	Vary the size of masses and elasticity of sheet. Was more discussion required? Is this analogical model best used as an advance organizer, an embedded activator, or to summarize the concept?

Science Content Standard B, Physical Science, Grades 9–12: "Interaction of matter and energy." This analogy involves motion and forces, gravity and matter-energy interactions (NAS, 1996, p. 180–1). The Gravity Warps Space-Time Analogy explains mass-energy interactions that support the idea that relativity is more universal than Newton's laws.

Suggested teaching strategies	Demonstrate a marble rolling past a heavy ball depressing a plastic or rubber sheet. Role-play demonstrations could include a student running past a group of students who grab the passing student, pulling the student toward them to change the running student's path. Or have students run across a downhill slope; their paths will curve down the slope. Another analogy is the way a young man's path deviates toward a group of girls.
Resources	Plastic or rubber sheeting, frame, large mass, small ball or marble. Description of the fact that large masses curve space-time and explanation of Eddington's (1922) experiment and its success. Take care not to claim that Eddington's experiment proved the general theory of relativity—it only provided strong supporting evidence.
Applications	High school physics.

The Supernova Cola
Analogy for Exploding Stars

Large stars end their life with a cataclysmic bang. This bang is called a supernova. A star of about 2 solar masses and upward produces so much energy and light when it dies that it momentarily outshines the galaxy in which it resides. Remember that galaxies like ours (the Milky Way) contain about 100,000,000,000 stars (or suns). A large supernova outshines all of these for a few moments.

A star greater than 1.5 solar masses (the Chandrasekhar limit) collapses into a black hole. Middling stars, above 1.5 solar masses, turn into neutron stars, and many of these are pulsars (stellar lighthouses, or better, stellar radio stations). Our sun will not blow up this way—it will turn into a red giant and then a white dwarf.

In a few milliseconds at its life's end, a star exceeding the Chandrasekhar limit collapses to roughly one one-hundred thousandth of its diameter. All the outer gas is blown away as a nebula, and the inner core collapses to become a neutron star. If our sun were to collapse this way (it's a bit too small to do so), it would shrink from approx 1,500,000km diameter to about 15km diameter.

The power that blows off the outer gas and crunches the inner core into a neutron star comes from the gravitational collapse that occurs when a star runs out of energy. This happens when most of the silicon fuses into iron. At this point, no fusible fuel is left to maintain the outward radiant energy pressure that balances the inward-acting gravity. The star loses its equilibrium and collapses on itself. The imploding shock wave (driven by intense gravity) hits the brick wall of maximum crunch (density) and bounces back outward, blowing away all the noncore gases. This is the stuff that rocky planets are later made of.

We can demonstrate a shock wave's power using a cola bottle (Figure 8.3). Fill the cola bottle with water, hold it in your hand 300–400mm above the bench, and bang it down bottom first on the bench. The water suddenly decelerates, creates a shock wave that continues on, hits the bottom, rebounds, and blows much of the water up and out the spout. Take care and use only a strong plastic bottle. You may need a raincoat.

This model can also be used to demonstrate momentum and longitudinal waves.

Figure 8.3   The Supernova Cola Analogy for an Imploding Star

The Supernova Cola Analogy for Exploding Stars

Focus	Concept	Shock waves are immensely powerful. Shockwaves occur when bombs go off, earthquakes happen and stars blow up as supernovas. Students are not familiar with wave power—they have heard of tsunamis, but few have seen the power of a small shock wave, much less a stellar one.
	Students	Students are familiar with the fact that if you bang an open can of cola or a full cup down on a table, some of the liquid spurts out the top.
	Analog	Exaggerating the experience shows what shock waves can do. If you bang a full bottle of cola (with the lid off) down on a solid bench, much of the liquid is ejected out the spout. You bang the bottle downward, but the liquid takes off in the opposite direction. Why? Because the liquid suddenly stopping moving downward generates a shock wave that reflects off the bottom of the bottle and blows the liquid upward. This is like a star blowing up when it runs out of energy and collapses inward.

Action	Likes—Mapping the Analog to the Target	
	Analog—Cola bottle fountain	**Target—Supernova explosion**
	Plastic cola bottle	Star bigger than our sun
	Cola in the bottle	Star's gases (mostly the outer half)
	Rapid downward motion	Star's gases collapsing under intense gravity
	Shock wave generated when bottle stops moving	Shock wave generated when gases can collapse no further
	Shock wave reflected off bottle's bottom	Shock wave reflected off maximum density
	Cola blown out of the top	Gases blasted off the star's outer half

The Supernova Cola Analogy for Exploding Stars (Continued)

	Unlikes—Where the Analogy Breaks Down	
	• Cola is a cool liquid; stars are made of very hot gases (or plasma). • Stars are many orders of magnitude bigger than a bottle of cola. • Cola just sprays out into the air; star gases become a nebula and can form planets.	
Reflection	Conclusion	Was the demonstration successful, and could the students visualize the downward momentum reflecting off the bottom of the can or bottle and blowing the cola upward? Can you bang the bottle down fast enough?
	Improvements	Should we play with ropes and slinky springs to show wave reflection before doing the cola bottle experiment? Can we apply these wave reflection concepts to tsunamis? Videoing an excellent cola demonstration and replaying it in slow motion will help.

Science Content Standard B, Physical Science, Grades 9–12: "Interactions of matter and energy." This analogy focuses on motion, forces, and gravity (NAS, 1996, pp. 180–181). The Supernova Cola Analogy demonstrates that when a star's forces are unbalanced, parts of it explode and are blown away.

Suggested teaching strategies	Establish that some stars blow off much of their mass as nebulae. Play with ropes and slinky springs and show that waves reflect. Carefully prepare and conduct the banged-down cola bottle experiment. Carefully map the process to star implosion. A videotaped version of the experiment is useful at this point.
Resources	Supernova and nebula diagrams, cola bottle full of cola or water, solid bench, strong student or teacher, video camera.
Applications	Astrophysics in high school; for showing the power of wave reflections

The Matches, Mousetraps, and Dominoes Analogies for Nuclear Fission

Nuclear fission belongs to the group of submicroscopic concepts that are best explained by analogy. Three analogies are popular: the block of matches, the mousetraps in an aquarium, and the lines of dominoes (Hewitt, 1999, p. 629).

When a high-speed neutron collides with a uranium-235 (U-235) nucleus, the new nucleus becomes unstable, deforms, and splits into krypton-91 + barium-142 + 3 high-speed neutrons. If, on average, one of these neutrons collides with another U-235 nucleus and it splits, then fission is sustained. This is how a nuclear reactor works. However, if two of the neutrons collide with two atoms of U-235, then one fission becomes two, two become four, and the process spreads exponentially. This is what happens in an atomic bomb. In a nuclear reactor, the U-238 is enriched so that it contains 3%–4% U-235, and at this concentration, the maximum rate is just over one neutron captured per fission. The reaction can run out of control (e.g., Chernobyl), but the fission rate cannot turn into a bomb (e.g., Hiroshima). If 90% of the uranium is U-235, an explosive chain reaction is possible.

If you stick 100 matches into a block of plasticine so that the match heads are 5mm apart and you ignite the match on the corner, the whole lot bursts into flame (see Figure 8.4). Take care or you can get burned. Do this in a sand tray, and of course be vigilant for the students' safety. Many children have done this by striking the end match in a book of matches—it all catches fire.

If you set 30–40 mousetraps and place them side by side in a small, empty aquarium, you can simulate a chain reaction (see Figure 8.5). Roll up 100, 10cm squares of paper and place 2–3 on each mousetrap. The paper ball should sit on the wire U-shape—the piece that springs over and hits the mouse. When all the traps are set with paper balls, throw more paper balls into the aquarium until one sets off a trap. Many other traps will be set off in a chain reaction. This analogy is better than the matches analogy because not all the mousetraps are set off.

Branching lines of dominoes also are a useful analogy for nuclear fission. The advantage is that students can make their own models of fission, and this model is very safe. All you need is 1–2 sets of dominoes. See Figure 8.6.

Figure 8.4   The Matches Analogy for Nuclear Fission

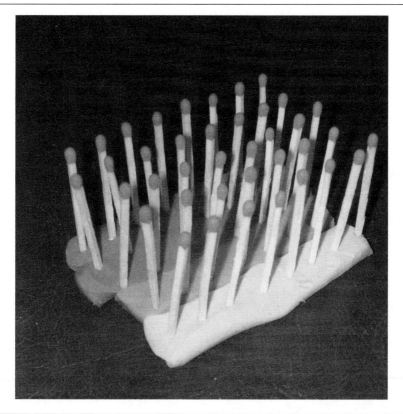

Figure 8.5   The Mousetrap Analogy for Nuclear Fission

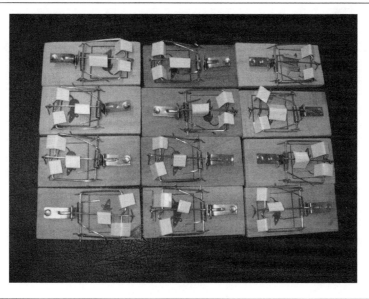

Figure 8.6   The Dominoes Analogy for Nuclear Fission

The Matches, Mousetraps, and Dominoes Analogies for Nuclear Fission		
Focus	**Concept**	Nuclear fission and chain reactions are nonobservable but key concepts—students are surprised how quickly an atomic reaction can spread. The reaction's speed and extent helps explain the vast amount of energy that can be released.
	Students	Students are interested in atomic bombs and nuclear power plants. Modeling a chain reaction is a great teaching moment. Children who have accidentally lit a book of matches know the power of a chain reaction.

	The Matches, Mousetraps, and Dominoes Analogies for Nuclear Fission (Continued)	
	Analog	Ignition spreads rapidly among closely packed match heads—this is like an exponential chain reaction. The same happens when one mousetrap among 30–40 traps goes off. You can liken falling dominoes to a chain reaction, especially if the dominoes branch out like a tree.
Action	**Likes—Mapping the Analog to the Target**	
	Analog—Matches, mousetraps, and dominoes	**Target—U-235 and neutrons**
	Matches can ignite rapidly.	U-235 hit by a neutron splits into pieces immediately.
	Matches must be close to ignite each other.	U-235 atoms must capture a neutron.
	Match ignition spreads exponentially.	U-235 fission spreads exponentially.
	Energy is released.	A huge amount of energy is released.
	Mousetraps are set off when bumped.	U-235 fissions when hit by a neutron.
	Close mousetraps can set off each other.	Close U-235 atoms can capture a neutron.
	Balls of paper	Neutrons
	Unlikes—Where the Analogy Breaks Down	
	• There are many, many more U-235 atoms than matches, mousetraps, and dominoes—the analogy is a gross oversimplification. • U-235 atoms release 3 neutrons; matches, mousetraps, and dominoes mostly affect just one other object.	
Reflection	Conclusion	Summarize with a conclusion like, "Nuclear fission and chain reactions are like one match's ignition spreading to ignite all the nearby matches." Ensure that students know where this analogy breaks down because spectacular analogies often mask the unshared attributes.

	The Matches, Mousetraps, and Dominoes Analogies for Nuclear Fission (Continued)	
	Improvements	Do I need just the matches analogy or should I perform two analogies—matches to show how a fission bomb works and the dominoes to show how a nuclear power reactor is similar but nonexplosive.
Science Content Standard B, Physical Science: Grades 9–12, "Interactions of matter and energy" (NAS, 1996, p. 180). The Matches, Mousetraps, and Dominoes Analogies demonstrate a chain reaction in a critical mass of fissile material. Mass is converted to energy, but the matter-energy sum remains constant.		
Suggested teaching strategies	Ask if students have ever accidentally ignited a book or box of matches. Discuss chain reactions and how they can spread rapidly—add a video of an explosive grass fire. Take great care with the matches demonstration (do a risk analysis) and link it to the mousetraps or dominoes analogy. Discuss atomic bombs and nuclear reactor differences.	
Resources	Plasticine, 100 matches, aquarium, 30–40 mousetraps, 100 paper balls, several boxes of dominoes.	
Applications	Suitable for students in Grades 9–12 and is a useful and needed explanation in inquiry science.	

The Eye Is Like a Camera Analogy

The eye is like a camera in some telling ways (see Glynn, 1991) and is featured in a number of science books. Two assumptions are often made by teachers when this analogy is used: (1) that students know how cameras work and (2) that students understand image formation with pinholes and convex lenses. This was a reasonable assumption when cameras were simple, but that is no longer the case. Digital and video cameras are a world away from simple 35mm cameras.

Students will have prior knowledge of camera optics only if they have made a pinhole camera and had experience with lenses that form real images of lightbulbs and candle flames. It is important that students understand the optics of simple image formation. Without pinhole camera or image formation with convex lenses experience, the eye analogy should not be used. It is arguable whether the camera teaches about the eye or the eye teaches about the camera.

The prior conceptual knowledge that students need can be summarized as follows:

- Rays of light actually converge on the fine detail of an in-focus real image. For example, images are formed when lenses cause rays of light to converge onto a point on a screen (e.g., overhead projector).
- Only light sources can produce focused images (e.g., candle flames, lightbulbs, intense light through overhead transparencies, data projectors).
- Light rays are bent in an orderly way as they pass through convex lenses.
- The following table shows some of the ways a camera's functions can be used to teach about the eye.

Ways in Which a Camera Is Like an Eye	
Camera Structure or Function	*Eye Structure or Function*
Convex lens focuses light on film.	Cornea and lens focus light onto the retina.
Lens changes position to focus on near and distant objects.	Lens changes shape to focus on near and distant objects.
Aperture size controls exposure brightness.	Pupil controls brightness of light on the retina.
Black interior prevents multiple reflections.	Black interior prevents multiple reflections.
Lens cap protects the lens.	Eyelids protect the cornea.
Image captured on film or chip.	Image captured on the retina.

Ways in Which a Camera Is Unlike the Eye	
Camera Structure or Function	*Eye Structure or Function*
One lens at the front of the camera	Two lenses—cornea at the front (not adjustable) and adjustable lens behind it
Captures single or repeated images	Captures continuous images
Limited range of light brightness	Works in vast range of brightness

The Eye Is Like a Camera Analogy

Focus	Concept	Both the camera and the eye form images (on film and the retina, respectively). Real images are formed when light rays from a source point focus on an image point. This difficult concept can be demonstrated using a Hodson light box and thin convex lenses.
	Students	Do students understand how images are formed? Have they seen images of lightbulbs or candle flames in a pinhole camera? Are they familiar with cameras and know how they work?
	Analog	Light rays from a luminous or illuminated object passing through a convex lens can be focused onto a screen, film, or retina. This happens in both cameras and eyes.

Action	Likes—Mapping the Analog to the Target	
	Analog—Camera	**Target—Eye**
	Convex lens focuses light on film.	Cornea plus lens focus light onto the retina.
	Lens moves to focus on near and distant objects.	Lens shape changes to focus on near and distant objects.
	Aperture size controls exposure brightness.	Pupil controls brightness of light on the retina.
	Black interior prevents multiple reflections.	Black interior prevents multiple reflections.
	Lens cap protects the lens.	Eyelids protect the cornea.
	Image captured on film or chip.	Image captured on the retina.

Unlikes—Where the Analogy Breaks Down

- The eye has a fixed lens (the cornea) and a variable lens, whereas a camera can have 6–10 differently shaped lenses in its lens system.
- Cameras capture single or repeated images; the eye is a continuous imaging device.

	The Eye Is Like a Camera Analogy (Continued)	
	• The eye responds to a wider range of brightness than cameras; however, some charged couple device cameras are becoming more eyelike; especially when the image is transmitted along a wire (like the optic nerve).	
Reflection	Conclusion	Was the analogy structurally and functionally convincing? Were diagrams of eyes and cameras sufficient or do students need to make model cameras and dissect eyes (or take models apart)?
	Improvements	Depending on the age and sophistication of the students, is it useful to compare the structure and function of digital cameras to the eye. Which analogy works best: the camera is like the eye or the eye is like the camera?
Science Content Standard B, Physical Science, Grades 5–8: "Transfer of energy," light interacts with matter (NAS, 1996, p. 155) and Content Standard C, Life Science: Grades 9–12: "Matter, energy and organization in living systems" (p. 186). The Eye-Camera Analogy shows how light rays are bent to form images.		
Suggested teaching strategies	Students should be familiar with convex lenses. They could make pinhole cameras and model eyes (round-bottomed flasks with convex lens stuck onto the front and filled with fluoroscein solution). An eye dissection could be added. At some stage the comparison between the camera and the eye should be elaborated. Eyes and cameras are analogies of each other.	
Resources	Model eye, materials to make model eye, cow's eye, dissection equipment, a selection of cameras (pinhole, box, SLR, digital, video).	
Applications	High school.	

The Pair of Wheels Analogy for the Refraction of Light

Mrs. Kay was using a light box to show that rays of light change direction when they pass from air to glass and vice versa. When light entered the block vertically, it passed straight through without bending; when it entered the glass obliquely (top image of Figure 8.7), it bent to the left and when it left the glass it bent to the right.

The concept states that when a ray of light passes from a less dense to a more dense transparent substance, the ray of light bends toward the normal. When a ray of light passes from a more dense to a less dense substance, it bends away from the normal. Mrs. Kay went on to say,

> Let me show you an analogy. I'm going to coat this pair of wheels with orange fluorescent paint. The wheel tracks will represent the ray of light. The wheels are like the two edges of the ray of light as it starts off; it's deliberately wider because it's hard to see the reason for the bending if it's too narrow [she points to the light ray bending through the glass block]. When the track's wider it's easier to see the reason for the bending.
>
> First we'll roll the wheels from the paper onto the carpet at right angles. The wheels are like the ray of light going straight through the block along the normal [path]. Push it straight . . . both wheels slow down at the same time, so it doesn't change direction. It's the same with a light ray; if the light ray goes through at right angles, it slows down, but it doesn't change direction.
>
> Now push the wheels . . . so the wheels roll from the paper onto the carpet at an angle. . . . See, it's bent, and the light did much the same thing, didn't it? When the light passed through our block at an angle, the light also bent. Why does it bend like that?

Discussion:

Sally: When the wheel is on a smooth surface, it's going faster.

Mrs. Kay: It's to do with speed. That's the point I wanted to make. When the wheels cross from the card to the carpet, which wheel slows down first?

Fiona: The one on the carpet.

Mrs. Kay: The one going onto the carpet slows down first because there's more friction on the rough surface. If you can think of the ray of light as being not quite as thin as it looks, one edge of the light would hit the block before the other side.

Beth: Yes. Yes.

Mrs. Kay: It's the same with light: one edge of the ray slowed down before the other, so the wheel that hit the carpet first slows down first, so it's covering less distance than the faster one

Figure 8.7   The Pair of Wheels Analogy for Refraction of Light

A RAY OF LIGHT BEING REFRACTED AS IT PASSES
FROM AIR TO GLASS.

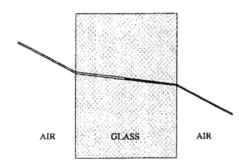

AIR   GLASS   AIR

IS LIKE

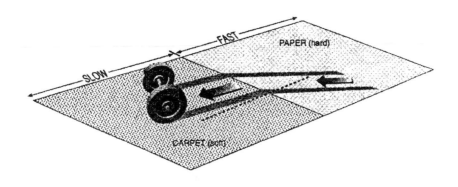

still on the paper, and when that one hits the carpet as well, the lines become parallel again because they return to the same speed. So the path bends because the wheels and the light travel more slowly in a dense medium, or in this case, on a rougher surface.

The Pair of Wheels Analogy for the Refraction of Light

Focus	Concept	Students are familiar with the bending of light as it passes through glass or water. Refraction is easily demonstrated with a glass block, a prism, and a light box. The phenomenon itself, however, is difficult to explain.
	Students	Students may be aware that light is wavelike, and they may have seen waves change direction at the beach or in a ripple tank. They may know that this bending is related to waves slowing down or speeding up. Some students will confuse reflection of light and refraction of light.
	Analog	Many students have experienced the change of direction that results when one wheel of a stroller, toy car, or car rolls off a hard surface onto a soft surface, like sand, carpet, or grass. The change of direction occurs because the wheel on the hard surface rolls easily while the one on the soft surface slows down. This phenomenon can be demonstrated (and practiced by the students) by rolling a pair of Lego wheels obliquely from a hard surface onto a softer surface. As one wheel slows, the pair of wheels changes direction. To show the change of direction, coat the wheels with bright poster paint.

Action	Likes—Mapping the Analog to the Target	
	Analog—Wheels	**Target—Refracted light**
	Wheel tracks	Ray of light
	Perpendicular path shows no deviation	Vertical ray does not change direction
	Oblique path bends toward vertical	Oblique ray bends toward normal

The Pair of Wheels Analogy for the Refraction of Light (Continued)

	Tracks change direction as one wheel slows	Ray bends because it slows
	Wheels slow because the carpet increases friction.	Light slows because glass is optically more dense than air.

Unlikes—Where the Analogy Breaks Down

- Light rays are very narrow, whereas wheels are quite wide.
- Two wheels are needed to represent one narrow ray of light.
- Optical density of glass slows the light, whereas friction slows the wheels.
- Photons of light are not connected to each other, but the wheels are joined by an axle.

Reflection	Conclusion	Was the model of refraction clear to the students; did they find it convincing? A good test of understanding is whether they can use the model to explain bending away from the normal as light leaves glass.
	Improvements	Do I need to show water waves bending in a tank or on a video before using this model? Should I perform the analogy in both directions? Should I leave them to think through the reverse process?

	Science Content Standard B, Physical Science, Grades 9–12: "Interactions of energy and matter" (NAS, 1996, p. 180); light waves change speed and direction when they interact with matter. The Pair of Wheels Analogy and its associated modeling is inquiry science and supports Science Content Standard A: "Abilities necessary to do scientific inquiry" use explanations and models and "cognitive . . . skills [to formulate] scientific explanations" (p. 175).
Suggested teaching strategies	If there is enough equipment, let the students repeat the analogy in groups. Show bending toward the normal as a demonstration and ask the students to find what happens when they roll the wheels the opposite way. Be sure the wheels turn easily on their axle.
Resources	Light box, square and triangular prisms, paper, and carpet (both A3 size, or about 11.5 by 16.5 inches), poster paint, shallow tray, Lego wheels.
Applications	High school: refraction of light and inquiry: how do we know how phenomena like refraction work?

Bridging Analogies for the Balanced Forces of a Book on a Table

When holding a book, most people agree that the book applies a downward force (weight) that is balanced by the upward push from their hands. The forces are balanced if the book does not move. When the book is placed on a table, many people say that there is now only one force acting, namely, the downward weight of the book. This alternative conception agrees with Aristotle's idea that objects seek stable and passive positions. The table is like the earth's surface, the place where everything belongs and comes to rest. Newtonian physics insists that stationary objects, like books on a table, do not move because the upward and downward forces are balanced: The table applies an upward force equal to the book's weight.

John Clement (1993) found that "76% of a sample of 112 high school students indicated that a table does not push up on a book lying at rest on it"; but "96% of these students believed that a spring pushes up on one's hand when the hand is pushing down on the spring" (p. 1243). He suggested that knowing that hand and spring forces are balanced could be used to explain why the table must apply a reaction force to a book sitting on it.

But students don't readily connect the forces they can feel when squeezing a spring with the book sitting on a table. After all, they can feel the spring pushing back on their hand, and the hand and spring tend to move a small amount. The book sits still.

Clement (1993) suggested that a series of analogies would help students connect their experience with their hands on the spring (called the *anchoring concept*) with the problem of the book on the table. The series of analogies he used works like the pillars of a bridge—each holds up a small part of the idea—hence he called the strategy a bridging analogy. The pillars of the bridge are shown in Figure 8.8. Students experience each analogy in order and the result is that most do connect the balanced forces of the hand and spring to the book on the table.

Start with the book-on-the-table problem: is there an upward force from the table balancing the book's weight? When most disagree or are not sure, introduce the anchoring concept using bulldog clips and rubber bands. Students feel their push and pull and the reaction forces. The book on a pillow can be done by the whole class—use freezer zip bags half-full of air and science books. Make the model table using thin plywood and then show how it's like the book on the table. It works for most students.

Bridging analogy strategies can be applied to friction, cells, genes and DNA, particles, concepts in math, and acid-base models, to name a few. When we first met bridging analogies, we thought that they were rare, but examples keep cropping up. Why do they work so well? Because they are scaffolds that help students work from an anchor to an abstract problem solution in small steps.

Figure 8.8 Balanced Forces Between a Book and a Table Is Like the Balanced Forces Between a Hand and a Spring

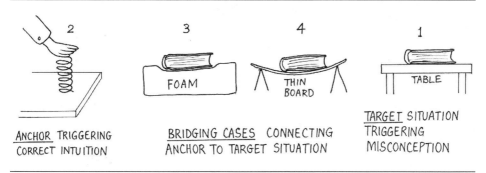

		Bridging Analogies for the Balanced Forces of a Book on a Table	
Focus	**Concept**	Objects like rigid chairs and tables exert an upward reaction force on objects sitting or placed on them. Objects such as books do not move because the upward and downward forces are balanced.	
	Students	Most students recognize the balanced forces involved in squeezing a spring or holding up books in their hands and situations where a load deforms its underlying support (e.g., a flexible table or padding).	
	Analog	Balanced forces in squeezing a spring and stretching a rubber band act as anchors for sequential analogical supports (book on a cushion or air-filled bag, flimsy table bending under book's weight). In a stepwise way, each analogy bridges (scaffolds) the gap between palpable forces of spring and hand and those of a book on the table and the table, which must be imagined.	
Action	**Likes—Mapping the Analog to the Target**		
	Analog—Spring held between fingers		**Target—Book on a table**
	A compressed spring exerts force back on a hand (balanced forces are felt).		Book has downward weight but no deformation can be seen or felt.

Bridging Analogies for the Balanced Forces of a Book on a Table (Continued)

	Stretched rubber band has balanced forces that can be felt.	Book's weight acts downward on table; table pushes back.
	Book's weight deforms an air bag; shows balanced forces.	Book's weight acts downward on table; table pushes back.
	Flimsy table bends under book sitting on it.	Table must push back on the book on it.
	Unlikes—Where the Analogy Breaks Down	
	• The table exerts a reaction force but does not visibly bend under the book's weight. The analogies could be called examples.	
Reflection	**Conclusion**	Were the bridging analogies carefully sequenced? Do I need to include more examples? Did I let the students tell me how they interpreted the bridging analogies? Did I give them adequate thinking time?
	Improvements	Did I demonstrate what the students could have done themselves? Do I need to revisit this idea in later lessons? If bridging analogies worked with reaction forces, can I use them elsewhere for other science concepts, say concepts in mathematics?
	Science Content Standard B, Physical Science, Grades 5–8: "Motions and forces" (NAS, 1996, p. 154). This analogy helps students understand "forces in equilibrium, especially if the force is associated with static inanimate objects, such as a book resting on the desk" (NAS, 1996, p. 154).	
Suggested teaching strategies	This is an excellent example of scaffolding and agrees with Vygotsky's (1986) sociocultural learning theory. In what other situations can effective sets of bridging analogies or examples be strung together?	
Resources	Table, book, chair, students, springs, bulldog clips, rubber bands, freezer zip bags, thin plywood and supports	
Applications	Middle school where balanced forces are not obvious; understanding action and reaction forces is a desired outcome.	

Electricity Analogies for Current, Voltage, and Resistance

When planning inquiry science, teachers choose topics that are interesting, raise curiosity, and are open-ended. Electricity meets all these criteria and is safe when done with batteries. Building electric circuits therefore is an excellent inquiry context for students in Grades 1–12.

Inquiry Science

There are three ways inquiry science can be open-ended: Ideally, students should

1. Suggest the problems to study and investigate;

2. Design the experimental methods and collect the data; and

3. Interpret the data and propose some theories and models (Hackling & Fairbrother, 1996).

Building analogical models helps students focus on the concepts being studied. Repeated cycles of proposing, testing, and revising analogical models is authentic science. While some science topics are too far removed from everyday life for students to suggest the problems and methods and interpret the results; electricity is different. Students use various electronic devices, play with battery-powered toys, dismantle flashlights— and some make electric gadgets.

Teachers like electricity because it is cheap to run, the materials are easy to obtain, and students can't hurt themselves with lightbulbs, wires, switches, and batteries. Young students (Grades 1–4) are really excited when their circuits work, and older students (up to Grade 12) are challenged when circuits do unexpected things. Electricity provides opportunities to test many different connections and introduces concepts like voltage, current, and resistance. Making sense of these concepts involves high-level thinking, especially when the students know that they can experiment, see expected and unexpected things happen, try again, and revise their models.

Some of the problems you can encounter when teaching electricity, and the strategies for dealing with them, are described in Osborne and Freyberg (1985) and Driver et al. (1994).

Electric current, voltage, and series and parallel circuit differences are hard to explain, so teachers regularly use analogies and models to help students understand what is happening. Like inquiry activities, analogies work best when the students are involved in the planning and thinking. Learning gains are high when the students develop and map their own analogies (Cosgrove, 1995; Zook, 1991), but students need guidance if they are to avoid common alternative conceptions. Electricity analogies mislead students when the analogy is taken too far. This is why it is better to use multiple analogies than stretch only one. This holds for both teacher and student analogies.

Common Electricity Analogies

The analogies and models that appear in the following pages are

1. The Water Circuit Analogy for a simple series circuit

2. Voltage is like water pressure

3. The analogy of doors in the assembly hall for parallel circuits

4. The Continuous Train Analogy to show conservation of current

5. The student circuit that runs on M&M's

6. The Shared Water Flow Analogy for multiple lightbulbs and motors in a series circuit

7. The Field Analogy for multiple lightbulbs in a series circuit

Three of these analogies—the water circuit, continuous train, and M&M's—are multiple analogies that address the common alternative conception that current is used up in electric circuits, as has been touched on earlier. Many science teachers have studied this problem (e.g., Grayson, 1996; Tasker & Osborne, 1985) and the analogies we have chosen can change students' conceptions. Some of the analogies are our own; others we've collected and brought together in this book.

What Students Know

Students know that batteries in flashlights, toys, and handheld electronic games go flat. They know that something is used up, and when they look for something to have been consumed, what's more obvious than the electric current flowing around the circuit? It's right that students should think that something is used up because batteries have to be replaced or recharged. Consequently, most of our analogies and models are designed to show that the electrons or electric current is conserved rather than consumed. When we say that the energy is used up, we mean it in the sense that the battery loses energy. Energy can only be changed into another form; it's never used up. It's important to discuss and clarify the expressions we use.

But students are hard to convince, and that's good, because that's how they learn and remember concepts. Effective analogies that show that current is conserved and energy is converted also need to be accompanied by explanations of why the current decreases as battery energy is used up.

The Water Circuit Analogy
for Electric Current

Think about this conversation between John and his teacher. Miss Davis asks John, "Can you put these [electricity terms] and ideas together and explain how an electric circuit works?" John: "Ah, no. That's the problem. I can't get a picture in my head of how this electricity stuff works" (Glynn, 1991, p. 186). As they talked, Miss Davis reminded John of the water circuit in the class aquarium, and she used the water circuit as an analogy for an electric circuit. Instead of retelling the whole story, we have sketched the aquarium water circuit and summarized Miss Davis's conclusions.

Figure 8.9 models a classroom aquarium—the pipes, pump, and filter all enlarged. The pump draws water from the aquarium through a pipe and pushes the water under pressure through another pipe into the filter containing a fine mesh that resists the water flow. The water flows through another pipe back into the aquarium.

The aquarium is the familiar object for the analogy and can be replaced by a swimming pool and its filtration system. Both use a closed water circuit that can be understood by the students. If your students cannot visualize the filtration circuit, show them a functioning aquarium, use an overhead transparency, or talk about swimming pool filters.

This is an effective analogy for a simple series circuit, provided the teacher and students realize that water is a liquid substance and electricity is not. Three alternative conceptions can arise from this analogy. Students see a fixed amount of liquid coming out of the pump; they may conclude that a battery produces a fixed flow of electricity and may also come to the following conclusions:

- Electricity will leak out of a switched-on power outlet if no appliance is plugged in to it.
- Two parallel circuits connected to the same battery share the electric current from the battery and each get half the current (in fact, twice as much current flows when two parallel circuits are connected to one battery).
- Two or three lightbulbs in series receive the same current (they do) and will glow equally brightly (they do not, because they share the voltage).

Figure 8.9   The Aquarium Water Circuit Analogy for a Simple Series Circuit

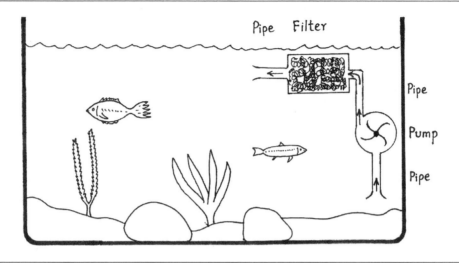

The Water Circuit Analogy for Electric Current		
Focus	**Concept**	Electricity only flows in complete, unbroken circuits. The electron flow is not used up, and work is done as the electricity flows around the circuit.
	Students	Up to 40% of the class may think that current is partly used up in a circuit. Most students have seen an aquarium with a water filter in it. Their teacher may have explained the need to circulate water through a filter to keep the water clean and the environment healthy. They may know how a swimming pool filtration system works.
	Analog	An aquarium filter system draws water in through a pipe, a pump pushes it through another pipe into a filter that resists water flow, and then the water exits through another pipe into the aquarium.

The Water Circuit Analogy for Electric Current (Continued)

Action	Likes—Mapping the Analog to the Target	
	Analog—Aquarium water circuit	**Target—Simple series circuit**
	Water	Electricity
	Flowing water	Electric current
	Pipes carrying water	Wires carrying electricity
	Pump pushing water (pressure)	Battery pushing electrons (voltage)
	Pump pressure	Battery voltage
	Filter (resists water flow)	Thin wire in lightbulb—resistance
	No water lost	Current is conserved
	Unlikes—Where the Analogy Breaks Down	
	<ul><li>Water is a material liquid; electricity is a flow of charge in an electric field.</li><li>Water can flow in an incomplete circuit; electricity always needs a complete circuit.</li><li>Water flow depends on the pump output and pressure; electric current flow is determined by the entire circuit (the circuit must be looked at as a whole).</li></ul>	
Reflection	**Conclusion**	Did the students understand the ways a water circuit is like an electric circuit and the ways in which it is different? Do I need to check their knowledge next class? Did I emphasize the need to see the circuit as a whole?
	Improvements	Next time, I could set up a working aquarium for the students to examine; I could use the water circuit alongside the students sharing M&M's analogy or the Continuous Train Analogy.

Science Content Standard B, Physical Science, Grades 5–8: "Transfer of energy" (NAS, 1996, p. 155); "energy is an important property of substances and . . . most change involves energy transfer" (NAS, 1996, p. 154). The Water Circuit Analogy shows that current is conserved and energy is transformed throughout an electric circuit.

The Water Circuit Analogy for Electric Current (Continued)	
Suggested teaching strategies	Students make simple circuits: 1 battery + 1 lightbulb; 1 battery + 2 lightbulbs (series & parallel). Agree on what happens. Examine (even set up) an aquarium with water filter—can the students say what is needed to analogize the electric circuit? Prepare cues and questions to compare electric circuit to a functioning aquarium or pool filtration system. Discuss how the water circuit and electric circuits are similar and how they differ.
Resources	Lightbulbs, batteries and wires; aquarium with filtration circuit or parts to make one; overhead transparency.
Applications	Middle school. Best used to develop the concept of complete circuits and current conservation. Most effective when used as part of a set of multiple circuit analogies.

The Water Pressure Analogy for Voltage

Voltage in electric circuits is difficult to visualize and explain. Batteries are labeled in volts: 1.5V, 6V, 12V, and so on. This is a measure of the force with which the battery can push electrons around a circuit. Scientists prefer to talk about potential difference (PD) and PD is measured in volts (V). The potential difference between two points in a circuit measures the potential of the current to flow between the points. The higher the PD, the better the current flows. PD is sometimes called *electrical pressure*.

Voltage affects the work an electric current does when it passes through a lightbulb, motor, or heater. If you double the PD with which a current is pushed through a lightbulb, you double the amount of work it does. Likewise, if you have a 12V battery and double the current flowing, you also double the work done or energy released. A circuit's capacity to do work is a multiple of the volts times the amps (the energy released is a multiple of amps × volts × time).

So how do we describe and explain PD (and voltage)?

A common model is The Water Pressure Analogy. Figure 8.10 shows a tall water bottle with holes at four levels. The pressure in the water depends on the depth: If the depth is doubled, the pressure is doubled. The pressure controls the amount and force with which water flows through the holes, assuming all the holes are the same size.

Similarly, if you have a circuit that is driven by a 6V battery, a certain current flows. If you double the PD to 12V, the current doubles (provided the bulb does not blow out).

Figure 8.10   The Water Pressure Analogy for Potential Difference and Voltage

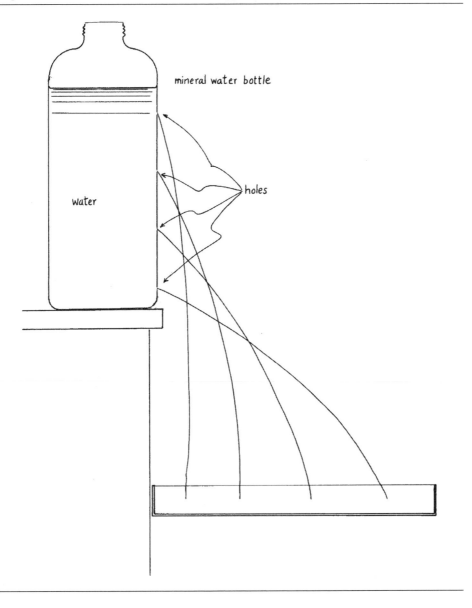

In the water bottle model, the direction of the outflow and how far it spurts can be likened to PD or battery voltage. The greater the depth, the higher the pressure, and greater the flow. Electricity works like this—but remember, electricity isn't a fluid substance.

Another use of this analogy is to compare the bottle to four flashlights—each with one, two, three, or four batteries. This comparison can mislead, however, unless you negotiate the variation in the brightness or the length of time the flashlight will shine. Perhaps this is a problem you could ask the class to work on in groups, report back, and debate the conclusions.

The Water Pressure Analogy for Voltage

Focus	Concept	PD is measured in volts and is difficult to visualize. Understanding PD is crucial when working with electric circuits because it is a key element in Ohm's Law and in energy and work calculations.
	Students	Students are familiar with water pressure and depth, and this concept is easily demonstrated. They know that a hole low down in a tank or bottle leaks water faster than a hole higher up.
	Analog	Different batteries have different PDs (volts). This is like a water tank or bottle with holes at different levels. The greater the PD, the greater the current flow; the deeper the hole, the more water it lets out.

Action	Likes—Mapping the Analog to the Target	
	Analog—Water flows out holes at different depths at different rates	**Target—PD (volts) determines circuit current**
	Water tank or bottle	Battery, dynamo
	Hole for water to escape	Battery in a circuit so current can flow
	Deeper the water over the hole	Higher the PD or voltage
	Deeper hole, more water flows	Higher PD, more current flows
	Flow rate proportional to depth	Current flow proportional to PD

Unlikes—Where the Analogy Breaks Down

- The water flow analogy encourages students to think of electricity as a material substance—it is not.
- Water flow rates decline as the tank or bottle empties; a battery may demonstrate reduced PD across its terminals but it is not empty.

The Water Pressure Analogy for Voltage (Continued)		
Reflection	Conclusion	Were the likenesses between PD and pressure (depth and voltage) clear? Were middle ability students able to use the analogy to restate the concept of PD in their own words? Did formative assessment help the students map the analogy and recognize where it broke down?
	Improvements	Do I need better cues, questions, and need-to-know information? Should I look for a better analogy next time?
Science Content Standard B, Physical Science, Grades 5–8: "Transfer of energy" (NAS, 1996, p. 155). The Water Pressure Analogy is useful for explaining electrical pressure or PD (voltage) in all or part of a circuit. PD is like water pressure but the analogy breaks down when the fluid flow idea is taken too far.		
Suggested teaching strategies	Students should experience differing currents in circuits with differing PDs (volts); make circuits and develop student models that need to explain PD, then introduce the model. Given the opportunity, students may suggest a depth and pressure model. If you have enough bottles, allow groups to make and measure water flow.	
Resources	Batteries or power packs with different PDs, ammeters, voltmeters, lightbulbs, motors, and bottles with 3 or 4 holes (see Figure 8.10).	
Applications	Suitable for middle school and secondary students. Encourage older students to develop quantitative definitions for PD.	

The Shared Water Flow Analogy

Imagine a crowd of people walking along a two-lane road—there are many pathways for each pedestrian and few people cut across each other's path. The wide road is like a thick wire and electricity flows easily with little resistance. If a short length of the road is narrowed by sewer construction and people can only pass two abreast, this section is like a thin filament in a lightbulb that has a high resistance. Less electricity flows along a thin wire in the same way as fewer people can pass the sewer construction.

As the flow becomes congested, people jostle and bump each other, and they have to walk faster so everyone can get through. This makes some people hot and angry and is like the thin filament heating up and glowing.

This analogy explains current flow in a one-lightbulb + battery simple circuit; but it does not adequately explain why, in a series circuit, the brightness of each globe diminishes as lightbulbs are added but not more batteries. Analogies that demonstrate a sharing of water flow are sometimes used, but these require great care as they contain strong alternative conceptions. The Shared Water Flow Analogy goes like this:

In summer our neighbor sometimes waters her lawn with a hose that has 3 or 4 sprinklers along its length (see Figure 8.11). If there are 2 sprinklers, the water spurts out 3.5m; if there are 3 sprinklers the water spurts 3m, and for 4 sprinklers, 2.5m. This is a bit like a circuit with 2, 3, or 4 lightbulbs connected in series with a 6V battery. If there are 2 lightbulbs, each glows brightly, if 3, the lightbulbs are medium bright, and for 4 lightbulbs, the light is dull. Sprinklers spray less distance when more sprinklers are on the hose, and when there are more lightbulbs in the circuit, the lightbulbs are less bright. The hose can supply only a fixed volume of water per second, and the battery can supply only a certain amount of energy per second. Increasing the number of sprinklers and lightbulbs means that each gets less water and electrical energy, respectively.

This analogy can mislead because more sprinklers increases the water flow in the hose (the resistance to water flow actually decreases), but in the electric circuit, each bulb delivers less light (because the electricity flow actually decreases with increased resistance). There is another weakness; it does not matter whether the sprinklers on the hose are in series or on side-by-side branches—the flow is the same in each. Lightbulbs in a line (series) glow much less brightly than lightbulbs side by side in parallels.

Figure 8.11   Resistance in a Multilight Series Circuit Is Like Multiple Sprinklers on a Hose

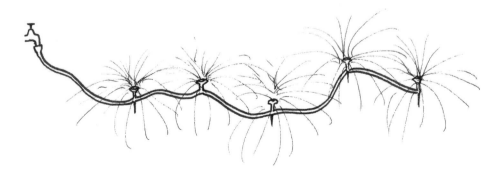

The Shared Water Flow Analogy

Focus	Concept	When you add lightbulbs to a series circuit, the current flow drops, and the current and energy are shared between the lightbulbs.
	Students	Students are familiar with water pressure and may have seen people watering their lawns using a hose with sprinklers placed along it. The sprinklers usually share the water flowing through the hose.
	Analog	Water flowing through a hose with 3–5 sprinklers is like a series circuit with 3–5 lightbulbs. Add sprinklers and the diameter of the spray reduces; add lightbulbs and the brightness of all lightbulbs diminishes.

Action	Likes—Mapping the Analog to the Target	
	Analog—Water flow from each sprinkler is an equal share of the water	**Target—Brightness of each globe is an equal share of the energy**
	Sprinkler	Lightbulb
	Water spraying out of sprinkler	Lightbulb glowing
	Diameter of the sprinkler's spray	Brightness of the bulb
	Add sprinklers, spray diameter reduced	Add lightbulbs, brightness drops
	Sprinklers share the water flow.	Lightbulbs share electric current and energy.

Unlikes—Where the Analogy Breaks Down

- The water flow analogy encourages students to think of electricity as a material substance—it is not.
- Increasing the number of sprinklers on a hose increases total water flow; adding lightbulbs to a series circuit reduces the total current and energy flow.

Reflection	Conclusion	Did students understand that The Sprinkler Analogy only shows that added lightbulbs share the current and energy in a series circuit? Did they realize that adding sprinklers makes the total water flow increase but adding lightbulbs reduces the total current and energy flow?

The Shared Water Flow Analogy (Continued)		
	Improvements	Do I need to demonstrate the sprinklers on a hose alongside a comparable electric circuit and show the effects of adding sprinklers and lightbulbs?
Science Content Standard B, Physical Science, Grades 5–8: "Energy is transferred" (NAS, 1996, p. 155); "energy is an important property of substances and . . . most change involves energy transfer" (NAS, 1996, p. 154). The Shared Water Flow Analogy shows that electric current does varying amounts of work throughout the electric circuit. Physical Science, Grades 9–12, benefit from this analogy when it is used to explain Ohm's Law and "moving electric charges" (p. 180).		
Suggested teaching strategies	Students need experience with 2, 3 or 4 lightbulbs in series with a 6V battery to see that increasing the number of lightbulbs leads to decreased brightness. Lead students to the question, Why does this happen? Intuition suggests the sharing of a finite resource, and The Sprinkler Analogy explains current phenomena in everyday terms. The main value of the analogy is its ability to raise the question, Why are the lightbulbs duller than expected? This paves the way for The Field Analogy.	
Resources	6V battery, lightbulbs and wires; hose with 3 or 4 sprinklers—best if sprinklers can be added.	
Applications	Suitable for middle and high school students. Most effective when followed by The Field Analogy.	

The School Gymnasium Analogy for Parallel Circuits

Compare Circuits 1 and 2: 1 battery + 1 globe and 1 battery + 2 lightbulbs in parallel. The lightbulbs are all equally bright, and the battery in Circuit 1 lasts twice as long as the battery in Circuit 2. Why do lightbulbs 2 and 3 glow as brightly as globe 1, and why does the Circuit 2 battery last only half as long as Circuit 1's? The opposite happened when lightbulbs 2 and 3 were connected in series. This can be explained using The School Gymnasium Analogy (see Figure 8.12).

Students can leave the gym with two open exits twice as fast as is possible with only one exit open. This analogy can be modified to have halls with

1 or 3 exits open, to model circuits with 1 and 3 lightbulbs in parallel, *or*

2 or 3 exits open, to model 2 and 3 lightbulbs connected in parallel.

Figure 8.12   The School Gymnasium Analogy for Parallel Circuits

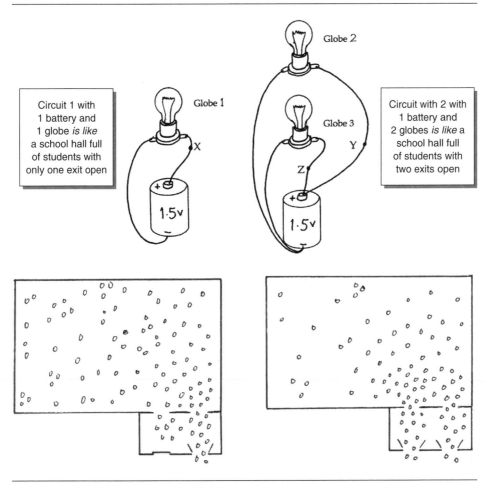

A variation on this analogy can be used to simulate a series circuit (or mixed parallel-series circuits). If there are a series of doors that each line of students has to pass through, the rate of escape drops off—the more doors, the slower the line flows. This is like several lightbulbs connected in a line (in series). The slower flow of students is analogous to the slower the current, the dimmer the lightbulbs.

Alternative Strategy

If you have an imaginative class that has regular experience with gym meetings and that has constructed parallel circuit lightbulbs and wondered why they are brighter than series lightbulbs, they may even suggest this analogy. My Grade 11 class did, and Mark Cosgrove's (1995) Grade 9 students also constructed a similar analogy. Don't underestimate student imagination.

The School Gymnasium Analogy for Parallel Circuits

Focus	Concept	Parallel electric circuits function as independent circuits. Two lightbulbs connected in parallel glow equally bright; each globe receives the battery's full voltage and they divide the current between them.
	Students	After a school meeting, students can exit the gym twice as fast if two doors are open than if one is open; open three doors and they exit three times as fast.
	Analog	This is sometimes called the teeming crowd analogy: the rate students leave a school gym depends on the number of doors open—this is like a circuit with lightbulbs connected in parallel.

Action	Likes—Mapping the Analog to the Target	
	Analog—Students leaving a school gym after a meeting	**Target—Parallel circuit lightbulbs receiving the full voltage and dividing the current**
	Gym full of students for a meeting	Fully charged battery
	Students exiting through 1 open door	One globe in the circuit
	Students exiting through 2 open doors	Two lightbulbs connected in parallel
	Speed of exit through each door the same	Each globe receives same voltage and current
	2 doors open hall empties twice as fast	2 lightbulbs in parallel, battery runs flat twice as fast

Unlikes—Where the Analogy Breaks Down

- Two lightbulbs often do not draw as much current as two separate circuits of 1 globe plus 1 battery.
- Depending on the number of exits, the emptying rate may be like or not like the circuit.
- People stop, talk and jostle each other as they leave a gym; electron flow is regular.

The School Gymnasium Analogy for Parallel Circuits (Continued)		
Reflection	**Conclusion**	Did the students link the rate of flow from a gym with the flow of electrons in an electric circuit? Do I need another explanation or a supporting analogy next lesson?
	Improvements	Do we need to simulate this in our classroom (if it has two doors)? Can I customize this analogy to our school gym next time I teach parallel circuits?
Science Content Standard B, Physical Science, Grades 5–8: "Energy is transferred" (NAS. 1996, p. 155); "energy is an important property of substances and . . . most change involves energy transfer" (NAS, 1996, p. 154). The School Gymnasium Analogy shows the rates at which electric current flows in series and parallel circuits. Physical Science, Grades 9–12, benefit from this analogy when it is used to explain Ohm's Law and "moving electric charges" (p. 180).		
Suggested teaching strategies	Role-play is an excellent way to establish this analogy's ideas; should I lead the role-play or let the students organize it (class age is a factor here)? Could an older or more able class derive this analogy from their own experiences with circuits and school life?	
Resources	Recent experience with a school meeting; ability to simulate this in the classroom. Overhead transparency diagram of two or three gym setups. Can this be modeled on a recent disaster where people had to escape from a dangerous building (older students only)?	
Applications	Works well with middle school and high school students	

The Continuous Train Analogy for Current Conservation in a Series Circuit

The idea that electric current is used up in an electric circuit is a common belief. After all, batteries go flat or die and flashlights gradually grow dim, and the current decreases with time. The current reduces, say students, because the current returning to the battery is less than the current going to the bulb: hence, current is gradually used up. Tasker and Osborne (1985) found this conception in up to 40% of 10- to 16-year-olds.

Various analogies and models have been used to help students understand that the current out equals current back and that current is never used up in a lightbulb or motor. It is energy that is used up, or better, transferred from the battery to the lightbulb or motor.

A useful analogy to address this intuitive idea is that of the continuous train; however, it is contrived because continuous trains do not exist except as toys. The version that Dupin and Johsua (1989) used is shown in Figure 8.13 and has workers pushing the train cars (representing the battery) and an obstruction on the tracks slows it down (representing the lightbulb).

Another version of The Continuous Train Analogy is shown in Figure 8.14, and this one shows people boarding the train at one station (battery) and alighting from the train at the other station (lightbulb). In this model, the train carriages represent the current and the people represent the energy.

Figure 8.13   Continuous Train Pushed by Workers (Bottom Box) Slowed Down by Sand Obstruction (Top Box)

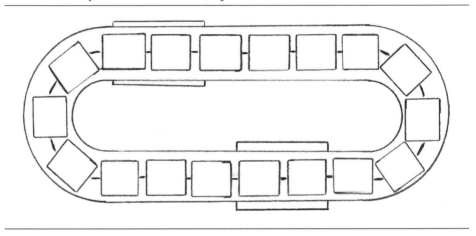

Figure 8.14   Continuous Train With People Boarding at One Station (Battery) and Alighting at the Other (Lightbulb)

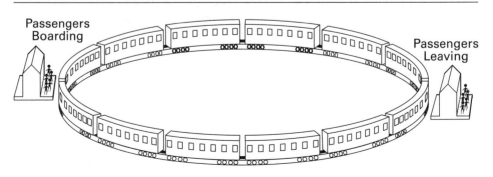

When using either analogy, discuss the artificial nature of the analogy with the students. If students are unsure of the analog or feel it is too artificial, then abandon the analogy. Aubusson and Fogwill (2006), however, show that even flawed analogies yield effective learning outcomes if the discussion is critical and comprehensive. The moral is, don't attempt an analogy you don't fully understand. Alternative current conservation–energy transfer models include The Escalator Analogy, The Bicycle Chain Analogy, and The Conveyer Belt Analogy (see Chapter 4). These three analogies use moving steps, chains, or belts to representing electric current, and they use people, work, and coal to represent energy transfer. These correspondences are drawn more fully in the following table.

Analogy or Model	*Electric Current Represented by*	*Electrical Energy Represented by*	*Battery Represented by*	*Lightbulb Represented by*
Continuous Train with People Analogy	Train carriages	People riding on the train	Station where people board	Station where people alight
Escalator Analogy	Moving steps in escalator	People riding escalator	Where people step onto escalator	Where people step off escalator
Bicycle Chain Analogy	The bicycle chain	Energy going from pedals to back wheel	Feet driving the pedals	Rotation of rear wheel
Conveyer Belt Analogy	Rubber conveyer belt	Coal, sand, rock	Mine rock face	Loading a train

The Continuous Train Analogy for Current Conservation in a Series Circuit		
Focus	**Concept**	Electricity only flows in closed circuits; energy is consumed (or more accurately, transformed) in electric circuits, but current is conserved. Remember, energy is hard to model.
	Students	Students think that current is consumed because batteries go flat and flashlights go dim. Some believe that the current

The Continuous Train Analogy for Current Conservation in a Series Circuit (Continued)		
		going from the battery to the bulb exceeds the current going from the bulb to battery. They are familiar with toy trains and escalators.
	Analog	A continuous train carrying people (energy) from one station to another. The train is not used up.
Action	**Likes—Mapping the Analog to the Target**	
	Analog—Continuous train	**Target—Current in a series circuit**
	Train carriages	Charge carriers or electrons
	Carriages moving	Electric current flowing
	Train track	Complete or closed circuit
	Passengers	Energy
	Station where passengers board train	Battery
	Station where passengers leave train	Lightbulb
	Unlikes—Where the Analogy Breaks Down	
	• People or cargo are used to represent energy, but energy is not a substance. • When one teacher used this analogy, her class concluded that the train slowed down as it passed through the "obstacle" representing the resistance. Current does not slow down when it passes through a resistance. • This analogy only works for simple series circuits.	
Reflection	**Conclusion**	Were my formative assessments of analog-target mappings appropriate? Should I recapitulate the analogy or use a further analogy next class?
	Improvements	If the continuous train caused problems, is the bicycle chain, escalator, or aquarium water circuit a better choice? Should I use a suite of complementary analogies next time?

The Continuous Train Analogy for Current Conservation in a Series Circuit (Continued)	
Science Content Standard B, Physical Science, Grades 5–8: "Energy is transferred" (NAS, 1996, p. 155); "electrical circuits provide a means of transferring electrical energy" (p. 155). The Continuous Train Analogy shows that current is always conserved in a circuit and energy is transferred from its source to devices that convert the electrical energy into heat, motion, or light.	
Suggested teaching strategies	As with all current conservation analogies, the problem should be grounded in experiences with simple series and parallels circuits. Use of the Tasker and Osborne (1985) quizzes is recommended. The analogy should only be introduced when students claim that current is used up or when they cannot explain circuit problems. Where possible, ask students to map the analogy and critique it. Once they understand The Continuous Train Analogy, can they construct another (e.g., Bicycle Chain Analogy, Escalator Analogy)?
Resources	Toy continuous train or, if not available, overhead transparency. Young classes can "play trains" (have a look at the M&M's analogy). Bicycle, picture of escalator, or real one, if easily available.
Applications	Suitable for middle and high school students—the mapping expected of students should increase with their ages.

The M&M's Circle Analogy for Electric Current

This model helps children make sense of the difference between energy that is consumed in an electric circuit and the current that is conserved. It's designed as a role-play so students can act out the circuit processes.

Clear away the desks and chairs and mark a large circle on the floor (use colored rope or ribbon). Place one colored piece of cardboard (labeled "Battery") on one side of the circle and opposite it another piece of colored cardboard called "Lightbulb." Note: this analogy is not perfect and the flaws are good opportunities to discuss the analogy's meaning.

Ask the students, "What do you think of when I say *energy*?" A popular answer is "food." Go on to say something like this: "Now electric circuits need energy to work, so we're going to pretend that each person is a little piece of electricity and these M&M's are the electrical energy. All these pieces of electricity (you students in the circuit) can move around, but you need something to make you move—that's what the M&M's are for." Students might even suggest this if you ask them.

Have the students stand on the marked circle (see Figure 8.15), ready to move. The circle moves in a direction decided by the students. Why does the circle move? It moves because the teacher or student standing at the Battery card gives students a small push as each passes the card. The Battery person also gives each student two M&M's. Continue your directions: "You can eat one of the M&M's to give you energy to move, and when you reach the Lightbulb card, you give the other one to Kerry, the Lightbulb person. When Kerry receives your M&M, she waves her hands over her head. What do you think this represents?" We sincerely hope the students will reply, "The lightbulb glowing." Another way to simulate the idea of the lightbulb glowing with energy is to put a box on the Lightbulb card. Students have to step onto the box and down again as they eat the second M&M (this model is more hygienic).

Two revolutions of the circle are enough for the students to get the idea. It's important to rehearse the analogy and discuss it again afterward. It's also essential to map out where this analogy works and where it breaks down. It's not perfect, and most electric circuit analogies are imperfect. This is an excellent discussion point for models and explanations.

In the discussion, pose questions like these: What do the Battery and Lightbulb people represent? Why did we draw a circle? Would it help if we linked arms? What do the two M&M's represent? (Is there a problem here? Yes, the M&M's do different things.) How can we improve the drama? Will the drama continue indefinitely? No. Why? (The hoped-for answer would be, "When we run out of M&M's, the battery's flat!")

Figure 8.15   The M&M's Circle Analogy for Electric Current

NOTE: The candy circle role-play is shown. For the M&M's Analogy, replace each lollipop with two M&M's per person.

The M&M's Circle Analogy for Electric Current		
Focus	**Concept**	Electricity only flows in complete circuits; energy is consumed (or transformed) in electric circuits but current is conserved. Energy is hard to model.
	Students	Students readily associate energy with food, and M&M's are well known and liked (and they're high energy food).
	Analog	Students in a circle receive two M&M's from the designated battery; one is used to make the electricity move and the other to make the bulb glow when they get to it.
Action	**Likes—Mapping the Analog to the Target**	
	Analog—Students moving in a circle eating M&M's	**Target—Circuit with one battery and one bulb transferring energy**
	Students in a circle	Electrons in a wire
	Student or teacher pushing circle	Electrons moving around a simple circuit
	M&M's	Energy
	Person giving out M&M's	Battery
	Student eating first M&M	Energy used to make electrons move
	Giving M&M to Lightbulb person	Electrical energy making the bulb glow
	Stepping onto box and eating M&M	Conversion of electrical energy into light
	Lightbulb person eats M&M	Lightbulb glows, producing heat and light
	Unlikes—Where the Analogy Breaks Down	
	• Circuit wires rarely consume as much energy as a lightbulb, but both representatives get an M&M • M&M's are not really energy (though they release energy), but electricity is energy. • Electricity is depicted as moving objects, whereas electricity is an interactive effect, not a substance.	

The M&M's Circle Analogy for Electric Current (Continued)		
Reflection	Conclusion	Did the role-play enable the students to differentiate between energy consumption (M&M's) and current conservation (students remaining intact)? If the students' ideas remain tenuous, will a parallel analogy like The Continuous Train Analogy help clarify the concepts?
	Improvements	If the role-play was teacher led, is it time to move toward a more student-designed drama?
Science Content Standard B, Physical Science, Grades 5–8: "Energy is transferred" (NAS, 1996, p. 155); "electrical circuits provide a means of transferring electrical energy" (p. 155). The M&M's Role-Play shows that current is conserved in a circuit and energy is transferred from its source to devices that convert the electrical energy into other energy forms.		
Suggested teaching strategies	Role-play engages students at many levels: from telling them the scenario through to allowing them to discuss circuit concepts and design the analogy. Role-play works best when students make circuits, identify the explanatory problems, discuss the conditions for an active circuit, and identify what they need to know.	
Resources	Batteries, light globes, and wires; M&M's, colored rope or ribbon, cardboard markers for Battery and Lightbulb, box or step stool (optional).	
Applications	Grades 5–8; for younger grades, teachers should lead the role-play, older grades can enact it as a project.	

NOTE: Ken Appleton is thanked for his rendition of this analogy. Ken acknowledges the input of the Children's Learning in Science group at Waikato University in New Zealand.

The Field Analogy for Electric Circuits

Gravity, magnetism, and electricity are forces that act at a distance. These forces spread throughout the space in which they operate, and we call this space a *field*. But just what is a gravitational, magnetic, or electric field? Where does the field metaphor come from? Michael Faraday invented field ideas to describe the sphere of influence of a magnet or electric charge. The problem in using this metaphor with students is that field concepts are rarely fully explained. Teachers assume students know when they really don't.

Fields take their name from specific areas that are used for agriculture, war, or sport. A soccer game is played on a field and the teams interact within this space and nothing of consequence to the game happens outside the field. The contest uses a ball, skills, and team players and is controlled by rules. Whether a team wins or loses is determined by the interaction of all the players. If you remove or restore a star player to the soccer team, that player usually affects every other player on both teams on the field. The field metaphor also applies to agriculture—the soil, plants, rain, fertilizer, and animals (if it is a grazing field) all interact to determine the farmer's profit or loss. The field concept is as an interaction, and the field's parts affect all other parts, or we can borrow from John Donne and say, "no *part* is an island, entire of itself."

Fields are used to explain force at a distance. It is an abstract idea, and lines of force is an analogy. The direction of a magnet's field is shown by the direction of its lines of force. The strength of the magnetic field is described by the closeness of the lines of force. But here's a problem: In weak fields, the lines of force are far apart. The diagram shown in Figure 8.16 implies that there is no force in the space between the lines, but there is. The analogy is often misinterpreted.

Figure 8.16   A Soccer Field Is Like a Complex Electric Circuit

Most of the difficulties with teaching electric circuits occur because teachers try to explain circuit properties in terms of their parts rather than their interactions. Think about an electric circuit with three or more light-bulbs connected in series and parallels. Expert teachers tell students, "Look at the overall circuit; don't concentrate on the parts, because it's the interactive whole that helps you work out currents and voltages."

The Field Analogy is a useful way to explain electric circuits when properly developed. Just like a magnet, batteries have lines of electric field joining the positive and negative terminals (Hewitt, 1999, p. 541). In a complete circuit, the conducting wires provide an excellent pathway for the lines of electric force to join the positive and negative terminals. Most of the electric field is confined to the conducting path. The battery, wires, filaments, and coils interact with each other to determine the field's strength and direction. The circuit functions as a unit. It is as if the field knows where every part of the circuit is, how they connect to and affect each other, and what they do. This is like a football team that interacts and plays together. No member of the team can do anything without affecting the other members.

The field concept explains how one bulb in a mixed series and parallel circuit seems to know that there is another bulb some distance along the wire that needs to share the electrical energy. The electric field takes the easiest path through the circuit, and the electrons flow best where the electric field is strongest.

The Field Analogy for Electric Circuits		
Focus	**Concept**	Electric and magnetic forces act at a distance, and their spheres of influence are described as fields. They exert their effect throughout the field, diminishing with distance from the source. Electric fields can be used to explain the flow of electricity in both simple and complex circuits.
	Students	Students know about playing fields and the team games that are played on fields (e.g., football, soccer). They know that a team succeeds if it functions as a whole and not as separate parts.
	Analog	In a football team, all the players function as a unit; in like manner an electric circuit functions as a whole and acts as if each part knows what every other part in the field is doing.

The Field Analogy for Electric Circuits (Continued)

Action	Likes—Mapping the Analog to the Target	
	Analog—A football team playing on a field	**Target—Complex electric circuits acting as a unit in an electric field**
	Playing field	Electric field
	Team members	Circuit components
	Game limited to the field of play	Electric circuit limited to conducting parts
	Rules of the game	Laws determining electric interactions
	Rules constraining player interactions	Laws constraining electric interactions
	All players affecting all others	Interaction of all parts together
	Players knowing what is happening everywhere on the field	Circuit parts functioning in accordance with the properties of all other parts
	Players taking the easiest route to the goal	Electrons flowing easiest where the field is strongest in the circuit

	Unlikes—Where the Analogy Breaks Down	
	• Team members know what each other person is doing and can communicate; circuit parts cannot: Interactions are governed by the electric field intensity at each point in the circuit. • Sport is totally confined to the field of play; electric fields are mostly confined to the circuit but weakly extend beyond the conductor.	

Reflection	**Conclusion**	Was the field metaphor well understood? Could average students explain The Field Analogy rules in their own words? Were they able to see the application to electric circuits?
	Improvements	Perhaps this concept should be revisited next period. Ask students to retell the analogy. Would a short video of a team sport or a discussion of a recent game help introduce the idea?

The Field Analogy for Electric Circuits (Continued)

Science Content Standard B, Physical Science, Grades 9–12: "Interactions of energy and matter" (NAS, 1996, p.180). The Field Analogy explains how an electric field (in a conductor) applies motive force to the charge carriers, which flow easily and create an electric current.

Suggested teaching strategies	Introduce this metaphor when students are having trouble with a series or complex circuit. The sports field analogies work best when the students realize they can't explain a phenomenon (e.g., how does the first bulb "detect" that there are others in the circuit? Discuss a recent popular big game to introduce the field concept.
Resources	Lightbulbs, batteries, and wires, newspaper or video accounts of a recent game. Demonstrate a magnetic field or have an OHT (remember that a magnetic field is an analogy for the electric field).
Applications	Grades 9–12. This is a powerful analogy, but be sure you can work it through. This analogy is best used as a culminating explanation for electric circuits. The analogy emphasizes the fact that electric circuits are rule-based interactions—a circuit is an interactive process, not bits acting on their own.

9

Effective
Earth and Space
Science Analogies

Neil Taylor

Terry Lyons

There are several good reasons why Earth and Space Science should be a part of any science curriculum. Nearly everything we do each day is connected in some way to the earth: to its land, oceans, atmosphere, plants, and animals. It is estimated that by 2025, eight billion people will live on earth. If we are to continue extracting resources to maintain a high quality of life, then it is important that our children are scientifically literate in a way that allows them to use the earth's resources in a sustainable way. People who understand how earth systems work can make informed decisions and may be able to help resolve issues surrounding clean water, urban planning and development, global climate change, and the use and management of natural resources.

Earth Science is a subject that has seen significant changes in recent times. The focus has moved from the surface geology of mapping and mining to global change and earth systems. The subject that was once dominated by historical explanations, like the "story in the rocks," now concentrates on understanding how human activity effects global change.

Thus the subject matter and skills needed to engage in earth science inquiry have shifted. The Internet is playing an increasing role in the teaching of some aspects of Earth Science. For example, the Kids as Global Scientists Project (www.biokids.umich.edu/projects/kgs.html) allows students to download daily weather information and satellite images and analyze these, while the Worldwatcher Project (www.worldwatcher .northwestern.edu) allows students to learn about the factors that contribute to the controversial global warming debate.

These new tools can clearly provide rich and exciting experiences for children in Earth and Space Science. However, in order to be able to use these new resources effectively, students need to have a good understanding of the underlying concepts, and there is considerable evidence that serious misconceptions are common in this area. For example, according to the U.S. National Research Council (1996), students in Grades 5–8 should have a clear idea about the direction of gravity when standing on the earth, the shape of the earth, and relative size and distance between the earth, sun, and moon. However, several studies have shown that many students in this age group have a weak understanding of these concepts (e.g., Stahly, Krockover, & Shepardson, 1999). According to Pfundt and Duit (2000), over 116 studies have reported that students of all ages enter science classrooms with explanations of earth and space concepts that conflict with those accepted by the scientific community.

Within Space Science, children often have difficulty developing an understanding of the complex relationships between objects in three-dimensional space. This is partly because most of the resources available to students are in the form of two-dimensional charts and images in textbooks. Furthermore, students have only one perspective in which to develop their understanding of the astronomy concepts—namely that of the earth. As a result, it has always been difficult to develop learning activities that offer students a broader perspective.

Osborne (1991) also points out that it is easy to underestimate the difficulty children have with concepts relating to the earth and other planets because they have to replace their own theories, which are reinforced by observation, with a scientific view that is often counterintuitive.

So while it is clearly important that students develop a good understanding of Earth and Space Science concepts, this presents many challenges. Earth and Space Science is a vast subject area, but the analogies that follow have been selected to help clarify some of the key underlying concepts, while other analogies are included because they illustrate complex concepts that students traditionally have difficulty understanding.

The first five analogies are related specifically to Earth Science while the latter five concern Space Science. Where possible, they have been sequenced to provide appropriate links. For example, the Analogy for Day and Night is followed directly by the Analogy for Arc of the Sun, a more complex idea, for which the earth's rotation is an enabling concept.

The Earth and Space Science analogies presented here are as follows:

Earth Science

- Modeling Dryland Salinity
- The Greenhouse Effect
- Visualizing Deep Time
- Continental Drift
- Convection Currents and Tectonic Plate Movement

Space Science

- Day, Night, and Time Differences
- The Arc of the Sun
- The Motion of the Planets
- The Scale of the Solar System
- Dancing With Black Holes

Modeling Dryland Salinity

Dryland salinity is a serious problem in many countries, including Australia, Canada, India, the United States, and various parts of Africa. In Australia, for example, nearly 14 million acres are at risk or affected by dryland salinity, an area that could triple in the next 50 years. It is not surprising that the problems associated with soil salinity now feature in many science curricula.

Students' understandings of the mechanics of dryland salinity are often fraught with misconceptions. For a start, many students think that groundwater refers to underground rivers or lakes or that there is no relationship between groundwater and surface water. Students may also be surprised to learn that a higher water table can actually be bad for crops or that inland soils contain large quantities of natural salts. In addition, research in the United States (Lee, Eichinger, Anderson, Berkheimer, & Blakeslee, 1993) showed that students hold alternative conceptions about how salt behaves in solution, with many believing that it disappears or that salt particles sink in fresh water because they are heavier. Students with such ideas will find it difficult to understand how salt can move upward through soil.

The model that follows is designed to help students understand both the concept of a *water table* and the process of capillary action by which salt is drawn to the surface (see Figure 9.1). The prior conceptual knowledge that students need can be summarized in these statements:

- Rain and irrigation water percolates down through soil, pooling when it reaches layers of rock or dense clay. The surface level of this water is called the water table.
- Deep-rooted trees absorb water from the soil, stopping the water table from rising too far.

- Heat and wind evaporate water from surface soil.
- When salt water is evaporated, any dissolved salts remain behind.
- Natural soils often contain salts (mainly NaCl) that come from the erosion of rocks, or are carried by wind from the ocean.

Figure 9.1   Model Demonstrating the Capillary Action of Saline Water in Soil

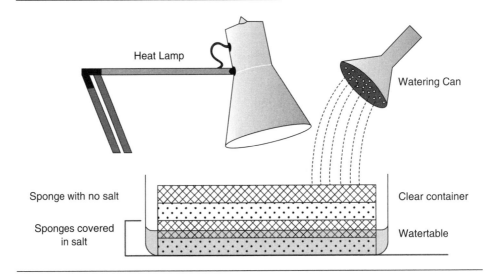

Modeling Dryland Salinity		
Focus	**Concept**	In areas where the water table is close to the surface (< 2m), saline water rises up through soil by capillary action. When this water reaches the surface, it is evaporated by the sun and wind, leaving the salt behind. Over time, the salt accumulates in the surface soil, limiting plant growth.
	Students	Students can confuse the concepts of the water table, capillary action of water through soil, and what happens when solutions are evaporated.
	Analog	A model of the water table, soil, and surface evaporation demonstrates capillary action and salination.

	Modeling Dryland Salinity (Continued)	
Action	**Likes—Mapping the Analog to the Target**	
	Analog—Salt in sponges	**Target—Soil salinity**
	Sponges in layers in a plastic container, two lower sponges covered in salt	Soils occurring in layers, deeper layers of soil containing natural salt
	Water on the top sponge percolating through the layers to pool at the bottom of the container	Rain and irrigation water percolating through the soil and pooling above nonporous materials, forming the water table
	Heat from the lamp evaporating the fresh water from the top sponge	Wind and sun evaporating fresh water from the surface soil
	By capillary action, the top sponge drying out and sponges slowly drawing water up from below	If the water table is close to the surface, water slowly drawn up to the drying surface soil by capillary action
	The rising water dissolving the salt and carrying it up through the sponge	The rising water dissolving the salt and carrying it up through the soil
	As salty water evaporates from top sponge, crystals of salt left behind	As salty water evaporates from the surface soil, crystals of salt left behind
	Unlikes—Where the Analogy Breaks Down	
	• Sponges are more absorbent than soil, and therefore speed up the capillary action. • The water table is usually much farther below the surface than can be shown by sponges.	
Reflection	**Conclusion**	By observing the model, students should be able to explain the salination processes. Then ask students to elaborate on why land clearing and irrigation can lead to salinity problems.
	Improvements	In suitable conditions, the model can be placed outdoors in sunlight. Students can also investigate the effects of lowering the water table by using more sponges.

Modeling Dryland Salinity (Continued)	
Content Standard D, Earth and Space Science, Grades 5–8: Structure of the Earth System (NAS, 1996, p. 159). The Dryland Salinity Model shows the impact of weathering and erosion on land forms.	
Suggested teaching strategies	Use at least four new sponges of different colors to represent soil layers. At the start, the sponges should be wet but not soaking. A dark-colored sponge must be on top so the salt crystals will be easier to see. Spread about 50g of salt between the lower three sponges. Salt can be sprinkled in the bottom of the container. No salt should come in contact with the top sponge. Slowly pour in fresh water until all four sponges are soaked and the water table covers the bottom sponge. When the level of the water table has stabilized, turn a lamp on directly over the top sponge. Evaporation takes several hours, it may be necessary to leave the model overnight.
Resources	Australian Broadcasting Corporation (2002). Department of Natural Resources (1998). Web resource—The All Schools Science Fair (www.all-science-fair-projects.com/science_fair_projects_encyclopedia/Soil_salination)
Applications	Earth and Science, Grades 5–8.

The Greenhouse Effect

Many students find the concepts of the greenhouse effect and global warming difficult to understand, particularly as they easily confuse this concept with the hole in the ozone layer. This probably happens because both problems are associated with our atmosphere, and chlorofluorocarbons (CFCs) and ozone are involved in both phenomena. Furthermore, in recent years both have received a good deal of media attention, some of which is conflicting. The analogy that follows is designed to help students understand the greenhouse effect by linking it to a very common experience, particularly in parts of the world with a high level of sunshine—that of a closed car's interior heating up when sitting in the sunshine (see Figure 9.2). It is particularly pertinent to countries like the United States and Australia where per capita greenhouse gas emissions are extremely high.

Figure 9.2   Radiation Entering a Car Becomes Trapped and Heats the Interior

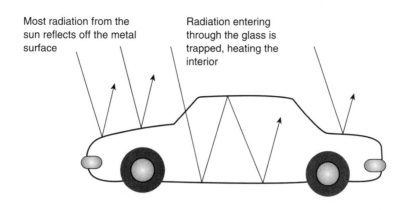

Most radiation from the sun reflects off the metal surface

Radiation entering through the glass is trapped, heating the interior

The Greenhouse Effect		
Focus	**Concept**	The increasing buildup of certain gases in the atmosphere is helping to trap heat, and this gradually raises the temperature on the earth's surface
	Students	The greenhouse effect is often confused with the hole in the ozone layer.
	Analog	Relating the greenhouse effect to a familiar event like the heating of a car's interior when parked in the sun helps students understand the concept. Heat entering a parked car's windows is trapped and raises the car's interior temperature in a way that is analogous to the greenhouse effect.
Action	**Likes—Mapping the Analog to the Target**	
	Analog—Interior of the car	**Target—Earth's atmosphere**
	Heat entering the car through the windows	Heat entering the earth's atmosphere
	The glass windows and windscreen	The layer of gases in the atmosphere
	Heat not able to easily escape from the car	Excess heat trapped in the atmosphere
	Air within the car warming up	Atmosphere warming up

The Greenhouse Effect (Continued)		
	Unlikes—Where the Analogy Breaks Down	
	• The speed at which the interior of the car warms up is very rapid, unlike that of the Earth's atmosphere, which heats up very slowly (over many years). However, it should also be pointed out to students that in terms of geologic time, the earth is warming quite rapidly. • Heat is trapped by gases in the atmosphere but not in the car, which has a solid skin acting as the insulator. • Reradiation and the resultant lengthening of the wavelength of the electromagnetic rays is a much more significant factor in the greenhouse effect than it is in the heating of a car's interior. • It is easy to cool the interior of a car by driving off with the windows down; however, reducing the greenhouse effect on earth is an extremely complex scientific and political problem.	
Reflection	**Conclusion**	Students can deconstruct this analogy and link its various components to those of the greenhouse effect. In so doing, they can also identify the limitations of the analogy.

	Improvements	Senior science students can research how heat is trapped by our atmosphere as a result of wavelength changes as it is reradiated from the earth's surface.
		    Students look at or debate the political aspects of the greenhouse effect, in particular their government's position on the Kyoto Protocol.
		    Students use thermometers or data loggers to investigate to compare internal and external temperatures of cars sitting in the sun.
		    Extension activity: compare and contrast the greenhouse effect with the car analogy (see http://www.letus.nwu.edu/projects/gw/pdf/C09.pdf)

Suggested teaching strategies	Group challenge: If students know why the interior of a parked car heats up, the analog can be used as a hint, and they can be challenged to work out why increased greenhouse gases result in increased atmospheric temperatures.	

	The Greenhouse Effect (Continued)
	Content Standard D, Earth and Space Science, Grades 9–12: Energy in the Earth System (NAS, 1996, p. 189). The Greenhouse Effect Analogy shows how global climate is determined by energy transfer and the impact of carbon dioxide on energy levels at the Earth's surface.
Resources	A BBC Web site provides a straightforward explanation of the greenhouse effect and has a link to an animated representation that offers a good visualization of the phenomena for children: http://www.bbc.co.uk/climate/evidence/greenhouse_effect.shtml
	An online quiz allows older students to test their knowledge of the greenhouse effect at http://news.bbc.co.uk/hi/english/static/in_depth/sci_tech/2000/climate_change/quiz/default.stm
	This Web site provides answers to a range of questions about the greenhouse effect: http://www.abc.net.au/science/planetslayer/greenhouse_qa.htm
Applications	Biology, Physics, General Science, and Earth and Space Science—Grades 9–12

Visualizing Deep Time

The concept of *deep time*, like deep space, requires students to work in an unfamiliar and perhaps unnerving frame of reference. Like adults, they have little real conception of the 4.6-billion-year history of the earth. As Stephen Jay Gould (1990) noted, the measuring rod of a human life is far too small a unit to appreciate and measure geological time.

Students' grasp of deep time can influence the quality of their engagement with important scientific issues, including sea level change, asteroid impacts, volcanic activity, and mass extinctions (Trend, 2001). However, they face two problems in conceptualizing deep geological time. First, they tend to merge or confuse events occurring at vastly different times. For example, the big bang is often confused with asteroid impact and ice ages with global climatic cooling. Some students even construct causal links between unrelated events—for example, believing that the big bang led to the extinction of the dinosaurs.

Students also find it hard to appreciate that 85% of the planet's history had already passed before mammals appeared, and that *Homo sapiens* has only been present in the last 0.003% of this history. Students need to visualize these intervals on some kind of analogous scale, and they are not helped by the time lines found in most textbooks, which generally use different scales for the first 4 billion years and the past 600 million years.

In this class activity, students construct a single-scale time line using a long roll of perforated paper toweling. Teachers can decide on the scale of the time line. For example, one in which each sheet represents 50 million years will require 92 sheets and take up just over 21m. The model can be created and displayed in a variety of ways, depending on the students, time allocated, and resources (see Figure 9.3). The prior conceptual knowledge that students need is as follows:

- The earth was formed around 4,600 million years ago.
- The atmosphere, hydrosphere, and lithosphere have changed dramatically over that period.
- A great variety of living things emerged over that period, some of which have become extinct while others have evolved into different species.
- Rock strata, fossil records, dating techniques, and DNA mapping provide us with a guide to geological and evolutionary history.

Figure 9.3   Students Creating a Time Line on the School Playing Field

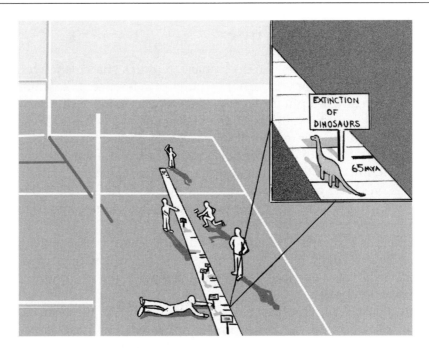

Visualizing Deep Time		
Focus	**Concept**	Scientists believe that the history of the earth covers about 4.6 billion years and that this history was punctuated by pivotal geological and evolutionary events, many of which occurred only in the past 500 million years. Humans and other mammals have been present in only very recent (geological) times.
	Students	Many students have difficulty visualizing the magnitude of time intervals involved in geological history relative to their own experiences.
	Analog	Pivotal geological or evolutionary events can be recorded on a long time line using a consistent scale.
Action	**Likes—Mapping the Analog to the Target**	
	Analog—Paper strip	**Target—Deep time**
	A long strip of perforated paper toweling pegged to a playing field or the classroom walls	The earth's 4,600-million-year history
	Markers, diagrams, or objects placed on the time line to represent pivotal geo-events	Pivotal geo-events intervals occurring at irregular intervals over a long period of time
	Long intervals on the paper showing few events contrasting with short sections crowded with activity	Long periods of little biological development contrasting with the evolution of a great variety of living things in a relatively short period of time
	Unlikes—Where the Analogy Breaks Down	
	• Marks on the model give the impression that periods and eras had distinct starting and finishing points. Boundaries between geological periods are approximate, and geographical changes were generally very gradual. • The model gives the impression that particular life forms appeared or disappeared at particular times, instead of being the product of gradual evolutionary processes.	

Visualizing Deep Time (Continued)		
Reflection	Conclusion	One way of assessing the usefulness of the project is to play a game in which one group places some events in an incorrect order. Other students would then have to correct the order.
	Improvements	As the outdoor model will be short-lived, it may be useful to photograph it being made and when complete. Students may produce a short film of geological-evolutionary history using an application like iMovie.

Content Standard D, Earth and Space Science, Grades 9–12: The Origin and Evolution of the Earth System (NAS, 1996, p. 189). The Deep Time Analogy helps students visualize geological time scales.

Suggested teaching strategies (Outdoor Activity)	Choose a dry, windless day and a time when the grass is dry. Discuss ways to show the position of events on the time line (e.g., colored markers, pegs, models of plants, dinosaurs, insects). Make the events on the time line visible from a distance. Students could be allocated specific jobs: pinning, counting, marking, drawing, writing, and so forth. Groups can also be responsible for marking particular events. Paper can be pinned to the ground using colored sports field markers. If the markers hold labels, they may even be used to indicate periods or eras. Start at the "Present" mark, walk beside the time line counting the sheets until you come to a position representing a period, era, or event. Mark this and date it.
(Indoor Activity)	The time line can be fixed to the classroom walls, just below the ceiling. The scale of the time line needs to suit the available wall space. Students can draw or represent events on pieces of paper. These sheets can be attached to the time line at appropriate positions.
Resources	Trend (2001).
Applications	Biology and Earth and Space Science—Grades 9–12

Continental Drift

Although the concepts of plate tectonics and continental drift are central to the modern view that the earth is a very dynamic place, the fact that the continents are so large and apparently stationary makes it very difficult for students to comprehend that they are gradually moving. Even when students have accepted that the continents are moving, there is often confusion about the mechanism that produces this movement and the way in which the tectonic plates are arranged. Marques and Thompson (1997) found that a large number of upper secondary science students believed that continental drift was caused by the rotation of the earth or that it resulted from the gradual cooling of the earth. Furthermore, some students believed that the tectonic plates are arranged in stacks and that they rotate around their center.

The following model (adapted from Van Cleave, 1991) provides students with a simple representation of the mechanism that drives continental drift at the mid-Atlantic Ridge, where convection currents cause the ocean floor to spread. This results in the upwelling of magma and the gradual separation of the Americas from Europe and Africa (see Figure 9.4).

The prior conceptual knowledge that students need is summarized as follows:

- The earth's crust is made up of a series of interlocking plates.
- The central core of the earth is composed of molten rock.
- Molten rock or magma can well up and move into the earth's crust.
- Heating of a liquid results in convection currents.
- Plates move at approximately 100mm–600mm per year.

Figure 9.4   Modeling Sea Floor Spreading at the Mid-Atlantic Ridge

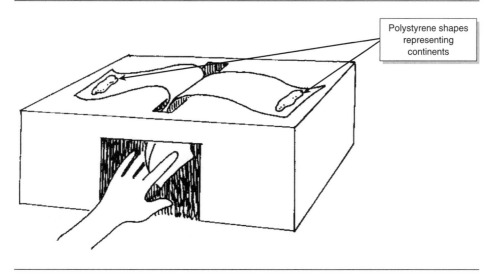

Polystyrene shapes representing continents

Figure 9.5   Modeling Folding and Mountain Formation Using Continental
Drift

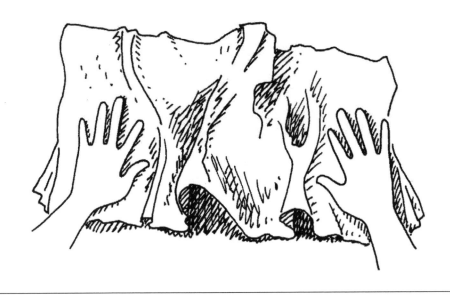

Continental Drift		
Focus	**Concept**	Throughout geological time, the continents have drifted over the earth's surface as rigid plates. Today they continue to move relative to each other as a result of convection currents within the mantle.
	Students	Students are unaware of the mechanism that drives continental drift or think it is due to the earth's rotation, a progressive cooling of the earth, or the plates rotating around their center.
	Analog	A useful model consists of a folded paper sheet pushed upward so that it spreads in two directions. This represents the spreading ocean floor on either side of the mid-Atlantic Ridge. Polystyrene blocks represent the two continents that are being forced apart. The hand represents the forces resulting from convection currents in the earth's mantle.

Continental Drift (Continued)		
Action	Likes—Mapping the Analog to the Target	
	Analog—Paper strip pushed upward	**Target—Continental drift**
	A student pushing the paper up through the gap in the model of the Earth's crust	Upwelling magma (deep convection currents) forcing the earth's plates apart
	Spreading paper	The movement of the earth's crust in response to convection currents
	The polystyrene shapes	Continents of the Americas and Europe and Africa on either side of the Atlantic Ocean
	Unlikes—Where the Analogy Breaks Down	
	• There is no representation of the subduction of the earth's surface in other parts of the world, such as the coast of South America. Continental drift is a balance of rising and sinking. • The model operates much faster than continental drift. • The model gives the impression that the upwelling magma and the tectonic plates are the same. • There is no representation of the folding of the earth's crust and the development of major mountain ranges.	
Reflection	**Conclusion**	Ask students to list the limitations of this analogy and explain these to their peers. Research what happens to the surplus surface area of the earth as a result of new rock produced at the mid-Atlantic Ridge. Explanation requires careful research and balanced processes
	Improvements	Use striped rather than plain paper, as the stripes show the changes in direction of the Earth's polarity in rocks on either side of the mid-Atlantic Ridge. 　The polystyrene blocks could be shaped to illustrate how the west coast of Africa is a good fit for the east coast of South America. 　Adapt the model to show how continental drift is associated with the folding and pushing up of mountain ranges like the Himalayas (see Figure 9.5).

Continental Drift (Continued)	
Content Standard D, Earth and Space Science, Grades 5–8: Structure of the Earth System (NAS, 1996, p. 160). The Continental Drift Analogy helps students visualize the nature of lithospheric plates and their movement with time.	
Suggested teaching strategies	Challenge students to develop the model to include folding or subduction. This requires research and reconceptualization of the model. It will show whether students had grasped the overall concept of continental drift.
Resources	Continental Drift? Do the continents really move? http://chiron.valdosta.edu/djudd/ljreyn012.html On the move . . . Continental Drift and Plate Tectonics http://kids.earth.nasa.gov/archive/pangaea/ evidence.html Plate tectonics and continental drift: http://members .aol.com/bowermanb/tectonics.html Geology: Plate tectonics: http://www.ucmp.berkeley .edu/geology/tectonics.html
Applications	Biology and Earth and Space Science—Grades 5–8

Convection Currents and Tectonic Plate Movement

Here is another analogy that also helps students develop a better understanding of the mechanism driving continental drift. This analogy can be used as an alternative to the one outlined previously or as a way of reinforcing the overall concept. In fact, having seen the first analogy, students might be asked to predict how this analogy will behave once heat is applied (see Figure 9.6).

Figure 9.6   Convection Currents Separate Two Foam Continents

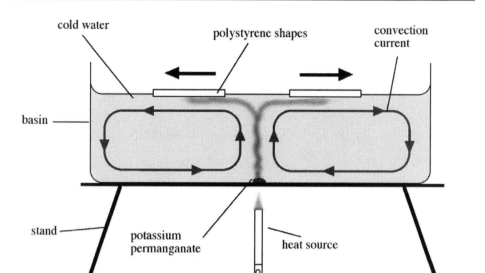

Convection Currents and Tectonic Plate Movement		
Focus	**Concept**	The continents move relative to each other as a result of convection currents within the mantle.
	Students	Students are often unaware of the mechanism that drives continental drift, or they hold alternative conceptions that link it to the earth's rotation or a progressive cooling of the earth or believe that the plates rotate around their center.
	Analog	The model consists of a tank of water with potassium permanganate crystals at the bottom and chalk powder on the surface of the water. Heat is applied directly below the potassium permanganate crystals, resulting in convections currents that students see as the crystals dissolve. The model shows how convection currents within the earth's mantle cause the crust to move apart in continental drift.

Convection Currents and Tectonic Plate Movement (Continued)

Action	Likes—Mapping the Analog to the Target	
	Analog—Convection currents in water	**Target—Upwelling magma**
	Purple liquid moving up from the area of heating	Upwelling of magma into the earth's crust
	Bunsen burner (or similar) heat source	Radioactive reactions that generate heat in the earth's core
	Spreading chalk powder on the surface of the water	The movement of the earth's crust in response to convection currents
	Purple liquid subsiding at the edges of the tank due to cooling	The sinking of the magma at the edges of tectonic plates (subduction)

Unlikes—Where the Analogy Breaks Down

- The speed at which the model operates bears no relationship to the actual speed of continental drift.
- Features such as the mid-Atlantic Ridge are not well represented.
- There is no link to the folding of the earth's crust and the rise of major mountain ranges.

Reflection	Conclusion	Ask students to compare this and the previous model of continental drift and decide which had the most limitations and why.
	Improvements	Add floating polystyrene blocks shaped to illustrate the west coast of Africa and the east coast of South America. This provides a more realistic model of continental drift and its underlying mechanism.

Content Standard D, Earth and Space Science, Grades 5–8: Structure of the Earth System (NAS, 1996, p. 160). The Continental Drift Analogy helps students visualize the nature of lithospheric plates that result from movement of the mantle.

Convection Currents and Tectonic Plate Movement (Continued)	
Suggested teaching strategies	Ask students to identify what would speed up the process of continental drift and to test this using the model.
Resources	Some thoughts about how to start teaching about convection: http://ethel.as.arizona.edu/~collins/astro/subjects/convection1.html
Applications	Biology and Earth and Space Science in Grades 5–8, Grade 5–8 Science.

Day, Night, and Time Differences

According to Sharp (1996), many children will provide explanations for the cause of day and night if asked. How scientific these are depends on the extent to which each child is aware of the earth's shape, its axis, its daily rotation on its axis, and its journey around the sun once a year.

Some children have problems explaining day and night: five- to seven-year-olds typically explain night as the sun covered by clouds or hidden by the moon, or they use anthropomorphic terms like "it goes to bed" (Osborne, 1991). However, a number of authors (e.g., Nussbaum, 1985) have demonstrated that many students in upper primary and lower secondary school also lack the enabling concepts that they need to explain day and night properly.

This analogy provides students with a strong visual representation of how the rotation of the earth in relation to the sun produces day and night. It develops an understanding of why shadows shorten and then lengthen during daylight. It is linked to an activity based on an Internet site (Earth and Moon Viewer at www.fourmilab.ch/earthview/vplanet.html) that allows teachers to assess if their students can apply their knowledge of day and night appropriately.

The analogy starts with students illuminating a globe of the Earth on one side and then rotating it slowly to model how different places enter night and day. The model can then be developed by securing a mini sundial to the globe and demonstrating that the length and direction of the shadow produced by sundial changes is a result of the earth's rotation (see Figure 9.7). The students can use the Earth and Moon Viewer Web site to apply their knowledge of day and night by predicting whether various cities around the globe will be experiencing day or night and checking this using the Web site. The Earth and Moon Viewer is a real-time representation of day and night around the globe, so when the Web site shows a satellite image of, say, Sydney during daylight, the images of London and Los Angeles will show them at night.

Figure 9.7   A Mini Sundial Casts a Shadow on the Globe

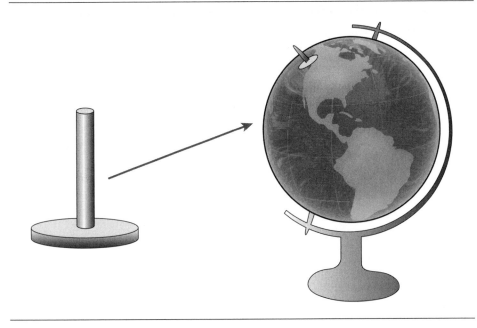

The enabling knowledge that students need can be summarized as follows:

- Shadows are formed when an opaque object breaks a beam of light.
- The Earth is spherical in shape.
- The Earth rotates on its axis once every 24 hours.
- The Earth is part of the solar system and travels round the sun once every 365.25 days.

Day, Night, and Time Differences		
Focus	**Concept**	The Earth is a spherical body illuminated by the sun on one side and rotating on its axis once every 24 hours. This causes day and night. Shadows vary in length because the rotation of the earth seems to change the elevation of the sun during the day.
	Students	Some students hold conceptions about the shape of the earth that are inconsistent with a scientific view of day and night. Others believe that the earth remains stationary while the sun moves from east to west.

Day, Night, and Time Differences (Continued)

	Analog	A model consisting of the sun (light source), earth (globe), and a mini sundial (matchstick and adhesive) secured to the globe can be used to demonstrate day and night and the changing length and orientation of shadows associated with this.

Action	**Likes—Mapping the Analog to the Target**	

Analog—Globe of earth and light source	**Target—Day and night**
A stationary light sources, a torch/flashlight, lamp, or overhead projector, illuminates half the globe.	Light from the sun illuminates half of the Earth.
A matchstick represents a sundial on earth that produces a shadow that varies in length as the globe rotates.	A sundial casts a shadow that varies in length and direction as the earth rotates from west to east.

Unlikes—Where the Analogy Breaks Down

- The matchstick is much taller relative to the globe than any sundial on the earth.
- Students rotate the globe much faster than the earth rotates.

| **Reflection** | **Conclusion** | Assess students' understating of day and night by asking them to predict which cities around the globe will be experiencing day or night at a particular position of the globe. Students can locate the cities in question using their globe, make their prediction, and check this using the Earth and Moon Viewer.
The Web site for the cities is www.fourmilab.ch/earthview/cities.html |
|---|---|---|
| | **Improvements** | Students can observe the shadow of an actual object at different times of the day and measure the position and length of the shadow. Have them compare this to the changes in matchstick shadow produced on the illuminated globe as it rotates. |

Day, Night, and Time Differences (Continued)		
		More able students could use this analogy and the Web site in an activity on precise time difference. Use longitudes to calculate the time in another part of the world. This is particularly relevant if they have a relative living in another country whom they can phone up to check the time and their calculation.
Content Standard D, Earth and Space Science, Grades 5–8: Earth in the Solar System (NAS, 1996, p. 160). The Mini Sundial Analogy helps students appreciate that objects in the solar system, including the earth, move in regular and predicable ways.		
Suggested teaching strategies	Shining a low-intensity flashlight on the face of a student while he or she rotates around a fixed position allows students to experience day and night at a more personal level. Students can then compare and contrast the components of this activity with those of the foregoing analogy. Students can develop a role-play involving being the earth, moon, and sun.	
Resources	Globes of the world and flashlights, lamps, or an overhead projector. Matchsticks cut in half and adhesive. Access to one or more Internet-linked computers and the Web site http://www.schoolsobservatory.org.uk/uninow/dayngt/	
Applications	Earth and Space Science—Grades 5–8	

The Arc of the Sun

Children often have difficulty understanding the relative motions of the earth and sun. Because of our frame of reference, it seems natural to assume that we are stationary while the sun, moon, and stars move across the sky. Many students begin astronomy units with a range of alternative conceptions about the motions of these bodies (Duit, 2004a, 2006; Pfundt & Duit, 2000; Sunal & Sunal, 2002). The challenge for the teacher lies in helping students visualize the motions of these bodies from different frames of reference.

To demonstrate the apparent rising and setting of the sun, teachers often use a light source, such as an overhead projector (OHP), and a globe of the earth. However, this type of presentation is not always effective. For one thing, students are asked to observe the relative positions of the bodies from their seats in the classroom (as so-called extraterrestrial observers) while simultaneously imagining what they would see from the surface of the earth. Assimilating views from two frames of reference at the same time represents quite a cognitive load for students.

The following model (from Mant, 1993) helps students see the sun stand-in from two frames of reference at the same time. The teacher uses temporary adhesive to fix a dome to the surface of the globe above a certain city or town. The dome represents a person's view of the sky from this location, with the base of the dome defining the horizon. When the OHP representing the sun is turned on, its light will be reflected in the dome as a bright spot (see Figure 9.8). This spot represents the position of the sun as seen by a person looking up from beneath the dome. As the globe is rotated from west to east, the light will appear to move from east to west, until it disappears below the horizon. In fact, a student can use a marker to plot the positions of the bright spot as the globe is turned. By joining these marks, students can trace the apparent arc of the sun as seen from the earth (see Figure 9.9). However, from their desks in the classroom, the extraterrestrial-observer students can see that the sun itself, as represented by the light, has not moved.

The prior conceptual knowledge that students need can be summarized as follows:

- The earth rotates on its axis every 24 hours.
- The direction of rotation is from west to east.
- The earth is tilted on its axis (23.5 degrees).

Figure 9.8   Views of the Dome in Three Positions

NOTE: As the globe is rotated west to east, the reflection of the OHP light (the sun) traces an arc from east to west on the dome. The figure shows the position of the sun from noon (A) to sunset (C), as seen by an observer on the earth.

Figure 9.9   The Arc of the Sun

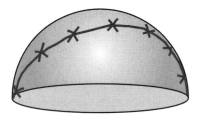

NOTE: The arc of the sun, from sunrise to sunset, can be plotted on the dome as the globe is rotated.

The Arc of the Sun		
Focus	**Concept**	The apparent movement of the sun across the sky from east to west is due to the rotation of the earth from west to east. The trajectory of this arc varies with the seasons due to the tilt of the earth's axis relative to its orbit around the sun.
	Students	Some students think that the earth is stationary and the sun moves from E→W. Giving students an extraterrestrial frame of reference can help them change this conception. Seasonal variations in the arc of the sun can also be understood using this frame of reference.
	Analog	A model consisting of the sun (light source), earth (globe), and a transparent dome represents the sky at a particular place.
Action	**Likes—Mapping the Analog to the Target**	
	Analog—Plastic dome	**Target—Arc of the sun**
	Light source (e.g., an OHP) illuminates half the globe	Light from the sun illuminates half the earth
	Transparent dome placed on the globe above a town represents our view of the sky.	Our view of the sky from any point on the earth is shaped like a dome and has a circular horizon.

The Arc of the Sun (Continued)

As the globe rotates from W→E, the dome emerges from the dark side, and a bright dot (reflection of the OHP bulb) is seen at the base of the dome.	As the earth rotates from W→E, we move from the darkened hemisphere into the light. Our first view of the sun is on the eastern horizon. This is sunrise.
As the globe rotates further, the bright dot appears to move across the dome in an arc. The curve of this arc depends on the position of the dome on the globe and the tilt of the globe.	As the earth rotates, the sun appears to move in an arc across the sky. The shape of this arc depends upon the location of the observer on the earth and on the season.

Unlikes—Where the Analogy Breaks Down

- The earth orbits around the sun, and the tilt axis of the earth is always aligned in the same direction, no matter where the earth is in its orbit. In the model, the globe is stationary, and the tilt axis is aligned in various positions to represented seasonal changes.
- Because of various landforms, the horizon is rarely visible as a circle.
- The domelike shape of the sky is only apparent. There is no real dome.

Reflection	Conclusion	Assess whether students have understood the principle by asking them to demonstrate the relative motion of the sun using the model. Ask students to draw arcs on the dome and explain why the arcs differ with latitude.
	Improvements	The position of the students relative to the model requires planning. They need to be able to see the reflection of the light source on the dome. Avoid domes that are too small or distort the reflection at their base.

Content Standard D, Earth and Space Science, Grades 5–8: Earth in the Solar System (NAS, 1996, p. 160). The Arc of the Sun Analogy helps students appreciate that objects in the solar system, including the earth, move in regular and predicable ways. in particular, it shows the relationship between the movement of the moon and earth.

The Arc of the Sun (Continued)	
Suggested teaching strategies	The dome can be attached to the globe using a temporary adhesive. Turn the globe so that the dome is on the dark side, away from the OHP. As you rotate the globe 30 degrees at a time, a student records the positions of the bright spot on the dome using a marker. Connect these marks to trace the sun's apparent path as seen from below the dome. The curve of the arc depends on the latitude and the tilt of the globe. Repeating for different positions allows students to plot arcs of different shapes. Changing the tilt of the globe models different seasons.
Resources	A dome between 7 and 10 cm; temporary adhesive.
Applications	Earth and Space Science—Grades 5–8

The Motion of the Planets

Astronomy is well established in most science curricula. The three-dimensional nature of astronomy can be difficult for students to understand, as many resources are in a two-dimensional format. A study of 42 sixth-grade students in a UK school showed that only 25 chose a sphere to represent the sun. Others chose discs, cylinders, or hemispheres or were unsure. When these students were asked to draw the paths of the earth, moon, and sun in relation to each other, only 20% were able to do so. Some of the students believed that the earth and the moon were stationary while the sun traveled around both every 24 hours (Sharp, 1996). These alternative conceptions were associated with familiar and visible planets. This might suggest that students could encounter greater difficulties when learning about planets that are not normally visible. According to Taylor, Barker, and Jones (2003), mental model building is an important skill in astronomy education. Physical models can help students develop mental models, but as with any type of analogy, there is a problem when students take them too literally.

Many schools have a physical model of the solar system, or parts of it, called an *orrery*. Orreries are named after the Earl of Orrery, Charles Boyle, who was a keen astronomer. They can vary considerably in quality and sophistication. Some simply involve the earth, moon, and sun, while others represent the whole of the inner solar system. Only rarely do they represent the whole solar system. The more advanced versions are automated, with the model planets revolving around the sun at speeds relative to the actual planets'. Orreries can be useful models for showing children the sequence of the planets, the shape of their orbits, and in some cases the relative speeds at which they orbit the sun. For example, the circular path of the earth around the sun in these models helps to avoid misconceptions

Figure 9.10   A Mechanical Orrery

about the reason for the seasons. Such alternative conceptions are often the result of children seeing two-dimensional diagrams of the earth's orbit that attempt to give a three-dimensional perspective.

Like most models of the solar system, orreries suffer from the problem of relative size and distance, and if the orrery is taken too literally, there is a chance that learners may think the sun is only slightly larger than the earth.

The prior conceptual knowledge that students need can be summarized as follows:

- The solar system is made up of the sun (a star) and eight planets.
- The planets are generally spherical in shape.
- The eight planets revolve around the sun.
- Each revolution of the sun by a planet represents one year on that planet.

The Motion of the Planets		
Focus	**Concept**	The planets orbit the sun at different speeds and times and in different orbits
	Students	Children have difficulty visualizing the dynamics of the solar system
	Analog	An orrery can provide children with a strong visual representation of the relative position of the planets in relation to the sun and the relative speeds at which they travel around the sun.

The Motion of the Planets (Continued)

Action	Likes—Mapping the Analog to the Target	
	Analog—Orrery	**Target—The solar system**
	Model planets	Actual planets
	Sequence of model planets from the sun	Sequence of actual planets from the sun
	Relative speeds at which planets orbit the sun	Relative speeds at which actual planets orbit the sun
	Unlikes—Where the Analogy Breaks Down	
	• The sizes of the planets cannot be to the exact scale of those in the solar system. • The planets in the orrery orbit the sun more rapidly than those in the solar system. • The relative distances between the planets in the orrery cannot be on an exact scale of the solar system. • The planets in the orrery have circular orbits; solar system orbits are elliptical	

Reflection	Conclusion	Ask students to explain the limitations of this analogy. This can be done directly after the analogy has been presented or after they have done further research on the solar system.
	Improvements	Use the analogy in combination with Web sites (listed in Resources). These allow students to conduct further research into the planets in terms of such things as the daytime and nighttime temperatures and the makeup of the atmosphere. Students could also draw up a table comparing the length of different planetary years or days or both.

Content Standard D, Earth and Space Science, Grades 5–8: Earth in the Solar System (NAS, 1996, p. 160). The Orrery Analogy helps students appreciate that objects in the solar system, including the earth, move in regular and predicable ways. In particular, it shows the motion of the planets.	
Suggested teaching strategies	Groups of students could be allocated a particular planet within the solar system and be asked to research it and present their findings to the rest of the class. Students can model the orbits of the different planets through role-play activities that indicate their relative positions and speeds.

The Motion of the Planets (Continued)	
Resources	Some virtual orreries: http://www.schoolsobservatory.org.uk/uninow/orrery/ http://www.fourmilab.ch/solar/solar.html http://www.harmsy.freeuk.com/orrery.html
Applications	Earth and Space Science—Grades 5–8

The Scale of the Solar System

This model can be used after children have seen the orrery. It reinforces knowledge of the sequences of the planets but gives a better impression of the relative sizes of the planets and the distances between them. For example, use the following materials:

Planet	Scaled planet diameter	Suggested Model	Distance
Sun	30 cm	Yellow beach ball	
Mercury	1mm	Poppy seed	12 meters
Venus	3mm	Dried pea	23 meters
Earth	3mm	Dried pea	32 meters
Mars	2mm	Pepper corn	49 meters
Jupiter	30mm	Tennis ball	167 meters
Saturn	26mm	Tennis ball	300 meters
For schools with access to more space			
Uranus	10mm	Marble	about 600 meters
Neptune	10mm	Marble	about 900 meters

For most schools it is relatively easy to model the inner solar system (sun to Saturn), as the distances here are not too great. However, in a school with a very large playing field, a long beach, or a unused airstrip in the area, it may be possible to model the outer planets as well, although a vehicle may be needed to transport the students representing these planets. Distances between the inner planets can easily be measured with a trundle wheel. A flag or whistle is useful in managing students at a distance.

The students simply take up their positions at the appropriate relative distance from the representative sun and hold up their seeds or balls. This analogy is a representation of the vast distances between the planets relative to their sizes and provides an indication that most of the solar system is empty space.

The Scale of the Solar System		
Focus	**Concept**	The planets of our solar system vary enormously in size, and the distances between them are vast compared to the sizes of the planets. Furthermore, most of the solar system is empty space.
	Students	Some students hold alternative conceptions about the shapes of planets, and many have difficulty conceptualizing their relative sizes and the distances between them.
	Analog	A model consisting of a number of different-sized spheres demonstrates the relative sizes of the planets and the distances between them.
Action	**Likes—Mapping the Analog to the Target**	
	Analog—Spherical objects	**Target—The planets**
	Spheres of different sizes	The planets of the solar system
	Relative distances between the spheres	Relative distances between the planets
	Unlikes—Where the Analogy Breaks Down	
	• There is air and possibly wind blowing between the models for the planets, while in space there is a vacuum • The model is generally presented as a straight line of static planets—rotation of each planet and its solar orbit is difficult to convey	
Reflection	**Conclusion**	Ask students to explain the limitations of this analogy. This can be done directly after the analogy has been presented or after they have done further research on the solar system.

The Scale of the Solar System (Continued)		
	Improvements	Instead of being given the scale, senior science students could be provided with data on the actual planet sizes and distances and asked to develop a scaled-down model of the solar system using a range of seed types separated by the appropriate distances—in effect, the reverse of this analogy. The positioning of the children as the planets could be video-taped and the video used for revision purposes.
Content Standard D, Earth and Space Science, Grades 5–8: Earth in the Solar System (NAS, 1996, p. 160). The Scale of the Solar System Analogy helps students appreciate the makeup of the solar system. In particular, it develops an appreciation of the relative sizes of the planets compared with earth.		
Suggested teaching strategies	Ask students to draw the planets of the solar system in sequences before the analogy is used. This could be done individually or in small groups. After using the analogy, further research could ask the students to redraw their diagram and compare it to their original effort.	
Resources	Seeds, balls, and spheres. A large open space in which children can spread out to demonstrate the relative distances between the planets (e.g., parkland, a beach, or a unused airstrip). The following Web site provides a great deal of information about the individual planets in our solar system, including some very interesting animations of planetary movement. There are also links to other useful solar system Web sites: http://www.bbc.co.uk/science/space/solarsystem/index.shtml	
Applications	Earth and Space Science—Grades 5–8	

Dancing With Black Holes

Students are fascinated by exotic astronomy phenomena. From supernova to comets, the more mysterious the object, the greater the interest—and few celestial objects generate more interest than black holes. However, in classroom discussions it is not long before someone asks the question, "If black holes are invisible, how do we know where they are?"

Most black holes are detected due to the large amounts of X-rays produced as they swallow up material from a binary partner (see Figure 9.11).

Figure 9.11   A Black Hole Swallowing Material From Its Binary Partner

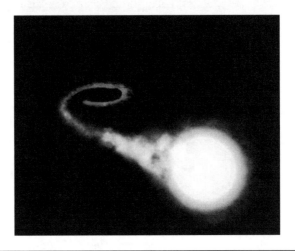

Figure 9.12   Waltzing in the Dark

However, black holes can also be detected by their influence on the motion of this companion star. The analogy described here can help students understand how the motion of a visible star can betray the presence of an invisible partner.

A binary star system revolves around a point located somewhere between the two partners. A binary system in which one partner is a black hole can therefore be likened to a couple waltzing in a darkened ballroom, where one partner, dressed in black, is invisible to an observer (Figure 9.12). However, the observer can deduce the presence of the invisible partner through the motion of the visible partner.

In astronomy, the orbital velocity of the companion star tells us something about the mass of the invisible partner and thus whether it is a black hole, rather than a neutron star, for instance.

The prior conceptual knowledge that students need can be summarized as follows:

- Black holes were created by collapsed stars and consist of matter so dense that even light cannot escape the gravitational pull. (For a senior class, the teacher might explain this in terms of distorting the fabric of space-time.)
- Most stars in our galaxy exist in groups of two or more. In a binary system, the partners orbit around a point between them.
- Objects have uniform motion unless acted upon by a net force.

Dancing With Black Holes			
Focus	Concept	Black holes are invisible to us because not even light can escape their gravitational field. However, their presence can be detected by the effect they have on other stars.	
	Students	Students often wonder how astronomers are able to detect black holes when they are relatively small and invisible to optical telescopes.	
	Analog	By using the image of a couple waltzing in a dark ballroom, students will appreciate that the motion of a visible partner can betray the presence of an invisible partner.	
Action	Likes—Mapping the Analog to the Target		
	A man and woman waltzing in a dark room: the woman is dressed in white while the man is dressed completely in black.		Some binary systems in the galaxy consist of a visible star and an invisible black hole.
	The man and woman waltz around the room in a circular motion, pivoting around a point between them.		The binary system rotates around a point somewhere between the two bodies.

Dancing With Black Holes (Continued)

	Because they are holding on to each other, they do not fly apart as they spin around.	Despite the centrifugal force resulting from their motion, the black hole and its companion star are held together by gravity.
	Although invisible in the dark room, the man's presence is deduced from the motion of the woman.	The presence of the black hole is deduced because of the motion of its companion star.

Unlikes—Where the Analogy Breaks Down

- Most black holes are detected by X-ray emissions rather than by anomalous motion.
- It is possible for a woman to change direction on the dance floor without the influence of a partner. Therefore she could be dancing alone. However, a star cannot have an orbital motion unless influenced by another body.
- The man is invisible because his dark coloring does not reflect any light. The black hole is invisible because light cannot escape its gravitational field.

Reflection		
	Conclusion	Assess student understanding of the concept by asking students to draw a diagram of a binary system containing a black hole. Cut out the diagram, pin it to a board, and demonstrate and discuss the rotation of the binary system.
	Improvements	If you can obtain video footage of couples dancing, the color, brightness and contrast controls on the television can be adjusted until only bright objects, such as the ball gowns, are visible. From the motion of the light ball gowns, deduce the presence of partners.

Content Standard D, Earth and Space Science, Grades 9–12: The Origin and Evolution of the Universe (NAS, 1996, p. 190). The Dancing With Black Holes Analogy helps students understand the history of the universe. In particular, it shows the composition of different stars.

Resources	QuickTime animations of binary systems containing a black hole can be found at http://imagine.gsfc.nasa.gov/Videos/XTE/xray_binary3.mov and http://imagine.gsfc.nasa.gov/docs/science/know_11/binary_stars.html
Applications	Physics and Earth and Space Science—Grades 9–12

References

Andersson, B. (1990). Pupils' conceptions of matter and its transformation. *Studies in Science Education, 18*, 53–85.

Aubusson, P. J., & Fogwill, S. (2006). Role-play as analogical modeling in science. In P. J. Aubusson, A. G. Harrison, & S. M. Ritchie, *Metaphor and analogy in science education* (pp. 93–104). Dordrecht, the Netherlands: Springer.

Australian Academy of Science. (1981). *Biological science: The web of life, students' manual* (Part 2, 9th ed.). Canberra: Author.

Australian Academy of Science. (1991). *Biology: The common threads, teacher's resource book* (Part 2). Canberra: Author.

Australian Broadcasting Corporation. (2002). *The silent flood* Video. ABC Education.

Ausubel, D. P. (1968). *Educational psychology: A cognitive view*. New York: Holt, Reinhart & Winston.

Bronowski, J. (1973). *The ascent of man*. London: British Broadcasting Corporation.

Bucat, R. B. (Ed.). (1976). *Elements of chemistry. Earth, air, fire, & water* (Vol. 1). Sydney: Australian Academy of Science.

Bucat, R. B. (Ed.). (1984). *Elements of chemistry* (Vol. 1). Canberra: Australian Academy of Science.

Butts, B., & Smith, R. (1987). HSC chemistry students' understanding of the structure and properties of molecular and ionic compounds. *Research in Science Education, 17*, 192–201.

Clement, J. (1987). Overcoming misconceptions in physics: The role of anchoring intuition and analogical validity. In J. Novak (Ed.), *Proceedings of the Second International Seminar on Misconceptions and Educational Strategies in Science and Mathematics* (Vol. 3, pp. 84–97) Ithaca, NY: Cornell University Press.

Clement, J. (1993). Using bridging analogies and anchoring intuitions to deal with students' preconceptions in physics. *Journal of Research in Science Teaching, 30*, 1241–1258.

Coffman, J., & Tanis, D. O. (1990). Don't say particle, say people. *The Science Teacher, 57*(8), 27–29.

Coll, R. K. (2006). The role of models, mental models and analogy in chemistry teaching. In P. J. Aubusson, A. G. Harrison, & S. M. Ritchie (Eds.), *Metaphor and analogy in science education* (pp. 65–77). Dordrecht, the Netherlands: Springer.

Coll, R. K., France, B., & Taylor, I. (2005). The role of models and analogies in science education: Implications from research. *International Journal of Science Education, 27*(2), 183–198.

Cook-Deegan, R. (1994). *The gene wars: Science, politics, and the human genome*. New York: Norton.

Cosgrove, M. (1995). A case study of science-in-the-making as students generate an analogy for electricity. *International Journal of Science Education, 17*(3), 295–310.

Crane, S. C., & Liu, R. S. H. (1986). Models for demonstrating organic structures to a large audience. *Journal of Chemical Education, 63*(6), 516–517.

Curtis, R. V., & Reigeluth, C. M. (1984). The use of analogies in written text. *Instructional Science, 13*, 99–117.

Dagher, Z. R. (1995a). Analysis of analogies used by science teachers. *Journal of Research in Science Teaching, 32*(3), 259–270.

Dagher, Z. R. (1995b). Review of studies on the effectiveness of instructional analogies in science education. *Science Education, 79*(3), 295–312.

Dahsah, C., & Coll, R. K. (2007). Thai Grade 10 and 11 students' conceptual understanding and ability to solve stoichiometry problems. *Research in Science and Technological Education, 25*(2), 227–241.

Darwin, C. D. (1967). *The origin of species* (6th ed.). London: Dent.

Dawkins, R. (1989). *The selfish gene.* Oxford, UK: Oxford University Press.

Department of Natural Resources & Environment. (1998). *The saltbook.* Melbourne, Australia: VIC.

Driver, R., Squires, A., Rushworth, P., & Wood-Robinson, V. (1994). *Making sense of secondary science.* London: Routledge.

Duit, R. (1991). On the role of analogies and metaphors in learning science. *Science Education, 75*(6), 649–672.

Duit, R. (2004a). *Bibliography: Student's alternative frameworks and science education* (6th ed.). Kiel, Germany: University of Kiel Press.

Duit, R. (2004b). *Students' and teachers' conceptions and science education.* Kiel, Germany: University of Kiel Press. Retrieved April 4, 2007, from http://www.ipn.uni-kiel.de/aktuell/stcse/stcse.html

Duit, R. (2006). *Bibliography: Student's alternative frameworks and science education* (updated ed.). Kiel, Germany: University of Kiel Press.

Dupin, J. J., & Johsua, S. (1989). Analogies and "modelling analogies" in teaching. Some examples in basic electricity. *Science Education, 73*, 207–224.

Eddington, A. S. (1922). *Theory of relativity and its influence on scientific thought.* Oxford, UK: Oxford University Press.

Evans, B. K., Ladiges, P. Y., & McKenzie, J. A. (1995). *Biology two* (2nd ed.). Melbourne, Australia: Heinemann.

Feynman, R. P. (1994). *Six easy pieces.* Reading, MA: Helix.

Friedel, A. W., Gabel, D. L., & Samuel, J. (1990). Using analogs for chemistry problem solving: Does it increase understanding? *School Science and Mathematics, 90*(8), 674–682.

Gabel, D. L., & Samuel, K. V. (1986). High school students' ability to solve molarity problems and their analog counterparts. *Journal of Research in Science Teaching, 23*(2), 165–176.

Gabel, D. L., & Sherwood, R. D. (1980). Effect of using analogies on chemistry achievement according to Piagetian levels. *Science Education, 65*, 705–716.

Gentner, D. (1983). Structure mapping: A theoretical framework for analogy. *Cognitive Science, 7*, 155–170.

Gentner, D. (1988). Analogical transfer and analogical access. In A. Prieditis (Ed.), *Analogica* (pp. 63–88). Los Altos, CA: Morgan Kaufmann.

Glynn, S. M. (1991). Explaining science concepts: A teaching-with-analogies model. In S. Glynn, R. Yeany, & B. Britton (Eds.), *The psychology of learning science* (pp. 219–240). Hillsdale, NJ: Erlbaum.

Gould, S. (1990). The golden rule: A proper scale for our environmental crisis. *Natural History, 9*, 24–30.

Grayson, D. (1994). Concept substitution: An instructional strategy for promoting conceptual change. *Research in Science Education, 24*, 102–111.

Hackling, M. W., & Fairbrother, R. W. (1996). Helping students do open investigations in science. *Australian Science Teachers Journal, 42*(4), 26–33.

Harrison, A. G. (2001). How do teachers and textbook writers model scientific ideas for students? *Research in Science Education, 31*, 401–436.

Harrison, A. G. (2002, December). *Analogical transfer: Interest is just as important as conceptual potential.* Paper presented at the annual meeting of the Australian Association for Research in Education, Brisbane, Australia.

Harrison, A. G., & de Jong, O. (2005). Exploring the use of multiple analogical models when teaching and learning chemical equilibrium. *Journal of Research in Science Teaching, 42*(10), 1135–1159.

Harrison, A. G., Grayson, D. J., & Treagust, D. F. (1999). Investigating a grade 11 student's evolving conceptions of heat and temperature. *Journal of Research in Science Teaching, 36*(1), 55-87.

Harrison, A. G., & Treagust, D. F. (1994a). Science analogies. *The Science Teacher, 61*(4), 40–43.

Harrison, A. G., & Treagust, D. F. (1994b). The three states of matter are like students at school. *Australian Science Teachers' Journal, 40*(2), 20–23.

Harrison, A. G., & Treagust, D. F. (1996). Secondary students' mental models of atoms and molecules: Implications for teaching chemistry. *Science Education, 80*(5), 509-534.

Harrison, A. G., & Treagust, D. F. (2000). Learning about atoms, molecules and chemical bonds: A case-study of multiple model use in grade-11 chemistry. *Science Education, 84*, 352–381.

Hawking, S. W. (1988). *A brief history of time.* New York: Bantam.

Hewitt, P. G. (1999). *Conceptual physics.* Menlo Park, CA: Addison-Wesley.

Holyoak, K. J., & Thagard, P. (1996). *Mental leaps: Analogy in creative thought.* Cambridge: MIT Press.

Hunter, R., Simpson, P., & Stranks, D. (1976). *Chemical science.* Sydney, Australia: Science Press.

Ingham, A. M., & Gilbert, J. K. (1991). The use of analogue models by students of chemistry at higher education level. *International Journal of Science Education, 13*(2), 193–202.

Jarvis, T., Taylor, N., & McKeon, F. (2005). Promoting conceptual change in pre-service primary teachers through intensive small group problem-solving activities. *Canadian Journal of Mathematics, Science and Technology Education, 5*(1), 15–33.

Jones, S. (1993). *The language of the genes.* London: Flamingo.

Justi, R., & Gilbert, J. K. (2006). The role of analog models in the understanding of the nature of models in chemistry. In P. J. Aubusson, A. G. Harrison, & S. M. Ritchie (Eds.), *Metaphor and analogy in science education* (pp. 119–130). Dordrecht, the Netherlands: Springer.

Lee, O., Eichinger, D. C., Anderson, C. W., Berkheimer, G. D., & Blakeslee, T. D. (1993). Changing middle school students' conceptions of matter and molecules. *Journal of Research in Science Teaching, 30*, 249–270.

Lenton. G., & McNeil, J. (1993). *Understanding living things and the gases they need* (Pack 3 of the series Understanding Science Concepts: Teacher Education Materials for Primary School Science). Oxford, UK: University of Oxford Press.

Lewis, J., & Kattmann, U. (2004). Traits, genes, particles and information: Re-visiting students' understanding of genetics. *International Journal of Science Education, 26*(2), 195–206.

Licata, K. P. (1988). Chemistry is like a.... *The Science Teacher, 55*(8), 41–43.

Lorenz, K. Z. (1974). Analogy as a source of knowledge. *Science, 185,* 229–234. Retrieved April 4, 2007, from http://nobelprize.org

Mant, J. (1993). *Understanding the Earth's place in the universe* (Pack 5 of the series Understanding Science Concepts: Teacher Education Materials for Primary School Science). Oxford, UK: University of Oxford Press.

Marques, L., & Thompson, D. (1997). Misconceptions and conceptual change concerning continental drift and plate tectonics among Portuguese students aged 16–17. *Research in Science and Technological Education, 15*(2), 195–222.

McDermott, L. (1993). How we teach and how students learn. *Australian and New Zealand Physicist, 30,* 151–163.

Mezl, V. A. (1996). Using ones' hands for naming optical isomers and other stereochemical positions. *Biochemical Education, 24*(2), 99–101.

National Academy of Sciences. (1996). *National science education standards.* Washington, DC: National Academy Press.

National Land and Water Resources Audit. (2002). Retrieved 11 January, 2005, from http://audit.ea.gov.au/ANRA/docs/fast_facts/fast_facts_21.html

Nersessian, N. (1992). Constructing and instructing: The role of "abstraction techniques" in creating and learning physics. In R. Duschl & R. Hamilton (Eds.), *Philosophy of science, cognitive psychology, and educational theory and practice* (pp. 48–68). New York: State University of New York Press.

Nussbaum, J. (1985). The Earth as a cosmic body. In R. Driver, E. Guesne, & A. Tiberghien (Eds.), *Children's ideas in science* (pp. 10–33). Milton Keynes, UK: Open University Press.

Nussbaum J., & Novick, S. (1982). Alternative frameworks, conceptual conflict and accommodation: Toward a principled teaching strategy. *Instructional Science, 11,* 183–200.

Osborne, J. (1991). Approaches to the teaching of AT16—the Earth in space: Issues, problems and resources. *Secondary Science Review, 72*(260), 7–15.

Osborne, R., &. Freyberg, P. (1985). *Learning in science: The implications of children's science.* Oxford, UK: University of Oxford Press.

Otto, J. H., & Towle, A. (1969). *Modern biology.* New York: Rinehart and Winston.

Pendlington, S., Palacio, D., & Summers, M. (1993). *Understanding materials and why they change.* Pack 4 of the series Understanding Science Concepts: Teacher Education Materials for Primary School Science. Oxford, UK: University of Oxford.

Pfundt, H., & Duit, R. (2000). *Students' alternative frameworks and science education bibliography* (5th ed.). Kiel, Germany: University of Kiel Press.

Pimentel, G. C. (Ed.). (1970). *Chemistry: An experimental science.* San Francisco: Freeman.

Pogliani, L., & Berberan-Santos, M. N. (1996). Inflation rates, car devaluation, and chemical kinetics. *Journal of Chemical Education, 73*(10), 950–192.

Rayner-Canham, G. (1994). A student's travels, close dancing, bathtubs, and the shopping mall: More analogies in teaching introductory chemistry. *Journal of Chemical Education, 71*(11), 943–944.

Reingold, I. D. (1995). A concrete analogy for combustion analysis problems. *Journal of Chemical Education, 72*(3), 222–223.

Ritchie, S. M., Bellocchi, A., Poltl, H., & Wearmouth, M. (2006). Metaphors and analogies in transition. In P. J. Aubusson, A. G. Harrison, & S. M. Ritchie (Eds.), *Metaphor and analogy in science education* (pp. 143–154). Dordrecht, the Netherlands: Kluwer.

Sharp, J. G. (1996). Children's astronomical beliefs: A preliminary study of year 6 children in south-west England. *International Journal of Science Education, 18*(6), 685–712.

Shipstone, D. (1985). Electricity in simple circuits. In R. Driver, E. Guesne, & A. Tiberghein (Eds.), *Children's ideas in science* (pp. 33–51). Milton Keynes, UK: Open University Press.

Silverstein, T. P. (2000). Weak vs. strong acids and bases: The football analogy. *Journal of Chemical Education, 77*(7), 849–850.

Stahly, L. L., Krockover, G. H., & Shepardson, D. P. (1999). Third grade students' ideas about the lunar phases. *Journal of Research in Science Teaching, 32*(2), 159–177.

Stavy, R. (1991). Using analogy to overcome misconceptions about conservation of matter. *Journal of Research in Science Teaching, 28*(4), 305–313.

Sunal, D., & Sunal, C. (2002), *Science in the elementary and middle school.* Upper Saddle River, NJ: Prentice Hall.

Tasker, R., & Osborne, R. (1985). Science teaching and science learning. In R. Osborne & P. Freyberg (Eds.), *Learning in science: The implications of children's science* (pp. 15–27). Auckland, New Zealand: Heinemann.

Taylor, I., Barker, M., & Jones, A. (2003). Promoting mental model building in astronomy. *International Journal of Science Education, 25*(10), 1205–1225.

Thagard, P. (1992). Analogy, explanation, and education. *Journal of Research in Science Teaching, 29*(6), 537–544.

Thiele, R. B., & Treagust, D. F. (1994). An interpretive examination of high school chemistry teachers' analogical explanations. *Journal of Research in Science Teaching, 31*(3), 227–242.

Thiele, R. B., Venville, G. J., & Treagust, D. F. (1995). A comparative analysis of analogies in secondary biology and chemistry textbooks used in Australian schools. *Research in Science Education, 25*(2), 221–230.

Treagust, D. F., Duit, R., Joslin, P., & Lindauer, I. (1992). Science teachers' use of analogies: Observations from classroom practice. *International Journal of Science Education, 14*, 413–422.

Treagust, D. F., Harrison, A. G., & Venville, G. J. (1998). Teaching science effectively with analogies: An approach for preservice and inservice teacher education. *Journal of Science Teacher Education, 9*(2), 85–101.

Treagust, D., Harrison, A., Venville, G., & Dagher, Z. (1996). Using an analogical teaching approach to engender conceptual change. *International Journal of Science Education, 18*, 213–229.

Trend, R. (2001). An investigation into the understanding of geological time among 17-year-old students, with implications for the subject matter knowledge of future teachers. *International Research in Geographical and Environmental Education, 10*(3), 298–321.

U.S. National Research Council. (1996). *National science education standards.* Washington, DC: National Academy Press.

Van Cleave, J. P. (1991). *Earth science for every kid.* New York: John Wiley.

Venville, G., & Bryer, L. (2002). A sanitary problem. In J. Wallace & W. Louden (Eds.), *Dilemmas of science teaching: Perspectives on problems of practice* (pp. 159–163). London: Routledge

Venville, G., Bryer, L., & Treagust, D. (1993). Training students in the use of analogies to enhance understanding in science. *Australian Science Teachers' Journal,* *40*(2), 60–66.

Venville, G., & Treagust, D. F. (1993). Evaluation of a heart model. *SCIOS, The Journal of the Science Teachers' Association of Western Australia, 28*(1), 33–39.

Venville, G., & Treagust, D. F. (1996). The role of analogies in promoting conceptual change in biology. *Instructional Science, 24,* 295–320.

Venville, G., & Treagust, D. F. (1998). Exploring conceptual change in genetics using a multidimensional interpretive framework. *Journal of Research in Science Teaching, 35*(9), 1031–1055.

Venville, G., & Treagust, D. F. (2002). Teaching about the gene in the genetic information age. *Australian Science Teachers' Journal, 48*(2), 20–24.

Vosniadou, S. (1989). Analogical reasoning in knowledge acquisition. In S. Vosniadou & A. Ortony (Eds.), *Similarity and analogical reasoning* (pp. 413–437). Cambridge, UK: Cambridge University Press.

Vygotsky, L. (1986). *Thought and language.* Cambridge: MIT Press.

Watson, J. D. (1968). *The double helix: A personal account of the discovery of the structure of DNA.* London: Penguin.

Whitten, K. W., Gailey, K. D., & Davis, R. E. (1992). *General chemistry.* Sydney, Australia: Saunders.

Wilkes, W. (1991). A model to illustrate the structure and function of the heart. *SCIOS, The Journal of the Science Teachers' Association of Western Australia, 26*(4), 33–38.

Williamson, V. M., & Abraham, M. R. (1995). The effect of computer animation on the particulate mental models of college chemistry students. *Journal of Research in Science Teaching, 32*(5), 521–534.

Wong, E. D. (1993). Self generated analogies as a tool for constructing and evaluating explanations of scientific phenomena. *Journal of Research in Science Teaching, 30,* 367–380.

Yager, R. E. (1995). Constructivism and the learning of science. In S. M. Glynn & R. Duit (Eds.), *Learning science in the schools: Research reforming practice* (pp. 35–58). Mahwah, NJ: Lawrence Erlbaum.

Zook, K. B. (1991). Effect of analogical processes on learning and misrepresentation. *Educational Psychology Review, 3*(1), 41–72.

Zook, K. B., & Di Vesta, F. J. (1991). Instructional analogies and conceptual misrepresentations. *Journal of Educational Psychology, 83*(2), 246–252.

Zumdahl, S. S. (1989). *Chemistry* (2nd ed.). Lexington, MA: Heath.

Index

CORWIN PRESS

The Corwin Press logo—a raven striding across an open book—represents the union of courage and learning. Corwin Press is committed to improving education for all learners by publishing books and other professional development resources for those serving the field of PreK–12 education. By providing practical, hands-on materials, Corwin Press continues to carry out the promise of its motto: **"Helping Educators Do Their Work Better."**